# Forgotten Footprints

John Harrison's award-winning travel writing with *Cloud Road* and *Where the Earth Ends* has featured journeys in South America and Antarctica. He has won the Alexander Cordell Prize twice and the 2011 Wales Book of the Year. His next project is *1519: A Journey to the End of Time*, following overland the route of the Cortés expedition which destroyed the Aztecs. When not guiding and driving powerboats in polar regions, or travelling for his own interests, he lives in London and Cardiff.

# Forgotten Footprints

Lost Stories in the Discovery of Antarctica

## John Harrison

PARTHIAN

Parthian
The Old Surgery
Napier Street
Cardigan
SA43 1ED

www.parthianbooks.com

First published in 2012
© John Harrison 2012
All Rights Reserved

ISBN 978-1-906998-21-9

Editor: Kathryn Gray
Cover design by www.theundercard.co.uk
Cover photograph by John Harrison
Contemporary photographs by John Harrison
Maps drawn by Charles Aithie
Typeset by books@lloydrobson.com
and typesetter.org.uk
Printed and bound by Gomer Press, Llandysul, Wales

Published with the financial support of the Welsh
Books Council.

British Library Cataloguing in Publication Data

A cataloguing record for this book is available from
the British Library.

High defenition PDF versions of all the maps may
be viewed free online at John Harrison's website:
www.cloudroad.co.uk

For Celia, who found me there

# Who is this book for?

The history of Antarctica is largely written in magisterial biographies and coffee-table tomes that require three polar heroes to lift them. My own collection can swiftly be piled up into a fortress against the harshest blizzard. Some of the explorers are household names, bywords for bravery and suffering. But none of those heroes discovered Antarctica: neither Cook, Scott, Shackleton nor Amundsen. You would think it was a conspiracy. The Russians will tell you Admiral Bellingshausen discovered it, Americans make a claim for a sealing captain called Nathaniel Palmer. No.

It was a Briton no one has heard of. This book tells his tale and those of the other jobbing sailors who were the first to find Antarctica, and to start to chart its shape. There's a few heroes too, where they went to places we can visit. That is the second aim of the book: to describe the discovery and exploration of Antarctica through the places that feature in the visits of the cruise ships which now land over thirty thousand passengers a year on the last continent. It focuses on the Antarctic Peninsula down to the Antarctic Circle, the South Shetland Islands, and the fringe of the Weddell Sea; around 98% of tourists come here. There are some fine general histories but they give equal weight to expeditions and activities which took place on remote shores and in harsh interiors visited only by a handful of professional scientists and daring adventurers. This book gives the background to the things and places visitors actually see. Whether you are planning a trip, or you are just an armchair adventurer it will explain how mankind found the last continent and how we have treated it.

# Contents

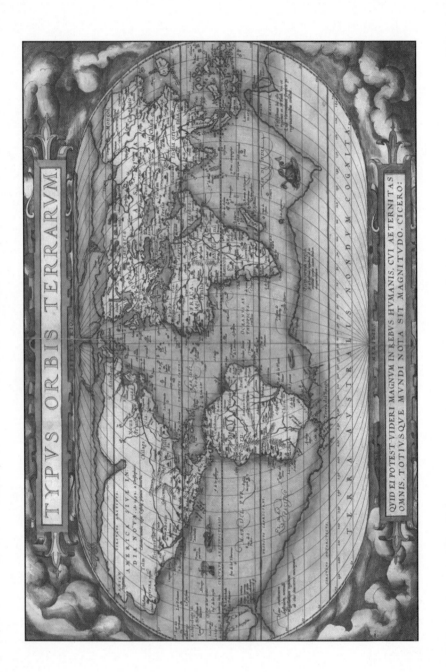

# PROLOGUE:

## The Ghosts of Detaille Island

I did not want to go ashore. We had never been asked to start an Antarctic landing at midnight. I'd get no sleep before and very little after. The Expedition Leader was showboating for the guests, perhaps because they included a Belgian Prince and Baron von Gerlache, the grandson of the Belgian explorer Adrien. Another guest owned tankers, six hundred of them. At Ushuaia, the Argentine gateway to Antarctica, their entourage brought the airport to a halt, as the authorities tried to find parking places for their fifteen private jets.

I climbed into my Zodiac, a five-metre-long open inflatable powerboat, and was lowered into the bay to ferry ashore the descendants of Adrien de Gerlache and their friends. The guests had spent the evening partying and celebrating their farthest south, just below the Antarctic Circle. We landed on a tiny block of rock on which stood the old British Detaille Base, and explored the huts by torchlight. The season was advanced and night had returned. The days had become mortal again; they had a beginning and an end.

Detaille Base seemed more authentic in the torchlight, and I enjoyed picking my way round. In its few years of active life from 1956 to 1959, it was lit by fitful generators and hot-handled hurricane lamps. It was a time capsule from my childhood. On a table lay the August 1953 edition of *World Sports* magazine. The middle-distance runner Christopher Chataway was on the cover, breasting the tape in a number 1 shirt. He was one of the athletes who would, the following spring, help Roger Bannister to run the first four-minute mile. Cupboard doors opened on tins whose primary-coloured fifties' cheerfulness was corroded by rust along the joints: the war was over, custard and porridge for all. The party enjoyed their visit; their boisterousness subsided to pleasant thoughtfulness. The Prince took off his mink-lined hat and absent-mindedly stroked the fur with his thumb. They left in trickles; I ran shuttles ferrying them back across the bay.

Each time I returned to the ship the bar sounds from the lounge high above the stern were more raucous. Each shore visit was more tranquil. The Expedition Leader asked if any of the Zodiac drivers wanted to be lifted. I said I was fine. I drove the last passengers back at 03:30, leaving the empty base to its ghosts, dropping the other staff at the gangway, before pulling away to prepare the Zodiac to be lifted by crane onto the top of the rear deck. I unfolded the web of three pairs of straps, coming to a central ring, then clipped the hooks onto the shackles at the front and centre of the boat. The back ones are fixed. I stowed my backpack where it would not tangle with them when I hitched the ring to the hook. Snug in my one-piece survival suit, I balanced, on my back, on the side pontoon of the boat. Above me, in the black blanket of sky, rents worked open, and the cover began to break up. Haphazard stars appeared. The radio crackled: 'John, we have slight problem with anchor.' When Polish officers speak English the articles disappear. 'Stand by fifteen minutes.'

She was an old Swedish ice-breaker built for coastal patrol, launched as the *Njord*, the god of the sea, but renamed the *Polar Star*. She does not go to Antarctica now. Under the delightful Captain Jacek Mayer, who taught me to use a sextant, and whose first command was a square rigger ('She is in a museum now, I am still sailing.'), she hit an uncharted rock off Detaille Base in 2011 and ripped her belly open. The company went bust as she sat in a Canaries dockyard and the repair bill mounted.

Now I had turned off the 60 HP Yamaha outboard engine, I could hear the fans and motors which keep the ship alive, the tinkling party, and the Filipino sailors I had worked with for six years, Alan, Lito and Dallas, calling to each other tiredly in Tagalog. The water cooling my engine piddled into the sea. I felt the wavelets ping the rubber hull. I saw the stars brighten and then fog in the confusion of the cloudless sweep of the Milky Way: the edge of the galaxy opening up with light from times when men walked in animal skins. The ship was a solitary pool of warmth and light. I let my Zodiac drift away from her into the darkness at the edge of the bay. Her deck lights were a cluster in the sky, a constellation without a name: a new, unpredictable star sign. The bar music faded and all I could hear was the creases of ocean slipping under the boat, the cold air hosing through my throat, and the thump of my heart. The Zodiac turned slowly as she drifted, and I was the only soul alone in an empty world. The only man abroad in a continent. The last continent. But who discovered it? I didn't care. I was unspeakably happy.

# 1

# The Master Craftsman:

## James Cook (1728–1779)

VOYAGE I (1768–1771)
VOYAGE II (1772–1775)
VOYAGE III (1776–1779)

*A ditch-digger's son becomes one of the greatest navigators of his own age, or any other age, and is sent out three times to look for the one land he does not believe exists.*

In a locked, unlit village shop, the gangly youth eased himself out from under the counter where he had slept the night. He was the son of a farm labourer who had left Scotland when it was reduced to desolation after the crushing of the Jacobite rebellion of 1715–16, and moved to the straggling hamlet of Marton in Yorkshire, in north-east England. Two years later, the labourer's wife gave birth to a son, James, who at eight years old was already helping his father clean ditches and cut hedges. A reputation for honest muscle earned the father a job as bailiff to the local Lord of the Manor, Thomas Skottowe, at a larger village: Great Ayton. Skottowe saw something in the boy and paid for him to attend school. To his humble parents, apprenticing James to a shopkeeper in the nearby fishing village of Staithes was a way to rise above a life of physical drudgery. But to Cook an apprenticeship to a draper-cum-grocer was just a genteel jail. One day a lady paid for goods with a brilliant silver shilling. When the shop closed, the youth read on it the letters SSC: South Sea Company. He put it in his pocket and replaced it with one of his own. The shopkeeper William Sanderson noticed it missing and accused Cook of theft. Cook's fervent denials were accepted, but Sanderson's lack of trust rankled, and Cook's pocket already held the shiny promise of another world. He asked to be released from the apprenticeship to go to sea. Sanderson agreed and Cook was bound as a seaman apprentice for three years with the Quaker family of John Walker of Whitby, a town famous for its ruined monastery, its whaling, and, for me, as the port where Dracula enters England.

The Walkers gave James a room of his own and paid his fees to attend sea school in the town. At this time London's hearths and furnaces devoured over a million tons of coal a year, much of it supplied by north-east England in a thousand sturdy, blunt-bowed colliers known as cats, carrying six hundred tons of coal. He first sailed in February 1747, aged eighteen, becoming a Master Mate in 1755, when he was offered his own command: the *Friendship*. But Cook's ambition had been shaped by reading the accounts of the great explorers of the Pacific. War with France was looming and he might be pressed into the Navy. With great courage he decided to meet fate on his own terms. He turned down promotion to a merchant captain and signed on as an Able Seaman in the Royal

Navy. The Navy was so short of experienced men that Cook made First Mate in less than a month. He learned surveying during the successful war to break French rule in Quebec, and after the war he was tasked with surveying the islands off Newfoundland which the peace treaty had ceded to France. A century later Admiral Wharton said of Cook's charts 'their accuracy is truly astonishing.'

In Cook's day, the supposed southern continent *Terra Australis Incognita*, lying in temperate latitudes and ripe for exploitation, was an idea that would not die. Cook doubted its existence long before he ever sailed south. The man described as 'one of the greatest navigators our nation or any other nation ever had' spent much of the rest of his life looking for something he doubted existed, but proving that conviction would re-write the map of the world and make him immortal. The Antarctic passages of his voyages would be forceful expeditions pressing as far south as was humanly possible, but he did so in a period of history when the earth was suffering a miniature Ice Age and it was the worst time in two centuries to be doing it.

The first problem he faced was the envy of a rival: Alexander Dalrymple. He was the creature of the Astronomer Royal, Nevil Maskelyne, the man who had so frustrated clockmaker John Harrison, the genius who solved the longitude problem. Maskelyne recommended that the expedition should be led by Dalrymple, a scientist and East Indiaman captain who was later the first Chief Hydrographer; he was also vain, cussed, and a man with a genius for backing the wrong horse. He was convinced his career would be crowned by charting the *Terra Australis Incognita*, which his readings of old and often dubious charts and memoirs convinced him was a known fact.

Dalrymple shot himself in the foot by demanding absolute overall control of the expedition. The Navy had made one famous exception to the rule that the senior Naval officer was the overall commander. The first Astronomer Royal, Sir Edmund Halley, had been given absolute control to observe a transit of Venus in the Pacific. Chaos ensued and mutiny threatened. Halley was Maskelyne's immediate predecessor as Astronomer Royal, so it was idiotic to imagine the lesson had been forgotten. The First Lord of the Admiralty, Sir Edward Hawke, made his oppositions plain enough even for Dalrymple, declaring 'I would rather cut off my right hand than sign such a commission.'

Cook shared his cabin with the naturalist, the twenty-five-year-old son of a rich, land-owning agricultural improver who had made a fortune draining the marshy fenlands of east England: a man who had employed numberless ditch-diggers and labourers like Cook and his father without ever knowing their names. Young Joseph Banks owned an estate near Lincoln worth £6000 per annum. He could have bought both the expedition ships out of a year's income and still have had cash spare to live like a gentleman. At Eton College, bored with Greek and Latin, he walked home from a swim in the river through a flower meadow and decided to study the beautiful flora. Oxford had no botanist, so he paid for one to move there from Cambridge. The whim became a stellar career. Once on board he impressed Cook with his diligence. Nothing was beneath his attention. He even noted that the weevils in the ship's biscuits were three species of the genus *Tenebrios* and one of *Ptinus*, but the white Deal biscuit was favoured by *Phalangium cancroides*.

The orders governing the expedition read comically today, governing as they do transactions with people and places which often did not exist; it is the bureaucracy of Never Never Land. If Cook found Antarctica, he had to take possession 'with the consent of the natives.'

For a ship, he chose a Whitby cat, renamed the *Endeavour*. The cruise took them to the main island of Tierra del Fuego where Banks showed his disdain for superstition by shooting a wandering albatross. Despite this, the Horn was a millpond. They sailed for the heat of Tahiti where the astronomers would observe the transit of Venus across the face of the sun, a rare and irregular event that allows accurate calculations to be made of the distance from the earth to the sun. Their next orders were to go to 40° south, heading into the south-west sector of the Pacific. To appreciate how good Cook's gut instincts were about *Terra Australis Incognita*, you have to look at the diaries of the other officers on his two ships to see how long, and how longingly, they clung to the romance of a temperate continent. Every time they go ashore in New Zealand, Banks refers to it as a visit to the continent. He calls his party of believers 'the Continents' but refrains from calling the opposition the Incontinents. They all but circumnavigate the North Island, but the officers refuse to accept it is an island until Cook goes back north to Cape Turnagain where he had begun. Although the weather was poor for much of the time, making surveying difficult, when the explorer Julien Marie de Crozet, a fine navigator himself, sailed these waters with a Cook chart he 'found it of an exactitude beyond all powers of expression.'

When Cook reached home he had been 1074 days away from his wife Elizabeth, whom he had left pregnant and with young children. But he first visited the Admiralty, before going home to find their baby had been born and died, and another child was also dead. Within one month he was preparing to leave on a circumpolar trip. There were still southern latitudes where *Terra Australis Incognita* might have been skulking since the Flood. Cook didn't believe it was there but he reasonably conceded that there were latitudes to the west of Cape Horn so little visited that sizeable land masses could have been missed.

Cook made two more Whitby cats famous: the *Resolution*, 462 tons, with 118 men, accompanied by the *Adventure*, 336 tons, with 82 men under Captain Tobias Furneaux. There were names already famous on board, and famous names to be. The Able Seamen included George Vancouver, aged fifteen, later to explore the Pacific NW Coast. AS Alex Hood, aged fourteen, was cousin to two admirals: Hood and Lord Bridport. Dalrymple didn't even make the long-list, but he had been busy redrawing the world from his desk. While Cook was away he had published a new chart of the southern oceans showing the extent of *Terra Australis Incognita*, incorporating the few sightings of land which could be given any credence, such as the French navigator Lozier Bouvet's claim to have seen a snowy headland on the first day of 1739 and named it Cape Circumcision. Dalrymple's chart was shoddy work, based on a map by Abraham Ortelius: a masterpiece in its day, but now nearly two hundred years old. In his early thirties, Dalrymple was already a young fogey.

Their best chronometer was justifiably famous: K2, the commercial rebuild of the John Harrison masterpiece H4 that won him the £20,000 prize for solving the longitude problem. Its error was less than one second a day. One of the scientists was Johann Reinhold Forster, a fan of Dalrymple and an overpaid complainer with the sharp hunger for recognition and respect which only the truly insecure display. But his son Georg was altogether better company. The handsome Banks was missing; grown vain while he was the toast of London society, especially its women. He sulked about the choice of small ships again, and flounced off to botanise in Iceland. Cook's expedition would make four passes south and come within half a days' sailing of seeing Antarctica, never, of course, knowing it.

In Cape Town, they heard the sea gossip. The Breton noble Yves-Joseph de Kerguelen-Trémarec with two French ships had recently put into harbour, with orders similar to Cook's to hunt for the southern continent. They had returned from the seas where Cook was heading, and claimed to have discovered land at 48°S, and coasted along it for 180 miles. They had seen a bay in which they hoped to anchor but when their boats were sent in to sound for an anchorage, a gale blew up and the ships stood off, abandoning the men ashore. Cook's lieutenant Charles Clerke fumed that there existed no circumstance so bad that Kerguelen had to abandon his men. Clerke was a man whose candid diaries make you long to have worked with him. He comes across as witty, earthy, pragmatic and humane. One officer summed him up like this: 'Clerke is a right good officer, at drinking and whoring he is as good as the best of them.' Cook was too preoccupied wondering whether the French had stolen a march on him to criticise their personnel policies. Kerguelen, despite the distance between him and the shore, was sure it was a land of plenty. The motto of believers in the southern continent was *Often Wrong: Never in Doubt*.

On 22 November 1772, Cook headed for Bouvet's Cape Circumcision. Bouvet claimed to have sailed for twelve hundred miles along a shore covered in snow and ice but with land beneath. His pilot thought it was nothing of the sort, but fools make work for wise men. By late November Cook began to see icebergs. Nothing prepares you for your first sight of large icebergs. In dull light the turquoise blue shines out brilliantly. They can look as if violet lamps have been lit in the recesses. The largest I have ever seen took three hours to steam past; it was twenty-nine miles long (forty-six kilometres) but was only a broken fragment of a much larger one. In mid-December Charles Clerke reported horrible fogs 'so thick we can scarcely see the length of the quarterdeck' and out of the murk came bergs which towered over the ship. He reported one as big as St Paul's Cathedral. Even the taciturn Cook took a moment in his diary to appreciate the grandeur of seas so fierce they broke over the tallest icebergs, but his responsibilities soon resumed precedence over aesthetics: the scene 'for a few moments is pleasing to the eye, but when one reflects on the danger this occasions, the mind is filled with horror, for was a ship to get against the weather side of one of these islands when the sea runs high she would be dashed to pieces in a moment.'

It would soon be midsummer, but the weather was getting worse. Ice smothered the rigging; a rope as thick as two fingers became as broad as your wrist and would not run through blocks and pulleys, so sails and yards could not be moved. Men were continuously employed hacking off ice, and clearing it from deck. If they did not keep pace, the weight aloft would capsize the ship. At least most of the livestock died and everyone enjoyed fresh meat.

By 13 December they were at 54°S, the latitude where Bouvet saw his coast, but the weather had driven them 354

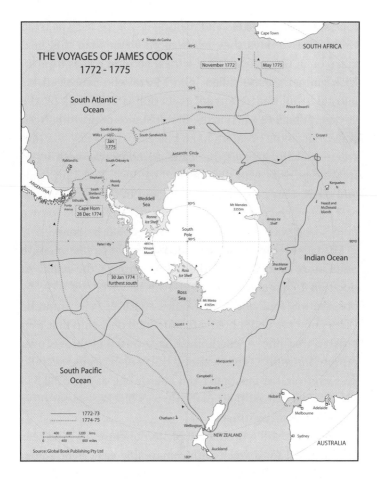

THE VOYAGES OF JAMES COOK
1772 - 1775

Tristan da Cunha
40°S

Cape Town
SOUTH AFRICA

November 1772    May 1775

South Atlantic
Ocean

50°S

Bouvetøya    Prince Edward I

60°S

South Georgia
Willis I    South Sandwich Is
Jan
1775

Crozet I

Falkland Is    South Orkney Is    Antarctic Circle

70°S

ARGENTINA

Elephant I
Moody
Point    Weddell
Sea

80°S

Mt Menzies
3355m

Kerguelen
Is

Heard and
McDonald
Islands

Ushuaia    South
Shetland
Islands

Punta
Arenas    Cape Horn
28 Dec 1774

Ronne
Ice Shelf    Amery Ice
Shelf

South
Pole
90°S

Peter I Øy    4897m
Vinson
Massif    Shackleton
Ice Shelf    Indian Ocean

30 Jan 1774
furthest south    Ross
Ice Shelf

90°E

Ross
Sea    Mt Minto
4165m

Scott I

Macquarie I

South Pacific
Ocean    Campbell I

Auckland Is    Hobart

Adelaide
Melbourne

1772-73
1774-75    Chatham I

0  400  800  1200 kms    Wellington    Sydney
0  400  800 miles    NEW ZEALAND

Source: Global Book Publishing Pty Ltd    Auckland    AUSTRALIA

180°

miles east of his location for Cape Circumcision, so Cook
tried to force his way south, into the pack. He tried for four
weeks before the weather eased on 15 January and he
enjoyed gentle breezes and serene weather for five
consecutive days. Fresh water was a problem; in Antarctica
most of it is frozen. He expected most of the sea ice would
be saltwater, but tested it by bringing brash ice on board in

rope slings and baskets and melting it. All the ice was fresh water. In two days they made more water than they had taken on at Cape Town. The wittiest account comes from an Irish gunner's mate called John Marra who concealed his journal from the enforced collection at the end of the voyage. 'I believe [this] is the first instance of drawing fresh water out of the ocean in hand baskets.' The reason is that when seawater freezes, the salts do not freeze with it, so freezing purifies water just as boiling does. By killing seals and birds, they could be self-sufficient in the south: vital if extensive voyages were to be conducted so far from known land. Cook was the first to prove this could be done.

His perseverance was rewarded when they pressed south once more and punched their way through the pack. At noon on 17 January, at around 40°E he wrote 'we were by observation four and a half miles south of [the Antarctic Circle] and are undoubtedly the first and only ship that ever crossed that line' – which must have raised eyebrows over on the *Adventure*. The next day thirty-eight icebergs could be seen from the masthead and later in the day at 67°15´S a wall of ice barred their path. He was blocked seventy-five miles from the continent.

There was still a Breton bubble to puncture. In good seas they cruised for a week with remarkable ease right across the land seen by Kerguelen the previous year. Charles Clerke relished it. 'If my friend Monsieur found any land, he's been confoundedly out in the latitudes and longitudes of it for we've searched the spot he represented it in and its environs too pretty narrowly and the devil of an inch of land is there.'

They headed east but on 8 February the two ships were separated in fog and forced to abandon searching for each other, and head for their agreed rendezvous in Queen Charlotte Sound, New Zealand. Captain Furneaux in the *Adventure* used the separation to head rapidly north and hightail it directly to New Zealand. Cook used it to push south once again, this time lacking a support vessel to come to his aid, but there are hints that Cook feels safer without Furneaux's assistance. On 10 February he was passing south through 50° of latitude when they saw many penguins in the water, raising hopes of land. A week later they were treated to shows of the *aurora australis*. Later in the month they suffered a gale which brought sleet and snow. It's the most miserable mix of all; few garments are warm when wet. The night had enough light for them to see huge icebergs all around and pray for daylight, but when it came they were even more scared as it spelled out just how dangerous their position was. One four times the size of the ship exploded into four pieces just as they were passing.

Forster Senior whined about the 'whole voyage being a series of hardships such as had never before been experienced by mortal man.' The rest reacted in the ambivalent way that typifies most first impressions of Antarctica: awe, fear and beauty.

Cook surveyed his men, and found their bodies and clothing were damaged and worn. Among the meagre livestock left on board the poor sow chose this time to farrow nine piglets. Despite efforts to help her care for them, all were dead by the end of the same afternoon. They sailed north to New Zealand, and found the *Adventure* had been and gone, but not before a shore party seeking water and greens had been killed by Maoris. Their cooked remains were later found in parts, in a basket. Not even this could prevent Cook being even-handed about the Maoris: 'Notwithstanding they are cannibals, they are naturally of a good disposition.' They stayed in warmer climes all winter but in the spring, on 25 November 1773, Cook turned the bow south again. On 12 December the first iceberg welcomed them back to the ice-realm. Soon ice jammed the blocks again and icicles an inch long were on each deckhand's nose. They crossed the Antarctic Circle a second time but were again soon blocked. On Christmas Day the crew stupefied themselves on hoarded brandy. Cook headed north east a while then turned back south on 11 January 1774, to make his third crossing of Antarctic Circle. They were desperate for land, willing it into view. Cook recorded that he 'saw an appearance of land to the east and south-east' and Wales: 'a remarkably strong appearance of land.' Next day Clerke soberly reassessed these hopes: 'We were convinced to our sorrow that our land was nothing more than a deception.' When the atmosphere lies in layers of differing densities it bends light back to earth showing images of land hundreds of miles away. At the end of the month they drove farther south than ever, reaching 71°10' S, 235 nautical miles beyond their previous best, though in this longitude, they were actually farther from the coast.

'We perceived the clouds over the horizon to the south to be of an unusual snow white brightness which we knew announced our approach to field ice. ... It was indeed my opinion as well as the opinion of most on board, that this ice extended quite to the Pole or perhaps joins to some land to which it has been fixed from the creation. As we drew near this ice some penguins were heard but none seen and but few other birds or any other living thing to induce us to think any land was near.' This may have been the poignant sound of penguins in water, where some species vocalise in a way they never do ashore, crying like a man lost.

He was 'now well satisfied no Continent was to be found in this ocean but what must lie so far to the south as to be wholly inaccessible for ice.' They headed for the warmth of Easter Island. Cook went down with a stomach illness. Perhaps it never left him, because his personality underwent a sea change, witnessed but not understood by all around him. The diary of one young officer, Trevenen, calls him a tyrant. They next headed west for Tierra del Fuego, reaching there just before Christmas, naming a dramatic double-turreted rock York Minster, after the great cathedral of Cook's native Yorkshire. The island they discovered on the 25th became Christmas Island. On Christmas Eve they shot six geese for Christmas dinner and Marine Bill Wedgeborough celebrated the birth of Christ with such fervour that he went forward at midnight to relieve himself and was never seen again.

They did some charting but it was half-hearted by Cook's standards, not even discerning that Cape Horn, whose whereabouts it was always nice to be sure of, was on an island. The men yearned to set course for home, but Cook turned south-east to explore the missing piece in the jigsaw of the Southern Ocean: the seas below and between Cape Horn and the Cape of Good Hope. This was the sector where Dalrymple, unknown to Cook at this point, had been publishing charts of the lands to be seen there. By 6 January they were sailing through the land Dalrymple had drawn around the mythical Gulf of St Sebastian. Cook sailed north to the place Dalrymple had argued was the peninsula marking the north-east limit of the gulf. This assignation had better provenance: a merchant, English despite his name, Antoine de la Roche, had seen land here in a storm exactly one hundred years before in 1675. Arriving at la Roche's co-ordinates he had taken, Cook found only fog. It cleared next day to reveal an iceberg, which in the mild latitude of 54°S suggested high and cold land was close by. It was first seen by Midshipman Willis, who was known for his heavy drinking, and possibly only on deck to relieve his bladder. The off-lying island he saw is named for him and soon there was more, a long run of coast, with high icy mountains towering into the clouds, separated by steep glaciers. Cook wrote: 'Not a tree or shrub was to be seen, no not even enough to make a toothpick. I landed in three different places and took possession of the country in his Majesty's name under a discharge of small arms.' They sailed down the dramatic north-east coast, Clerke discerning subtle variations in misery and desolation when comparing it to other God-forsaken places they had seen and concluding 'I think it exceeds in wretchedness both Tierra del Fuego and Staten Land (Island), which places till I saw this I thought might vie with any of the works of providence.' He didn't appreciate the 'sublime' nature of wild landscapes; that would become popular taste in the next century.

But as they went south-east and the shore continued, mile after mile, for a hundred miles, some of the men began to believe this was at last the ancient dream: *Terra Australis Incognita*. Then the coast began to turn; there were off-lying islands separated by reefs and rocky shoals which catch tabular icebergs blown north. The fjord now named Drygalski opened up, then a string of islands and rocks forced them further out and when they could come close again they saw the land running back north-west, the way they had come; it was an island. Cook named the southern tip Cape Disappointment, adding. 'I must confess the disappointment I now met with did not affect me much, for to judge of the bulk by the sample it would not be worth the discovery.' His sense of tact seemed to be wearing a little thin because he then named it after the King: South Georgia. It is still governed by Britain; it must be, there is a Post Office. Cook turned south-east and spent the first three days of February in conditions that appalled even his most experienced officers. The land they suddenly saw, when they could see at all, threw peaks straight from the sea some four thousand feet into the clouds. Cook was happy to declare it 'the most horrible coast in the world' then name it after his friend, the Lord of the Admiralty, the Earl of Sandwich. Unsure of whether they were looking at islands or a peninsula they called it Sandwich Land.

He declared:

I firmly believe that there is a tract of land near the Pole, which is the source of most of the ice which is spread over this vast Southern Ocean. The greater part of this Southern Continent (supposing there is one) must lie within the Polar Circle where the sea is so pestered with ice that the land there is inaccessible. The risk one runs in exploring a coast in these unknown and icy seas, is so very great, that I can be bold to say that no man will ever venture farther than I have done, and that the lands which may lie to the south will never be explored. Thick fogs, snowstorms, intense cold and every other thing that can render navigation dangerous one has to encounter, and these difficulties are greatly heightened by the inexpressibly horrid aspect of the country, a country doomed by nature never once to feel the warmth of the sun's rays, but to lie forever buried under everlasting snow and ice.

The natural harbours which may be on the coast are in a manner wholly filled up with frozen snow of a vast thickness, but if any should so far be open to admit a ship ... she runs a risk of being there forever.

Future travellers would read these words and feel an icicle enter their hearts.

Elizabeth Cook must have been delighted to have one of the most talked about men in the Navy back in her house, when he eventually got there after first visiting the Admiralty. She was also glad to be pregnant within two months, while he made plans to settle in London. He had nothing more to prove. After six months he was invited to a dinner with three of the most powerful men in the Admiralty to advise on the manning of an expedition to find the North West Passage by sailing across the Canadian Arctic to the spices and silks of the east. The prize equalled that for solving longitude, £20,000, much of which would go to the captain. By the end of the evening Cook had risen to his feet with his glass in hand and volunteered to lead it. It was probably just what their Lordships had intended would happen. What Elizabeth thought is another matter. In another six months he was gone. She would live to be ninety-one, but she would never see her James again. She would outlive all her children.

His orders were to take the latest cats, the *Resolution* and *Discovery*, to look for the land Kerguelen-Trémarec had claimed in the sub-Antarctic waters, then probe the west coast of North America, loosely claimed as New Albion by the British without actually having visited it. He was to press north into the Arctic through the Bering Straits, then retire to overwinter in Kamchatka, Siberia. In the spring he was to return to the high latitudes and look for the most promising passage to the east. One of his young sailing masters was a highly determined and skilful man called William Bligh.

The Antarctic element of his final expedition was modest. He checked the positions of Crozet and Marion Islands and found the French navigators had located them accurately. At the Kerguelen Islands, despite finding a bottle claiming them for France, they left a Union Jack and a counterclaim. The rest of the trip was spent carrying out orders in a slow and aimless way. It was not the Cook any of them knew. His temperament, once so sober and serious, began to be subject to violent fits of anger, bouts of indecision, and irrational attacks of urgency.

Ironically Cook's final discovery was Hawaii, where he was revered, arriving exactly how and when ancient myths predicted a God would, but when he was forced back to repair his ship he stepped outside the myth: the god did not return. He was clubbed to death in the surf, cut up and most of him eaten. Just a few remains were returned to a heartbroken Charles Clerke, already dying of tuberculosis at thirty-eight, for burial at sea.

In almost any other decade Cook would have met less ice and discovered Antarctica. He did so by inference; penguins, seals and icebergs all required land. Although he never saw Antarctica, he added much information about what it was not, and made it impossible for anyone of reason and judgement to believe that any large new land mass lay in the southern temperate zone. The area we know as Antarctica contains huge swathes of ocean he first sailed through, peppered with small islands as wild as the day he saw them. He concluded that there was nothing more to be gained by further exploration only because his vision of exploration was bound up with early ideas of empire: the utility of a place was all. He also failed to appreciate that another age would bring other young bloods eager to exceed their predecessors.

The boy who saw a silver world shining in a shilling piece set the gold standard. Yet he didn't discover the last continent. And if Cook didn't, who did? Navigators from all nations would follow like sharks behind a great ship, seeking glory. But their discoveries did not lead to conquest and empires, or to riches. The greater share of polar fame has gone to the heroic failures: Franklin, Scott and Shackleton.

Who discovered it in the first place? Who indeed.

# THE ANCIENT MARINER

Samuel Taylor Coleridge is often remembered for a cliché of poetic inspiration: he wrote *Kubla Khan* in an opium-inspired trance. It is a fine tale, but false. The inspiration for his epic poem *The Rime of the Ancient Mariner* is much stranger, and is completely true. The albatross of his tale was a real bird, shot in 1726 near Staten Island north-east of Cape Horn. However Coleridge did not begin intending the albatross would be a central motif and it was not even his own idea.

Poems are written for many reasons and his reason was money. He and his friends William and Dorothy Wordsworth were on holiday in the English West Country and finances were failing. On a walk along the coast near the small port of Watchet they hatched a project to publish a book of ballads, a form then bringing popular success to Robert Burns and Thomas Chatterton. Coleridge was turning over his mind a nightmare, dreamed by his friend and local bailiff John Cruickshank, of a spectre-ship that still sailed although all its planks were gone: a skeleton of a ship.

Wordsworth warmed to the idea. 'I suggested; for example, some crime was to be committed which should bring upon the Old Navigator, as Coleridge after delighted to call him, the spectral persecution. I had been reading Shelvocke's *Voyages*, a day or two before, that while doubling Cape Horn, they frequently saw albatrosses in that latitude. Suppose you represent him as having killed one of these birds on entering the South Sea, and that the tutelary spirits of these regions take it upon them to avenge the crime.' Coleridge seized the idea, and studied the original account. Shelvocke wrote 'we had not had the sight of one fish of any kind, since we were come to the Southward of the straits of *le Mair*, nor one sea-bird, except a disconsolate black *Albitross*, who accompanied us for several days, hovering about us as if he had lost himself, till Hatley, observing, in one of his melancholy fits, that this bird was always hovering near us, imagin'd from his colour, that it might be some evil omen... after some fruitless attempts, at length, shot the *Albitross*, not doubting (perhaps) that we should have a fair wind after it.' These words were reborn as:

> 'God save thee, ancient Mariner!
> From the fiends, that plague thee thus!-
> Why lookst thou so?' – 'with my cross-bow
> I shot the ALBATROSS.'

Behind this coming together of ideas another scarcely believable coincidence is hidden. Hatley's 'melancholy fits' had a cause. Some years before he had been sailing on a privateer called the *Cinque Ports* along the west coast of South America when they put in at the uninhabited offshore island group of Juan Fernández. The ship was in poor condition and the first mate, Alexander Selkirk, remonstrated with his young captain when he gave Selkirk orders to sail before repairs could be completed. Selkirk said the ship was unsafe and he would rather be left there, and he was. He survived four years and four months before being picked up by another privateer, Captain Woodes Rodgers. The *Cinque Ports* had sunk, but one of the survivors had been captured by the Spanish and worked for years as a slave in a silver mine. That man was Simon

Hatley. Selkirk was briefly a celebrity, but he was immortalised under another name by a writer who turned his adventure into a novel. The author was Daniel Defoe; the book was *Robinson Crusoe*. The otherwise unknown Hatley helped inspire two of the classics of his age.

The narrative of the *Rime* takes place in the cold south (Antarctica's discovery was still twenty-one years off) then the tropics, but nowhere is clearly recognisable. Coleridge didn't want it to be. The ship has no name nor does any character in it. There are no officers, no cargo and no ports. At the time he wrote the *Rime* the longest sea voyage Coleridge had made was to cross the River Severn near Bristol. The *Rime* is a spiritual journey; every section except the last ends with a direct or indirect reference to the Cross of the Sacrament. He employed two animal images, the killing of the albatross, for sin, and the blessing of the water snakes, for redemption. He used them to affirm that all life is part of one moral system.

# 2

# William Who?

## A Merchant Goes Astray

WILLIAM SMITH (1790–1847?)

*The captain of a small English merchantman sails far south of Cape Horn to avoid a storm and finds an unknown island on which a ghost ship has been wrecked, providing him with his coffin.*

You'd think discovering one of the seven continents would make you famous, although America preserves the name of the navigator Amerigo Vespucci, who definitely didn't discover it. Columbus long got the credit for discovering the Americas, despite two objections. Firstly Leif Erikson had already been there in the tenth century, and secondly Columbus spent the rest of his life denying it was a new continent; you can hardly discover what you deny.

The last continent to be discovered was Antarctica. Two hundred years ago – two human lives – no one knew it existed, although in summer it is the size of the USA and Mexico combined, and doubles in size in winter when the surrounding sea freezes. Surely its finder would become a historic figure on a par with Columbus. He didn't.

Odder still, the ancient Greeks named the continent long before it was discovered. They believed that the world must be in balance, so to counterpoise the vast earth, there must be an anti-earth, or *Antichthon*, moving unseen round the other side of the sun. As there were large temperate land masses in the north of the earth, there must be similar temperate continents in the south, beyond the broiling tropics. They called it the Unknown Southern Land, translated into Latin as *Terra Australis Incognita*. The southern land would be different, and must be separated from the world the Greeks knew by a strait of water, for these two worlds could not touch: like matter and anti-matter. Centuries rolled by; Europeans voyaged towards all points of the compass, but no one found a land that matched the ancients' ideas of a balmy southern continent. Yet belief never wavered; *Terra Australis Incognita* became a thirst for a southern world which the Americas, for all their riches and romance, did not slake. Every scrap of rock glimpsed through a gale became the tip of a peninsula reaching out from the southern paradise. In 1598 five Dutch ships sailed through the Strait of Magellan and one, under Dirck Gherritz, was first separated from the others by fog, and then driven south in a storm. Accounts said that at 64°S he had seen mountains covered in snow, looking very like Norway, which might have located him at the south end of the South Shetland Islands off the west coast of the Antarctic Peninsula. Until the nineteenth century he was given credit for sighting Antarctica. But his own writings made no such claim; only when they were translated in 1622 was that passage added.

In 1811, forty years after Captain James Cook concluded there was a frozen southern continent, a consortium of five businessmen was gathering funds to build a 216-ton brig. One of them was a young man called William Smith, born on 11 October 1790 in the coastal village of Seaton Sluice, Northumberland. In the baptismal register his name is sandwiched between those of babies born to pitmen, glass-workers, farmers and sailors. He grew up three miles farther north in the coal port of Blythe, where, judging from the standard of his letters, he received a competent education. Aged twenty-one he was the master and owner of the *Three Friends*. Williams had also worked in the Greenland whale fishery and was a confident ice-pilot: a specialist job. The brig was finished the next year, and since two of the other principal three shareholders were also called Williams, they imaginatively christened it the *Williams*. Within three years they were early players in the new trade with South America. Another four years on, she was in Buenos Aires with her twenty-two-man crew preparing to make a voyage which usually took around six weeks, sailing west round Cape Horn to Valparaiso in Chile. Chile was one of the new republics rising from the ruins of the Spanish Empire, declaring independence in 1818. Britain actively assisted the fledgling republics. It wasn't high-principled support for personal freedom which spurred Britain on; at this time no British woman had the vote, and only those men who owned property. It was eagerness to open up new markets for its trade goods, displacing Spain, its trading and colonial rival. Britain provided vital naval support under the brilliant maverick, Lord Cochrane. The busy man in Valparaiso charged with protecting British interests in Chile during this turmoil was Captain Shirreff of HMS *Andromache*.

However, Spain's New World empire had propped up her antique economy and European ambitions for three hundred years; she would not surrender South America without a fight. One of King Ferdinand VII's responses was to send out more troops from Spain in a squadron of four ships including the powerful seventy-four-gun warship *San Telmo* under Captain Joaquín Toledo. The squadron encountered terrible storms off Cape Horn and was driven far south of their usual sailing routes. Dismasted and rudderless, the *San Telmo* was towed until she began to imperil the towing vessel, and she was cut loose on 4 September 1819 at 62°S. The *San Telmo's* 644 men, coffined in the helpless hulk, drifted south.

Into the hold of the *Williams* went the usual miscellany of trade goods, including nine cases of pianos, five cases of hats, and one of eau-de-cologne, tobacco, medicine and cloth. There was also a consignment that typified how British manufacturing created dependent markets round the world. Samples of hand-woven ponchos had been taken back to England and replicated on northern steam looms for a fraction of the cost. Gauchos would now buy their ponchos from Yorkshire. Although it was still the southern summer, Captain William Smith met strong contrary winds south of Cape Horn and decided to head further south and take a calculated risk of encountering ice, whose dangers he was familiar with, rather than be at the mercy of a storm over which he had no control. He was not an explorer, adventurer or a geographer, he was a businessman reducing his risks.

What happened next is poorly documented. There is no surviving original document, just partial copies and contemporary reports referring to papers now lost. On

19 February, he found himself in a south west gale stiffened with sleet and snow. Coming up to daybreak at 06:00, where the charts showed open ocean, he saw land. He recorded in his log, 'Land or Ice was discovered ahead bearing SE by S distant about two leagues, blowing hard gales with flying showers of snow.' He logged his position as 62°15′S and 60°01′W. In the afternoon the weather improved: '4pm tacked ship, the land or islands bearing SEbE to ESE about 10 miles, the weather fine and pleasant, when discovered to be land a little covered with snow.' The skies soon told Smith the foul weather was ready to return; at 18:00 with whales and seals all around, he resumed his course to Valparaiso.

Smith anchored beneath the city's steep hills, only to find the British representative Captain Shirreff was in Santiago, so Smith spoke to the most senior officer, Captain Thomas Searle, of the forty-two-gun warship *Hyperion*. Searle was so startled at the news he forbade them to go ashore where grog would loosen sailors' tongues. When Shirreff returned, he quizzed Smith. Had he landed, explored any length of shore? – or at least taken soundings to prove it was real land, and not ice, or one of the many islands seen once at a distance and never again? (A century before, Jonathan Swift had lampooned such fugitive sightings when he invented the flying island of Laputa in *Gulliver's Travels*.) Williams had done none of these things. It wasn't that Shirreff didn't believe him, but in Chile he had many tasks of clear and pressing importance to British interests. He required solid evidence before pursuing other ends. Smith said he would sail a similar course on the way back, but when he got to the same area on 16 May, the weather was poor; winter had begun. The encircling ice began to rip off the expensive copper plating which protected the vessel against shipworms. He left without re-sighting land.

But Smith knew what he had seen. With his next cargo, in October, he swept south again and at 18:00 on the 15th, he reached the position where he had logged land, and saw it again. This time he was determined to prove his case. He was probably looking at King George Island, and he followed the land eastward and named features. On 17 October, at a place now called Venus Bay on Ridley Island, also known as Ridley's Island, 'Finding the weather favourable, we lowered down the boat, and succeeded in landing; found it barren and covered in snow; seals in abundance. The boat having returned, and been secured, we made sail.' That laconic, business-like record was the last time anyone could record finding a continent. He claimed it for Great Britain, and named it New South Britain. They turned and went 150 miles WSW along the coast of an island chain, and when they finally decided to turn north, still more land was in view. He was later persuaded that since the Scottish Shetland Islands occupied an equivalent latitude in the north, he should re-christen the group the South Shetlands. Smith invested a lot of time in this diversion. This trip took an extra six weeks, so he planned to come back and take seals, to recoup his investment. He also recorded that sperm whales, the most valuable whales of all, were abundant. There were no great words or thoughts on landing, as Antarctica was at last discovered; he had no way of realising the significance. On 18 October he wrote, 'I thought it prudent, having a merchant's cargo on board, and perhaps deviating from insurance, to haul off to the westward on my intended voyage.' He wasn't going to be an uninsured driver.

Alexander von Humboldt sarcastically observed that there were three phases in the popular attitude to a man who makes a great discovery. Firstly men doubt its existence, next they deny its importance, finally they give the credit to someone else. Smith suffered all these. Some British journalists were not convinced Smith's reports were genuine. *The Edinburgh Magazine* mocked: 'At first we treated it as an Irish or American report, both of which are generally famous for not being true.' Then, as soon as word of Smith's discovery spread, American newspapers proclaimed that these islands had already been discovered by US sealers. Baltimore's *Niles Weekly Register* for 23 November 1822 read: 'It is now well-known that some of these hardy people had visited what is regarded by the English as newly discovered land as early as 1800.' There was no written evidence but that, they said, was not surprising since sealers were secretive about their movements: knowledge was money. In which case why were the beaches still swarming with seals after twenty years' sealing? Rookeries were wiped out in two seasons. Tellingly, records of sealers in the period 1812–19 show that no vessel came home with catches exceeding expectations from known rookeries, but when the sealers followed Smith to the Peninsula, catches soared, and the Antarctic fur seal was all but exterminated by 1822.

The partially informed sharpened their quills and recycled old lies. The prestigious *Edinburgh Philosophical Journal* carried a report of Williams's discovery illustrated with a chart showing a southern continental mass labelled *Terra Australis Incognita* lying between 54-58°S and 40-53°W. They claimed this was the previously reported land mass which William Smith had merely re-discovered. This despite the fact that Captain Cook had sailed through that area and seen only ocean and ice. The chart was an old fraud, based on a Mercator map of 1569, copied in turn from a small world map of Oronce Finé drawn in 1531. But if there was money to be made, any pretext might do to claim prior discovery. What was really needed was an official voyage to formally take possession and claim it for their sponsor's country. Britain, handily established in Chile, was first off the mark. One factor which helped Shirreff make a case for diverting effort south was that Britain had no convenient base from which to help exploit the emerging trade markets in South America. The Falklands had been abandoned in 1774 and would not be effectively occupied again until 1833. Their nearest colonies were South Africa and Australia, too remote to help.

Smith's landing secured Shirreff's ear. Shirreff was only thirty-four but he had been in the Navy since he was eleven years old. He wanted to help and he could spare some men from the *Andromache*, but the vessels themselves were committed. The *Williams* had been chartered to an entrepreneur called John Miers to ship heavy technical equipment from Valparaiso to Concón. But Miers was also a man with strong scientific interests; he would later become a Fellow of both the Linnaean Society and the Royal Society, and bequeath over twenty thousand specimens to the British Museum. He kindly agreed to shelve his plans and let Shirreff charter the *Williams* to investigate the South Shetlands.

Command of the vessel was given to Captain Edward Bransfield, born in Cork, Ireland in 1785. He had been pressed into service when only eight years old. Now the word was out, it would be a race to go south and take the initiative in exploring the new territories. That summer, fifty British and American vessels followed the *Williams's* wake, over the toughest seas in the world, to see what money a man might make there. Shirreff's orders to Bransfield looked for a longer commitment. They read:

> You will ascertain the natural resources for supporting a Colony and Maintaining a population, or if it be already inhabited, will minutely observe the Character, habits, dresses, customs and state of civilisation of the Inhabitants, to whom you will display every friendly disposition.

It seems quaint to imagine native Antarcticans waiting to exchange diplomatic niceties, but at this time William Parry and John Ross were voyaging high above the Arctic Circle and meeting native peoples surviving in far harsher climates than Smith had reported. Might they not meet the southern equivalent? What's more, *The Literary Gazette* had reported William Smith as saying of the South Shetlands that 'firs and pines were observable in many places.' It continued: 'The climate of New Shetland would seem to be very temperate, considering its latitude; and should the expedition now sent out bring assurances that the land is capable of supporting population, – an assumption which the presence of trees renders very probable, the place may become a colony of considerable importance.' *The Literary Gazette* had exaggerated a line in William's log of an observation he made in thickening weather as he prepared to leave: 'could perceive some trees on the land the southward of the cape.' He was deceived. Antarctica's largest plant is a few inches high.

Captain Edward Bransfield, with William Smith and forty-three others on board, sailed from Valparaiso in late December and sighted Livingston Island in the South Shetlands on 16 January 1820. They made their way north-east along the northerly coasts of the large islands of the group, then round to the south side of King George Island, where Bransfield landed in what is now King George's Bay, after George III of England. It is one of the nice perks of being a monarch that you sit snugly on your throne while others suffer the discomforts of finding places to name after you.

These islands are a relatively warm part of Antarctica, their climate softened by the surrounding ocean; during their voyage, the lowest temperature recorded was −1°C. Because of this, and the ease and economy of servicing a base there, it is now the home of many Antarctic stations including those of nations with subterranean profiles in the annals of Polar history, such as Papua New Guinea. However it isn't hot, and many of the seamen transferred from the *Andromache* in Valparaiso had settled down to life in a Mediterranean climate and sold off all their warm clothes. They now suffered miserably from exposure.

Although they had taken ninety days' water, leaking barrels made them anxious to replenish stocks. From 22 to 27 January they anchored off a small island dominated by an extinct volcano and named it after the main inhabitants, Penguin Island, before beating them aside to go ashore. It is a short climb up from the beach, through soft ash and cinders, to the main crater, within which lies a smaller cone. There was still breath to spare for more words of possession and a volley of small arms. From the 170-metre-high summit, there is a breathtaking view across the narrow channel guarded on the far side by Turret Point on King

George Island, a cluster of three stacks linked to the land by a wishbone of shingle beaches. They crossed over and soon found a more convenient spring, and encountered elephant seals on the beach. They decided to kill some to make oil. At that time of year elephant seals, which weigh up to four tons, are moulting, which is uncomfortable and puts them in a bad mood. Although they are not agile on land, they are powerful and deceptively flexible. One sailor approached a seal from behind, but was caught flat-footed when it swivelled round and savaged his hand in its immensely strong jaws. The officers contented themselves with safer work: collecting mosses and stones for study.

They landed again the next day and killed twenty-one elephant seals in thirty minutes, startled at the quantity of blood which came from the carcases. Other wildlife didn't wait to be approached. Skuas are brown birds built like a heavy gull. Although they have webbed feet they act more like birds of prey, and are aggressive and skilled hunters. I have watched two knock down a large man by co-ordinated swoops on his head. When sailors came ashore with a dog, the skuas of King George Island were faced with two new species at once, and, true to form, decided to attack both. The dog was soon covered in blood, and the sailors had to fetch staves to defend themselves.

Unknown to them, on 27 January, as they left Penguin Island and cruised down the South Shetlands, King George III was released from his final madness by death. The news did not reach Valparaiso until May that year. So they continued south, and named and claimed new bleaknesses on his behalf. They passed Livingston Island again, a fiercely beautiful island of jagged peaks and ridges skirted with swooping snow slopes: 'every atom was covered with snow.' The talk on deck 'was the idea of having, by the direction the land took, found what might possibly lead to the discovery of the long-contested existence of a Southern Continent.'

We know about such chatter because of the survival of one original document from this trip: the journal of Midshipman Charles Wittit Poynter. He was baptised in 1798, the son of an East Indiaman Captain, and joined the Royal Navy in 1811 serving on HMS *Inconstant*. It was more common to name vessels after virtues rather than vices. It conjures up images of a whole fleet of disreputable ships and men: all the drunken sailors gathered on HMS *Inebriate*, enjoying adultery on HMS *Inconstant*, before retiring to HMS *Incontinent*. Poynter's journal comprises seventy pages of handwritten ink entries bound in red calf leather with marbled boards. We have few descriptions from the first two summers around the peninsula; making money from taking animals was uppermost in most minds. But there was a strong emotional reaction to these landscapes, and it is consistent in its nature: awe at beauty forged in desolation. Robert Fildes, shipwrecked in the sealer *Cora* in 1821, was forced to live ashore for a while, he and his men sleeping in barrels inside a tent. The ship's cat moved into an empty barrel and was promptly joined by two penguins, living together amicably. Fildes initially tried to be amusing about the landscapes, writing, 'Madam Nature had been drinking too much gin when she made this place.' But he soon became serious: it possessed 'an awfully grand though terrific and desolate appearance.' By the time he reached the shores of volcanic ash at gloomy cloud-capped Deception Island, he was seduced: 'the mind is forced into pious contemplation of the grandeur of the scene.' Just over sixty years before, the philosopher Edmund Burke had written *A Philosophical Enquiry into the Origin of Our Ideas of the Sublime and Beautiful*. Burke suggested, 'The sublime is the supreme, strongest emotion, [and] can be excited by terrible, painful and dangerous things. ... When danger or pain press too nearly, they are incapable of giving any delight, and are simply terrible; but at certain distances, and with certain modifications, they may be so capable.' This perfectly fitted these new Antarctic landscapes which, in the same moment, could be both breathtaking in their beauty and terrifying in their hostility.

They met no Antarcticans. It has never been inhabited by humans. On the stony shores of Desolation Island, where once I landed in bone-biting cold at dusk, with snow darkening the sky, a human skull was found next to a primitive stone hut. Simple stone and bone tools were found. Initial excitement cooled when they were studied carefully. The remains date to the early nineteenth century, and the artefacts are all from known cultures in Tierra del Fuego. The hut is a sealer's hut, and the skull was that of a woman around twenty-one years old. She was probably one of the Patagonian natives whom sealers were known to take on board for company and, doubtless, sex.

On 30 January, Bransfield and Williams saw what we now know is the continental land of the Antarctic Peninsula, though they had no way of knowing it. It looked no different from the islands. They named the strait between the South Shetlands and the new land after Bransfield. They thought it might be a gulf; it is now the Bransfield Strait. Penetrating to more than 63°S, they named some of this Trinity Land, after the maritime organisation Trinity House, which manages navigation in

British waters. Smith would soon need them. They went on, writing names on the whiteness of the land and the maps, sketching the coast. A map annotated with remarks from the log summarises the experience: 'supposed land', then 'lost in fog' and 'here the coast was lined with icebergs.' After reaching the limit of the land and naming it Hope Island (for the hope that the eastern shore they could not see extended away into continental land) the farewell was once again: 'lost in fog.' They reached Elephant Island where Shackleton would stagger ashore after his escape from the crushing of the *Endurance* in the Weddell Sea ice. They found a driftwood log and speculated where this old tree had once taken root and sent tender buds into the spring air. They took fur seals and found them tough to kill. As soon as the seabirds smelled blood, they swooped down and attacked both men and seals. Union Flags were scattered over the rocks and squirrelled away in protecting caves, then the first prospective colonisers returned to Chile. Winter returned to Antarctica, freezing all ambition. William Smith made a hazily documented fifth voyage in 1821. It was probably on this voyage that Smith suffered an eerie *memento mori*. Standing off in Blythe Bay, Desolation Island he saw ships' timbers on Half Moon Beach. Landing, he found spars, and sails tangled like winding sheets, all from the galleon *San Telmo*, the Spanish vessel abandoned in the Drake Passage. It had made a stubborn path south through the tempests, before the Furies riding the Antarctic winds broke it apart, and the sea and rocks had prised open its carcase like monstrous skuas. There were no bodies, so it is likely that it was broken up at sea, and the debris dispersed. Smith brooded over the ship's remains in melancholy mood. He found the anchor, a symbol of hope, its wooden stock hooped with iron and bolted with copper. Some inner demon made him order its removal, to be made into a coffin. He said he would be buried in the anchor that had waited for him in the cold rocks at the end of the world. Financially he was badly stretched, having lent his brother money for an unsuccessful project to build a steam vessel in Bristol, ironically called the *Hope*. But there was profit to be taken; Smith said the seals were so thick on the ground they looked as if they had been stowed in bulk. He returned to Britain on 17 September 1821 with thirty thousand fur seal skins. On the market they were worth £7,500, a rich return for him and his three partners. But while he was away, they had gone broke. The skins were seized by debtors and sold off cheaply, leaving him bankrupt.

Smith wrote a letter to the Admiralty, received on New Year's Eve 1821, begging a reward for the discovery, and claiming for Britain, of new territories. They offered him nothing. He continued to press the Admiralty for reward for sixteen more years. They continued to refuse. He was forced to sell the *Williams* on 13 June 1822, to a consortium in London's East End. The proceeds bought him release from bankruptcy two weeks later. For the next twenty years he would live in the same area, first at 3 Commercial Place in Whitechapel. His neighbours were tradesmen and the lower middle classes. None of them had discovered a continent. He worked in humble maritime jobs: from 8 June 1824 he was licensed as a Trinity House pilot on the Thames. The licence describes him as living in 54 Lucas Street off Commercial Road, and being five feet eight inches tall, with black hair and a dark complexion. He subsequently met James Weddell who was a partner in the Leith whaling firm of Messrs Wood, and secured him work as a master on the *William and Ann* whaling in the Davis Strait off west Greenland. In his first year he caught a respectable twenty-five whales. But every year his catches were lower, each one less than the season's average. In 1830 he returned 'clean': no whales caught; the following season the *William and Ann* had a new skipper. In 1837 he resided at 44 Jamaica Street, in the heart of Whitechapel. Next year he applied for one of the two Trinity House almshouses, pitiably not realising he was a year too young to qualify. A small courtyard of those almshouses still stands behind locked wrought gates on the Whitechapel Road, whispering of old dignities, beneath a weathercock in the form of a small brig. Next year his licence was withdrawn because he was 'a pilot greatly reduced by age and infirmity' though he was only forty-eight years old. He was pensioned off by Trinity House in 1839, but could not fully support himself financially. He petitioned the Admiralty again for a reward for his discovery of Antarctica. There is an extant letter asking for a statement from Captain Shirreff describing Smith's services in the discovery, but no record of further correspondence survives, and the following year he was admitted to the charity of the almshouses. His date of death is not known, but his will was proved in 1847, to the value of £100, about £6,000 in modern money. There wasn't much for the British Columbus to dispose of. His real bequest was Antarctica. In the *Dictionary of National Biography* there are twenty-three Williams Smith but not the man who discovered Antarctica.

## THE NAMING OF NAMES

Naming is powerful; it asserts control. Stories like Rumpelstiltskin and Turandot have at their core the power of knowing a name. Explorers often ask the locals the names of places. If they share no common language, confusion results, sometimes comic, occasionally poignant, memorials to the failure of two peoples to understand one another. Near Cape Horn is Tekenika Bay, *Teke unika* being the Indians' response when asked what it was called. The words mean 'I don't understand.'

Uniquely, Antarctica was huge and uninhabited when discovered. It was a blank to be written on: no locals to help. Antarctic place names reflect western values. If naming is power, the powerful want a share. Kings, princes, politicians, naval officials and sponsors of all kinds go nowhere and watch the world being inscribed with their names. South Georgia and King George Island still commemorate King George III of England. The Chilean name for the Peninsula, Tierra San Martín, commemorates the founder of their state, and their Antarctic bases González Videla and Frei record the names of the two presidents to have visited the continent. The Peninsula is also Grahamland, named in 1832 for Sir James Graham, First Lord of the Admiralty. Americans name part of the Peninsula Palmer Land after Nathaniel Palmer who did at least explore for himself. Money can buy immortality on a map. The world's largest glacier, Beardmore, is named for one of Shackleton's backers. The first man to overwinter below the Antarctic Circle, Adrien de Gerlache, remembered the generosity of sponsors in the beautiful (Paul) Errera Channel which threads its way between the

Peninsula and (Madame) Rongé Island. Luck also matters. Two sponsors of Shackleton, Messrs Stancomb-Wills and Dudley Docker, had the ship's boats named after them converted into huts and are remembered only by polar historians. The third boat, named after jute millionaire Sir James Caird, was sailed to South Georgia and into history; his name endures. The greatest price paid for a name is death. De Gerlache's seaman Carl Wiencke was washed overboard in the Gerlache Strait, and is now recalled in picturesque Wiencke Island. From the same expedition we have Danco Island, named after the geophysicist who tasted seal meat just once before announcing he would rather die than eat more. Soon the late Mr Danco had his memorial. And, of course, people name things after family, wives, sweethearts and each other. Adélie Land, like the Adélie penguin, is named for the wife of Dumont D'Urville, who, as well as charting parts of Antarctica, purchased for France a statue of Venus, patron of sweethearts everywhere.

# 3

## The Admiral
## and the Boy Captain:
### Thaddeus Bellingshausen (1778–1852)
### and Nathaniel Palmer (1799–1877)

*A teenage captain creeping across uncharted water in dense fog hears his small bell answered by two greater ones. He meets the leader of a Russian expedition. One of them has just seen the continental mainland of Antarctica for the first time, but which one?*

Poor Bellingshausen. He achieved success without fame, suffered toil without recognition. Even his name is a mouthful that needs rehearsing before you can remember it. He was one of two captains involved in the most famous sea encounter in Antarctic history: the polar equivalent of Livingston and Stanley. But in later life, the other man, embellishing yarns in his well-heeled retirement, got his name entirely wrong, in print.

Russia's defeat of Napoleon before the gates of Moscow in 1812 inspired her to view the world with the confidence of a great power. Her empire stretched from the borders of Europe, across all Asia, continuing so far east it crossed the International Date Line into the Americas and became the west again; modern Alaska was then Russian. But the east

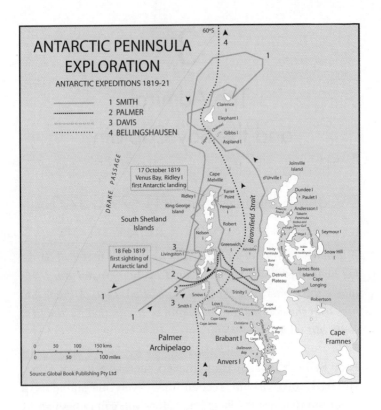

ANTARCTIC PENINSULA
EXPLORATION

ANTARCTIC EXPEDITIONS 1819-21

1 SMITH
2 PALMER
3 DAVIS
4 BELLINGSHAUSEN

60°S

DRAKE PASSAGE

17 October 1819
Venus Bay, Ridley I
first Antarctic landing

South Shetland
Islands

18 Feb 1819
first sighting of
Antarctic land

Palmer
Archipelago

Clarence
Elephant I
Gibbs I
Aspland I

Cape
Melville

Ridley I

King George
Island

Nelson

Greenwich
I

Livingston I

Snow I

Smith I

Low I

Cape Garry

Cape James

Turret
Point

Penguin
I

Robert
I

Astrolabe

Tower I

Trinity I

Houseson

Christiana
Is

Brabant I

Large I

Dallmann
Bay

Anvers I

Joinville
Island

d'Urville I

Bransfield Strait

Trinity
Peninsula

Bone
Bay

Detroit
Plateau

Cape
Herschel

Hughes
Bay

Dundee I
Paulet I

Andersson
I

Antarctic
Island
Tabarin
Peninsula
Erebus and
Terror Gulf

Seymour I

Mt Haddington

Snow Hill
I

James Ross
Island
Cape
Longing

Larsen Inlet

Robertson

Cape
Framnes

Source: Global Book Publishing Pty Ltd

0    50    100   150 kms
0         50        100 miles

was so remote it might as well have been on the moon.
Land transport was little farther advanced than at the dawn
of history. The only effective way to move bulk goods was
by water. Russia's coastline was huge, but practically every
mile of it was ice-locked from autumn to spring or even
summer. This changed just when Bellingshausen was born,
on a small island off modern Estonia, in 1799. Russia had
just won control of the mouths of three mighty rivers, the
Bug, Dnieper and Don, which flowed into the Black Sea
and gave Russia a gateway to the world. From there,
through the Hellespont, lay the Mediterranean, then the

Atlantic. But it was a world in which Russia had no chain of possessions 'establishing future permanent sea communications or places for the repair of ships', as the brief for a new circumnavigation of the world put it. They would look for such havens in the Southern Ocean. Their first choice for commanding officer didn't work out. Second choice was Fabian Gottlieb von Bellingshausen, usually known by his Latinised name: Thaddeus Bellingshausen. Despite receiving just six weeks' notice of departure, he sailed on time.

Bellingshausen had gone to sea aged ten as a cadet, and from 1803–06 had been a humble Fifth Officer under Admiral Krusenstern on Russia's first circumnavigation of the world. Krusenstern had served in the British Navy from 1793–97; this wasn't unusual. Russia knew it was not rich in maritime experience and had a policy of placing its officers in other navies and appointing foreign officers to its own ships. The second practice, putting foreigners in charge of the military, was not as reckless as it sounds, as a Russian captain was not the absolute ruler he was in other navies. Major decisions were referred to a cabinet of the senior officers on board in which native Russians were always in the majority.

At this time the government was still forcing the eastern governors to build wooden ships from local timber and fit them with anchors made in pieces in the west, and rope cut into fifty-foot lengths, then carried four thousand miles overland on carts, barges and sledges. The work employed four thousand horses. When Bellingshausen returned to Russia, he lobbied for vessels to be sailed round to the east and stationed in the north-west Pacific, independent of the overland transport. The problem with going away and broadening your mind is that your masters stay at home. His petitions fell on deaf ears until a new Czar, Alexander I, came to the throne, and one of Alexander's projects was opening up the east.

Bellingshausen's mentor Krusenstern idolised James Cook. Krusenstern copied the Englishman's obsessions with the sciences of navigation and charting, and his manias for accuracy and cleanliness. In his two ships, the *Nadezhda* and *Neva*, not one man died: an astonishing record for a vessel passing through every kind of climate, sea and tempest. Bellingshausen learned the same disciplines from Krusenstern. His devotion did not induce any special warmth from his mentor at the end of three years' work. In fact Krusenstern's account of the trip seldom raises itself above the narrative thrill of a laundry list. But he did manage to stir his pen for a sentence on Bellingshausen: 'His reputation as a skilful and well-informed officer in the different branches of navigation ... I found to be perfectly just.'

While Bellingshausen was being damned with faint praise, a seven-year-old boy called Nathaniel Palmer was playing in his father's shipyard at Stonington, Connecticut, 110 miles up the coast from New York City. When he was thirteen, learning to sail ships, the US was at war with Britain. To make life difficult for foreign mariners unfamiliar with the waters, all lighthouses were decommissioned and the buoys marking the channels were lifted. For six years he traded in unmarked waters, running the British blockade of the ports as a smuggler or a free-trader, depending on your passport. By nineteen, he was a captain. Like Drake and Cook, he had learned the skills of coastal sailing in diverse waters: invaluable when exploring.

Stonington was in the heart of whaling country, but Palmer's town prospered on sealing, killing fur seals for their skins and elephant seals for oil, rendered down from the fat layer beneath the skin to a product that was as fine as good whale oil. These ships typically paid no wages; crew members received a share of profits according to their rank on board. Sealing was as good an example of a ruinous free-market as you could devise. The seals came ashore each year to pup and mate on the rocky shores of islands so remote that no government actively governed them: it was a free-for-all. Any animals you leave to breed will not be there next year, they will be in someone else's warehouse. They killed the females then the males, often blinding the beachmasters in one eye so they would continue to force half of their harem of females to stay onshore, while the men on its blind side killed the rest with a blow to the head from a hickory club. They didn't bother killing the pups; the skins were too small. They just starved to death without mother's milk.

Sealskin is very warm, with an extremely dense layer of short, fine fur. This is protected by longer, tougher guard hairs that take the rough and tumble of rocks, stone beaches. Every visible hair covers up to forty under-hairs; there are 330,000 hairs per square inch. Americans and Europeans didn't know how to take off the guard hairs without damaging the fine fur. The Chinese did. In the 1780s the ship the *States* had gone sealing in the Falklands and brought back 13,000 skins which a New York dealer bought for 50¢ each. He took them to China where they were a high fashion object, especially in the north, with its bitter winters. They sold in Canton for $5 each, making a profit of $58,500 for a single voyage. In 1792 the *Eliza* of

New York took 38,000 skins to Canton. The voyage was long enough for the least numerate crew member to multiply $4.50 by 38,000 and get the answer: riches. When they got there they found the market was flooded; a skin sold for 50¢. It must have been a long trip home. In 1796 the London furrier Thomas Chapman invented a process for removing the guard hairs and the lure of sealing turned to lust. The trick is to shave the back of the skin close. The coarse guard hairs have deeper roots which are severed by this process, and can then be combed out.

The *Eliza's* failure didn't stop the New Englanders trying. In a voyage from 1797 to 1799, the *Betsey* went first to the Falklands, and then on to Más-a-Fuera in the Juan Fernández Islands, five hundred miles west of Valparaiso, Chile. On this rocky island, just a few miles across, they killed 100,000 seals. The *Betsey* sailed for Canton leaving men ashore to continue killing until they returned. The sealer Captain Amaso Delano guessed that three million seals were taken from this tiny island group in seven years. With the profits from the skins and the Chinese goods later sold in New York, the *Betsey*, a one hundred-ton ship which had cost only $3000 to build, made $52,300 profit. One trip could make a man. An ordinary deckhand's share bought him a 40% stake in a similar vessel. A bad trip would disgorge him onto a wooden pier in Connecticut, chill with the morning dew, after two years' hard, dangerous work, without a cent in his pocket, watching a wife's joyful smile collapse into a a bent pin of desperation. But he was alive to try again.

An early portrait of Nathaniel Palmer shows a confident-looking man who you would be pleased to share a beer with in a quayside bar. He was a man who would try again.

Returning to old sealing grounds didn't pay much. Sealers had to be prepared to take ever greater risks and sail further from safely charted waters. One neighbour of Palmer was Edmund Fanning, a sealer, and author of *Voyages Round the World*. When Palmer was a baby, Fanning took 57,000 fur seal skins to Canton. He was also a man who liked to spend time with dog-eared charts and ancient deep-water tales. One was the account of Dirck Gherritz in 1599. Driven far south of Cape Horn, he saw islands which he christened the Auroras. Or at least the part of the account added without his knowledge by a translator twenty-three years later said he did. Fanning didn't know about the fraud, but bad information can lead you to good things, like Columbus looking for China and discovering the Caribbean. Fanning eliminated from his search the sea areas reliable navigators had sailed through, and looked at the gaps. He concluded the Auroras were real, and lay in a window bounded by 60°-65°S and 50°-60°W, which, by chance, boxes off the tip of the Antarctic Peninsula and the more northerly of the South Shetland Islands. When sealing failed in 1817, for the unsurprising reason that they had killed all the ones they knew of, eyes turned south, and Palmer went with them.

Bellingshausen adopted his mentor's spare journal style; there is little fun in reading him, though he lacks the literary anaesthesia that makes Krusenstern so numbingly dull. He was only interested in learning as much formal science as could help navigation, but considering this, his speculations during the voyage on scientific matters were rich in sound insights. The log shows he was a disciplinarian, and lash-happy. Portraits show a man you wouldn't joke with unless you were extremely sure how the remark would be received.

His fellow commander Lt. Mikhail Lazarev was much more social and a more popular officer.

The ships were not ideal; they seldom are in Polar work. They were what was available and fit to sail. The *Vostok*, meaning East, was a frigate 129 feet long crewed by 117 officers and men. The *Mirnyi* (Peace) was a sloop under Lt. Lazarev crewed by seventy-three officers and men. The smaller, *Mirnyi*, was ice reinforced unlike her companion ship, but was so slow that *Vostok* had to sail the whole voyage under reduced sail.

Expeditions under military command usually receive standard pay for unusually demanding and dangerous exceptional work. Some private expeditions offered no pay at all: just experience and adventure. This one was different. All officers and crew received eight times their regular pay plus a year's extra pay. Their orders included studying the colour, stature and constitution of any inhabitants of new regions, plus details of their 'inner anatomy should it be possible to obtain bodies for dissection.' Natives resisting this unwanted contact often became museum specimens.

Pickled cabbage, a traditional food in Russia and Germany, would be good protection against scurvy. Other health measures went down even better; spruce essence and molasses were taken to make anti-scorbutic beer. 'As beer is the healthiest drink at sea, it would seem beneficial to give it frequently to the men.' If only all employers were as enlightened.

Bellingshausen's brief of 'establishing future permanent sea communications or places for the repair of ships' seems impossibly loose to build a voyage plan around it. In fact, the tropical and temperate latitudes and most navigable

Arctic seas were well explored and useful discoveries were unlikely. The real opportunities lay in the open spaces of the southern oceans. He would plan a course to complement Cook's, focusing on those coasts and seas which were not seen by him because of bad ice or weather, or simply because even Cook could not sail every mile of this vast space.

They sailed from Kronstad, near St Petersburg, on 16 July 1819. Only one civilian scientist was taken: the astronomer Simanov. They anchored off Portsmouth while officers went to London to buy charts, instruments and favourite and luxury foods. Bellingshausen wrote, as if from experience, 'there are more prostitutes in England than anywhere else, particularly in the chief ports.' As they entered the Atlantic, the surgeon examined the crew and to the officers' surprise found the crew free of sexual disease. At the equator, Bellingshausen was reminded just how parochial the Russian navy was; he was the only person on either ship who had previously crossed the Line. The ceremonies were civilised by the standards of the English navy which left men half-drowned, covered in tar and filth, and pole-axed by drink. The Russian officers were merely sprinkled with water; it was more like a decorous Mass in honour of Neptune. More seriously, only he, Zavodovski and Lazarev knew how to take astronomical observations. The rest now trained under severe eyes.

Bellingshausen's real work began on 27 December 1819 when they sighted Willis Island, off the north-west tip of South Georgia. Cook had charted the north-east shore but left for home after seeing just enough of the south-west coast to prove it was an island. Bellingshausen kept to port the stone pyramids of Willis Island, Bird Island and their guard islets, skirted with spume thrown up by the grey South Atlantic. They met elephant sealers, dropped in a cove to live under their boat from spring to autumn, killing and boiling down fat and flesh in crude iron cauldrons. One was a Russian Navy sailor who had jumped ship in England. If he had known Bellingshausen's reputation for flogging he might have remained ashore, but Bellingshausen let sleeping dogs lie. The men spent a short time on board remembering there was a world outside South Georgia, where cold had respite, and killing was not the only pastime. With gifts of grog, sugar and butter, they climbed down the rope ladder and cut away into the spray and back towards the loveless shore.

They went south to examine Cook's South Sandwich Land, where atrocious seas and weather had worn down even that Yorkshireman's resolve before he could establish with certainty what he was looking at. Naming it Sandwich Land, not Islands, was an act of faith and flattery to his sponsor, Lord Sandwich. Bellingshausen found more land than Cook had described, and made the first landings, including, on 5 January 1820, one on Zavodovski Island, named for Lt. Commander Ivan Zavodovski. If you remember David Attenborough, in one of the opening scenes of *Life in the Freezer*, standing amid volcanic fumes and one million chinstrap penguins braying like asses, that's Zavodovski Island. The Russians climbed halfway up the volcano until fumes of sulphur and hot guano drove them down. The place names say it all: Acrid Point, Stench Point, Fume Point, Reek Point, Pungent Point and Noxious Bluff. If the murk clears, you may glimpse its highest point, at 1805 feet: Mt Asphyxia. They stayed until 5 January labouring under weather much the same as Cook had suffered. By then he had proved South Sandwich Land was the South Sandwich Islands. They took live penguins back on board, where, despite being surrounded by an ocean full of fish, they fed the birds on pork. They all died. They pressed on south, passing the Antarctic Circle for the first time on 15 January.

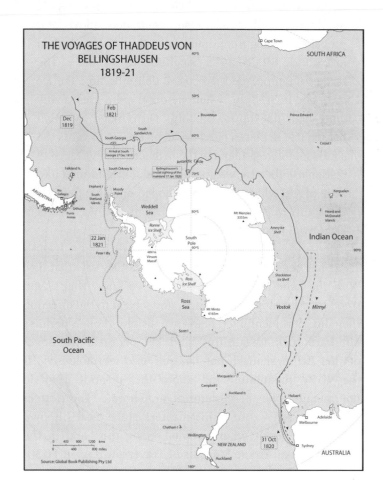

THE VOYAGES OF THADDEUS VON BELLINGSHAUSEN 1819-21

On 17 January 1820 Lazarev on the *Mirnyi* wrote of an 'ice shore of extreme height'. Bellingshausen recorded:

> At 6:00am the broken ice had become so dense and thick that the attempt to continue farther to the southward at this point was impossible. A mile and a half from there we could see blocks of ice piled on top of the other. In the farther distance we saw ice-covered mountains similar to those mentioned above and probably forming a continuation of them. We were then in Latitude 69°06´24"S Longitude 15°51´45"E. The farther we proceeded, the more dense became the ice until about 3:15pm, when we observed a great many large high flat-topped icebergs surrounded by small broken ice, in places piled up high. The ice towards the south-south-west adjoined the high icebergs which were stationary. Its edge was perpendicular and formed into little coves, whilst the surface sloped upwards towards the south to a distance so far that its end was out of sight even from the masthead.

There has been endless debate over what they saw that day. With the benefit of modern charts, we know that if you stood on their ships' mastheads, and looked in the direction they did, continental ice-fields are visible, though perhaps not bare rock to confirm land lay beneath. Moreover neither Bellingshausen nor Lazarev used words loosely. If they write 'mountains' and 'shore' they mean it. They do not mean 'like a mountain or shore'. The letters Bellingshausen wrote to his masters make clear his own convictions about what he was seeing then and in the following days. To the Marquis of Traversey, 8 April 1820:

'After midnight between February 5 and 6 we reached latitude 68°07´S and longitude 16°15´E. There, behind small ice floes and islands, the continent of ice was seen. It had edges broken perpendicularly and stretched beyond the limit of our vision, sloping up towards the south like a shore.' In the official journal for the Minister of the Navy for 24 January: 'I designate as continental the huge ice which, on approaching the South Pole, rises into sloping mountains, as I believe that when it is four degrees of frost on the best summer day, then further to the south the frost does not, of course, become any milder, and therefore I can conclude that the ice spreads over the Pole and must be immovable, touching the ground or islands in some places.' On 17 February he observed 'ice islands near that continent show clearly that pieces are broken off this continent, because they have edges and surfaces similar to the continent.' They then probed where Cook had achieved his farthest south, not to compete with the master, but to compare ice conditions in different years. They were halted sixteen miles short of his position.

A healthy diet kept both crews fit, but it was now thirteen weeks since they had left the warmth of Rio de Janeiro. That time had been spent almost entirely in cold and exposed waters. Bellingshausen had fostered good spirits by observing all the many Russian feast days, although in the cold, the officers might not always have appreciated being required to observe the holidays in formal dress uniform. They now sailed east, keeping south of 60° until the first week in March when, with the temperature at −13°C, the commander decided he had endured enough of 'dark, harsh climes: it seems as if men's hearts grow cold in sympathy with the surrounding objects, men become gloomy, depressed, harsh and to a certain extent indifferent to everything.' The two vessels separated, *Mirnyi* sailing a more northerly course, though it was still 150 miles south of Furneaux's timid route in the *Adventure* after he and Cook separated. The Russians tied up in Sydney at the end of March after 131 days at sea. All the livestock and two sailors were suffering from scurvy. He received a dispatch from the Russian ambassador in Rio describing William Smith's discovery of the South Shetlands. The news flew round the port. When they sailed, on 31 October, local sealers were just a few days behind their wake. The Russians made a bad start. The *Vostok* sprang a bad bow leak but they laboured on to Macquarie Island where one of the forty sealers they found had been living for six years. They were killing elephant seals; the fur seals had already been exterminated. Leaving there on 2 December, they sighted no land for the next two months. On 22 January 1821 they began to see terns and skuas when 250 miles further south than any previously sighted land. When land appeared, the first ever seen south of the Antarctic Circle, even Bellingshausen managed to let himself go a little: 'Words cannot describe the delight.' They named it after the Czar: Peter I Island. Their feet were itching to go ashore but the ice had other ideas, keeping them fourteen miles off. It was not landed on until whalers from the *Norvegia* made it ashore in 1929. Now the Russians were eager to follow up the news of Smith's South Shetlands. As soon as they arrived and anchored there, they had the strangest encounter. But first, we need to back-track a little.

The *Hersilia* was a new brig under Captain James A. Sheffield; Nat Palmer was second mate. In warmer climes, seal skins were cured for storage simply by drying them out. Where the *Hersilia* was heading, they doubted there would be enough fine weather for that, so they sailed via the Cape Verde islands off the tip of West Africa and took on six hundred pounds of salt: enough for ten thousand skins. They next called at the Falklands, then lawless and ungoverned, to obtain water, greens, and fresh meat from wildfowl and the abandoned cattle which thrived in huge numbers. Palmer and one sailor were dropped ashore to do this, while the *Hersilia* cruised the off-lying islands looking for seals. Another brig appeared on the horizon, and it headed for shore. It was the *Espirito Santo* out of Buenos Aires, with British owners and crew. The lack of clear written records of these early sealing voyages is often put down to sealers being secretive in the extreme, to protect their biggest trade secret: where the seals were. In fact knowledge was shared by word of mouth, but they did not need to justify their every action to the owners in writing so little down; the test of a successful voyage was skins, not good paperwork. They also felt a comradeship with all seafarers, and confided good anchorages, safe harbours and supplies of fresh water and food. Palmer and his shipmate helped the new crew re-provision from the land and probed for intelligence on the *Espirito Santo's* voyage. All they would confide was that they were provisioned for only a short voyage, and were following up reports of new islands sighted by William Smith. The English sailed first, Palmer watched them to the horizon, noting their course. All his life he was credited with excellent long-distance vision. But were they sailing a blind, knowing he would watch? He had three days to remember that course before the *Hersilia* returned. Captain Sheffield decided they would follow.

Four days later they saw land: the South Shetland Islands. The received a typical reception: two days in the lee of an island, cowering from vile weather. When it calmed enough to show their heads above deck they made for a harbour fleetingly glimpsed before the storm. Palmer claimed, and it seems rather too pat, that they found the *Espirito Santo* at anchor there. When the captain finished salting his own skins he guided Palmer to the rookeries, and the butchery began again. Antarctica has virtually no harbours where a ship can moor safely against the land. So the men were dropped ashore from whaleboats, slim wooden craft about twenty-five feet long and five feet wide, and lived on the exposed, narrow beaches, made huts from timber and canvas, and ate seal meat and more seal meat. As long as it is not overcooked, it has enough vitamin C to stave off scurvy. The heart and liver cooked up as haslet was said to be like pork haslet. Particularly if you hadn't had pork in a while. One man could kill and skin about fifty animals a day, rounding them up the beach and striking them on the head with the tip of the hickory clubs, sheathed in iron to stop them shattering on the rocks when a blow missed. It was then heavy work to scrape the blubber off the skin with a heavy beaming knife. Despite having six hundred tons of salt, they could see they would run out of it before they ran out of seals. They first tried to kill the non-breeding males, whose large fine skins fetched the highest prices. That season they sold in Stonington for $2 each, an 800% return on investment. Young Nat probably got the share of 1 skin in 35: a bonus of about $560.

Next year Stonington sent more ships. The roustabouts of New York, New Haven, Boston, Nantucket and Salem geared up for the plunder. The Stonington men even built a new ship specially. They agreed it would be useful to have a smaller, manoeuvrable vessel to fetch and carry once they were back in the South Shetlands, and to go off, lightly crewed, looking for new rookeries. For that work, they took a sloop, the *Hero*, fifty feet long and forty tons, with a shallow draught for the unchartered seas. First she had to sail across the worst stretch of water in the world: the Drake Passage. The *Hero's* log is a budget book bought from Samuel A. Burtus at his Book Store and Lottery Office on the corner of Water Street, in the south-east corner of Manhattan. A cover of old sail canvas and sail twine binds a few hundred sheets of soft writing paper. In it Palmer, skipper of the little sloop, would write history. The log begins: 'Commences with fair weather with breeze from WSW.' His writing is small, ornamented and clear; his spelling is usually sound. The two vessels left for the South Shetlands on 5 November. By the 9th they sighted Smith Island, at the south-west end of the Archipelago, and anchored in President's Harbour. The rest of the Stonington fleet was there, under the leadership of Captain Benjamin Pendleton. The area had rocks and the rocks had seals, but the 'harbour' was nothing more than space between two islands. Above them, usually hidden by cloud, Smith Island rose to 6,900 feet, the highest point in all the South Shetlands. This is an exposed area; I have landed fewer than half the times I have tried, rebuffed by surf crashing on steep shingle beaches. Their light wooden whale-boats whipped in, men jumped over the bows into the numbing waters, straining to hold the boat against the outward drag of the receding waves, then turning to stop the next roller throwing her up the beach and stranding or smashing her. The other men hurled gear beyond the waves' reach, scrambling to land everything quickly before the boat was stove. The second it was done, the boat was pushed out, the last man jumping up, weighed down with freezing water, throwing himself over the gunwale, his mates grabbing his shoulders and arms, hauling him unceremoniously into the bilges, laughing with relief when it was safely done. The shore party dragged everything to the top of the beach and turned a few pieces of lumber and old sail canvas into a hut: their home for months to come. Each evening was the same: arms, shoulders and back exhausted from the labour, the mind a little coarser from the killing, despite the gallows humour they used to escape the moment. Three oars would be crossed in a tripod, and a cast-iron pot hung over a fire. They savoured hot tea and coffee sweetened with molasses, full bellies, stinging mugs of grog. Never enough sleep.

Killing was done by rounding up a segment of the herd, and driving them up beach to stop the main herd becoming alarmed. They did this slowly, not out of kindness, but so as not to damage the fur. Then they clubbed them; seal skulls are not especially strong. The danger to the men came from charging males. I have been charged on a rough beach by a 250-pound male fuelled by a riot of hormones, moving faster than I could run. Knowing that they usually stop if I stand my ground lends me courage. But I would prefer something more certain than *usually*. At the last minute I take a step forward, raise my arms to look tall, and make some kind of loud grunt. By this time, grunting comes easily. If it doesn't stop, the seal will mow me down, and when I roll face down to protect my face and other favourite organs, pick me up by the buttocks with its long yellow teeth, and throw me in the air. The bite is filthy, and, before antibiotics, always became infected. Even if your immune system saw you through, you would eat standing up for weeks.

The work went on, boats returned through the surf to take the skins on board for salting. The fleet's commander Captain Pendleton thought the seals at President Harbour would not provide sufficient for the whole fleet. Nat Palmer was sent to look for new rookeries. The *Hero* now earned its keep. He departed at 14:00 on 15 November 1820. The story is famous. He headed south and west, and soon saw an island that, oddly, had less snow on it than its neighbours. He made his way along its eastern shore which was straight as a ruler but too rugged to land. At the southern end was the massive bluff of Bailey Head and beneath it a beach which, even today, in tough inflatable powerboats, is a trophy landing. I've managed it once, and even then, the surf was wild enough to make an able seaman miss his leap into the last departing boat and go swimming. The afternoon of 15 November 1820 was not a fine day. Snow was blowing up into a storm. Palmer felt his way down the coast and, at 20:00, finding no shelter, he stood off to ride out the night. At five next morning he continued to where the cliffs had a bite out of them, before they reared up again in gigantic cliffs teeming with pintado (painted) petrels with irregular white flecks over the wings looking like paint spills. In mid-morning, a slot-like gap opened in the coast and he turned to starboard, rust-red rocks to his left. Instead of ending in a gully where one or perhaps two small ships might take precarious shelter, he found he had sailed into one of the world's great natural harbours, up to five miles across. It is shaped like a horseshoe that has been bent until almost wholly closed, giving protection from bad weather, whatever point of the compass it comes from. He named the entrance Neptune's Bellows, and the island whose shape had fooled him Deception Island. In thick weather he went ashore and climbed the south-facing crags to the bite in the cliffs, and named it Neptune's Window. Mobbed by petrels, he collected eggs and trained his superb eyes on the south and the east. On the horizon he saw land. Soon he would sail there and find land which proved to be the Antarctic mainland. He christened the anchorage Port William. It was soon well-used by American sealers and a nickname, Yankee Harbour, stuck. To avoid confusion with another anchorage of the same name, it is now Whalers Bay.

It's a story I have told many times. My research for this book showed me it isn't true. His own log confirms it. Firstly he wrote that he was leaving President Harbour for Deception Island, which you can't write unless Deception had already been discovered and named. Palmer's biographer John Spears says the island had been named on 'the previous voyage' without explaining clearly what he means. The answer lies in the fourth voyage of William Smith. Under Captain Bransfield they landed at King George Island, claiming it for that monarch, and headed further south on 27 January 1820. Two days later worsening weather forced them to stand off south from the land they had in view, and they passed a group of small islands then a larger one. In that location it could only be Deception. Smith and Bransfield were there ten months before.

Secondly, Palmer's log suggests that in contrary winds he gave up trying to reach Deception. The log consists of spare notes with few place-names, many nautical terms and abbreviations and little useful punctuation; quoting it would not help clarify the point. But Edouard Stackpole in a paper entitled *The American Sealers and the Discovery of the Continent of Antarctica*, reads the log as taking him east to Livingston, to the bay that Weddell would later name Palmer's Bay (not its modern name, but lying immediately west of Livingston's most southerly limb: Barnard Point) and claims that subsequent log entries make much better sense if you read him as starting from there.

Wherever he was, Palmer's landing is also a suspect legend. Edmund Fanning's book says: 'From Captain Pendleton's report, as rendered on their return, it appeared that while the fleet lay at anchor in Yankee Harbor, Deception Island, during the season of 1820 and 21, being on the lookout from an elevated station, on the mountain of the island during a very clear day, he [that is Pendleton] had discovered mountains (one a volcano in operation) in the south; this was what is now known by the name of Palmer's Land.'

What did he see? I have climbed those cliffs two dozen times. If he climbed right to the top of Cathedral Crags, above the Bellows, he could see farther than me, because access to the very top is now prohibited to protect nesting birds. On two occasions I have seen a low snow hill far out to the south-east, scarcely distinguishable from an iceberg. Checking my compass bearing against the ship's charts, it was the nearest peninsula on the mainland, some thirty miles off: Cape Roquemaurel. It is possible he saw the mainland, though if he was on the south shore of Livingston, the distance was still farther. Palmer's own papers were later lost in a house fire, so unless luck throws more information our way, the evidence will remain ambiguous.

Nat reported back to the fleet in President Harbour. His news was timely; he found that the *Frederick* had dragged her anchors in the inadequate shelter of that anchorage and nearly been wrecked. Five vessels now relocated to the haven of Whalers Bay, Deception. They had leisure to realise that the reason there was less snow, and that the springs along the beach were hot, was that they were anchored inside a volcano. They dug pits in the black volcanic sand and luxuriated in the hot water, washing clothes and bodies caked with blood and fat. It is a caldera, a volcano that had collapsed after a fierce eruption, allowing the sea to come in, as he had, through the Bellows, and fill the crater. For the rest of the season, the larger vessels acted like factory ships, staying in shelter and salting the skins brought back by the *Hero*, which acted as a tender between the shore parties and Whalers Bay. Palmer found time to scout around Livingston Island, a short distance to the north-east. It is the most beautiful of the South Shetland Islands. Its high mountains rise in swooping ridges that are both wild and elegant. It is as though tents had been overtaken by a blizzard and fossilised in rock and ice. It was after sailing past Livingston that sealer Robert Fildes wrote, 'the mind is forced into pious contemplation of the grandeur of the scene.' Sailing alone into a narrow strait, Palmer grounded on a hidden rock, but managed to ease her off without damage. He then saw a whale swimming slowly ahead, declared 'Where a whale can go, I can go!' and followed it safely through to discover more rookeries. They now knew the whereabouts of sufficient seals to fill all the ships. It was late November, and the seals were arriving in ever greater numbers. On 26 November he picked up 465 skins from the shore-men. The log then falls strangely silent until 3 December when he records 905 skins ferried to Deception. On 7 December the log records ten thousand skins picked up, so many that he and his crew did not finish unloading at Deception until midnight. Then he weighed anchor and sailed back to President Harbour. Two vessels which had been working Livingston Island sailed into Deception with skins and grim news: their companion ship the *Clothier* had been driven ashore and although the men were saved, the ship was wrecked. The busiest period of all now followed, but Palmer still has time for one-line log entries. Then there are more silent days. What could have been happening, what kept him too busy to write a single line?

The sealers wrapped up the season taking elephant seals for oil, which they rendered in Whalers Bay. The *Hero* took it home, departing 22 February 1821, having ferried 50,598 skins to Whalers Bay. A quarter of a million skins were taken by all sealers in the 1820–21 season. The average return of all sealers was 8,333 skins per vessel but the Stonington fleet did best, averaging 11,000 per vessel. They also harvested fifteen hundred barrels of elephant seal oil at $10 a barrel. When they left Antarctica, they probably thought that the loss of one vessel was a cost they could afford to carry, but the full price had not yet been paid. Captain Sheffield in the *Hersilia* left their company to go fur-sealing at St Mary's Island off Chile, where he took fifteen thousand skins. He and his vessel were then seized by Spanish. All the hard-won skins were confiscated.

There is still the question of Palmer's missing days. The answer lies in the journal of another Stonington sealer, Edward Fanning. He wasn't on the voyage, but in later life he recorded Palmer's memories of those missing days. He might have forgotten a Russian name, but facts slip when feelings and impressions remain green, even in old age.

Palmer had sailed towards whatever he had seen to the south and east from the heights of Deception. He recollected, 'I pointed the bow of the little craft to south'ard and with her wings spread, the mainsail abeam, and the jib abreast on the opposite bow. She speeded on her way like a thing of life and light. With her flowing sheet she seemed to enter into the spirit which possessed my ambition, and flew along, until she brought into the sight of land not laid down on my chart.' Fanning wrote: 'To examine this newly discovered land, Captain N. B. Palmer, in the sloop *Hero*, a vessel but little rising forty tons, was despatched; he found it to be an extensive mountainous country, more sterile and dismal if possible, and more heavily loaded with ice and snow, than the South Shetlands; there were sea leopards on its shore, but no fur seals; the main part of its coast was ice-bound, although it was in the midsummer of this hemisphere, and a landing consequently difficult.' He reached land around what is now Mount Hope, and turned south. The leopard seals were of no interest; they are mostly solitary animals fortunate to have neither desirable fur nor thick blubber.

The *Hero* bumped her way to 68°S before the pack ice became impenetrable, and he turned the helm back north. Few modern cruise ships make it that far south in this area. As he passed Mount Hope once more, fog came. He lowered a line; it was too deep to anchor. He kept the minimum sail needed to manoeuvre and crept forward, fearful of sailing onto a reef or into ice. The wind softened away. They drifted. Such times have a special solace. When I work in Antarctica there are times when I stand by in a small boat until needed. It might be five minutes or an hour. I turn off the engine. If it's calm, there is a peaceful solitude I feel at such times which I ever never known anywhere else. In moments, the ship has ceased to be there. No time passes, there is just now. Just me and the universe, above, around and below me. Antarctica blows its crystals into your mind.

As night fell, a light breeze sprang up. Bow ripples and the gentle creak of cord and canvas replaced the faint dripping from ropes and spars. At midnight Nat relieved the Mate, Phineas Wilcox. At 00:30 he gave bell a single tap. He heard a second bell answer from off the bow. While he was still telling himself he was alone in the world and there could be no answering bell, he heard a third. Palmer said: 'The response startled me, but I soon resumed my pace, turned my thoughts inward, and applied myself to making castles in the air.' At one he struck two bells and heard two more answers. 'I could not believe my ears. Save for the screeching of the penguins, the albatrosses, the pigeons and Mother Cary chickens, I was sure no living object was within leagues of the sloop.'

Many of the crew thought the bell supernatural. At 03:30 Wilcox came on deck saying he had heard human speech. The voices were unfamiliar, speaking a strange language. Soon the fog lifted a little. It was only twenty-three years since the publication of *The Rime of the Ancient Mariner*. What spectre-barks had come to them in the night? Parts of the mist became darker and took shape. A frigate was seen off the starboard bow, and a war sloop off the port quarter, and ship's cutter coming towards them bearing a man in full uniform. Palmer hoisted the Stars and Stripes. The ships raised the Russian flag. The officer spoke good English. 'Capt Bellingshausen requests your company on the *Vostok*.' It was a strange embassy. The Russians wore naval uniform, Palmer a home-made sealskin coat and boots with a sou'wester. Bellingshausen's English was minimal. Palmer offered to guide him round the South Shetlands. He freely told them where they were sealing, and about his foray south past over 150 miles of coast, and sent the cutter back to fetch the *Hero's* chart and log. It wouldn't have helped the Russians much. Palmer was a businessman not an explorer, and because he had found no fur seals, he had not charted his route or the coast in any detail. A chart on which he soon after collaborated with the English sealer George Powell showed the known segments of what we now know is the Antarctic Peninsula. Powell's memoir on the chart shows he thought the Peninsula was like the South Shetlands: an archipelago but with the channels between blocked by ice.

American accounts stress Bellingshausen's admiration for the young adventurer whose little ship lay in the shadow of his frigate. In them the Russian mocks his own hopes of discovering and naming the neighbouring islands of the South Shetlands, as Palmer, this Yankee boy wonder, has come down in his cockleshell and done it all. Fanning wrote: 'His astonishment was yet more increased, when Captain Palmer informed him of the existence of an immense extent of land to the south, whose mountains might be seen from the masthead when the fog should clear away entirely.' Fanning claims Bellingshausen immediately named it Palmer Land. This is fiction. Firstly, flowery words were not Bellingshausen's style, especially on a cold foggy morning when discussing navigation in a language he knew poorly. Fanning's eulogy also forgets that Bellingshausen had come to the spot because he had already heard at Sydney that Smith had discovered islands in the area. He had no expectation of being the first.

Bellingshausen's account of the meeting is matter-of-fact. Well, dull would be more honest. Its focus is not a magical encounter in the fog (he doesn't mention there being any fog) but in the feverish activity of the sealers who had rushed south like gold prospectors. He was prescient about the short-sightedness of the massacre.

At 10 o'clock we entered the strait and encountered a small American sealing boat. I lay to, despatched a boat, and waited for the Captain of the American boat. Soon after Mr Palmer arrived in our boat and informed us that he had been here for four months sealing in partnership with three American ships. They were engaged in killing and skinning seals whose numbers were perceptibly diminishing. There were as many as eighteen vessels about at various points, and not infrequently differences arose among the sealers, but so far it had not yet come to a fight. Mr Palmer told me that the above mentioned Captain Smith, the discoverer of New Shetland, was on the brig *Williams*, that he had succeeded in killing as many as 60,000, whilst the whole fleet had killed 80,000. As other sealers were competing in the destruction of the seals there could be no doubt that round the South Shetland Islands just as at South Georgia and Macquarie Islands the number of these sea animals will rapidly decrease. Sea elephants, of which there had also been many, had already moved from these shores further out to sea.

More practically, it wasn't a place to linger. 'The anchorage was thin sand, and two British ships and one American one had dragged their anchors and been wrecked.'

71

Bellingshausen then rouses himself for some striking lines to encapsulate the momentous meeting of these two genuinely great men and put his finger on the emotional impulse of the moment. He wrote: 'Mr Palmer soon returned to his ship, and we proceeded along the shore.'

They sailed along the islands, charting. On 10 February they left the north shore of Elephant Island, with neighbouring Clarence, the most northerly islands in the chain, lashed by a blizzard. It is a wild shore facing thousands of miles of empty ocean, and a marvellous last sight of Antarctica. One dusk I jammed myself into corners of the deck trying to get enough shelter from the Force 12 katabatic winds screaming off the island's ice-cap to photograph the savage beauty of the scene, while the wind kept tearing the camera from my face. They headed for balmy Rio de Janeiro, reaching it on 11 March. The home port of Kronstadt was finally regained on 5 August 1821 after 751 days and 57,073 miles. Just three men had been lost, a record Cook couldn't have bettered. In his absence, Russian politics had moved on; land ambitions had overtaken marine. His brilliant voyage was forgotten; recognition has been little and late. It took ten years fighting bureaucratic obstruction to publish, and there was no English version of his voyage until 1945. There was no official visit to Antarctica by Russia or the Soviet Union until 1946. Bellingshausen remained in the Navy, was appointed Admiral in 1831, and became Governor of Kronstadt, where he died in 1852.

The year after the meeting in the fog, despite the warning signs that all the easy sealing had been done, Stonington geared up a sizeable fleet, giving Palmer a larger sloop than before; the *James Monroe*. Once in Antarctica, Palmer was again despatched south to scout. Once more, he reached 68°S before the pack ice barred his way. Next, in the company of the English sealer the *Dove*, Capt George Powell, he went farther north looking for new rookeries. North and east from the tip of the Antarctic Peninsula, they found barren islands lying around 60°S and between 044° and 047° W, and named them after Powell. Soon they were re-named the South Orkneys, because they lay in the equivalent latitude to the northern Orkneys.

Already, the big seal catches were just a memory. All told, the entire fleet took just fifteen hundred skins. The *Hero* was sold at Coquimbo, Chile, and its cargo was brought back by the *Alabama Packet*. Palmer never claimed he had seen continental land, but as the map of the Peninsula was filled in, it looked less and less like an archipelago.

The newly trained navigating officers of the *Vostok* and *Mirnyi* were zealous in the huge quantity and fine quality of their observations. The charts made of the South Shetlands set new standards for Antarctic surveying in this area. Right until the 1930s, the coastal sketches of South Georgia made by Paul Mikhailov were still used in the Admiralty's *The Antarctic Pilot*, the international handbook for sailing those waters.

A portrait of Nathaniel Palmer as an old man shows another face: a patriarch whose opinions are law. Even allowing for the immobile expression demanded by long photographic exposures, the jaw juts sullenly, and the mouth bends down in a grim bow. He seems to have repeated too often the dictum of the skippers who went south down and past the roaring forties, and begun to believe it: 'Up there you obey your captain and God

Almighty. Down here I am God Almighty!' He had helped Simon Bolívar in his wars of liberation against the Spanish, and escaped a firing squad by giving the officer in charge a Masonic handshake, and finding a fellow member. He led the packet trade to Europe and the Clipper trade to China, designing ships with slimmer hulls which flew through the sea. He loaded the *Samuel Russell* until the deck was only a foot above water; she then sailed from New York to San Francisco and beat the record. He rebuilt the biggest all-wooden ship ever made: the *Great Republic* of 4555 tons after she burnt out in Liverpool docks in 1853, but he never believed in iron ships. He stood up a hull plate on the dockside, fired a musket ball through it, and said, 'They'll never work.' He died on Midsummer's Day 1877. Iron ships took over the world.

# 4

## Charted in Blood:

James Weddell (1787–1834)

and Other Sealers

### JAMES WEDDELL'S VOYAGE OF 1822–24

*Seduced by Antarctica, Weddell puts business aside, passes
James Cook's farthest south, and finds an open sea. Ancients
were right: you can sail to the South Pole.*

James Weddell's no-nonsense approach is epitomised by his
writing. After the customary meandering title, *A Voyage
to the South Pole Performed in the Years 1822 – 24*, he
describes everything about the aims and resources of the
voyage in two sentences. 'Our adventure was for procuring
Fur-seal skins, and our vessels were the brig *Jane*, of Leith,
of 160 tons, and the cutter *Beaufoy*, of London, of 65 tons,
both fitted out in the ordinary way and provisioned for two
years. The former, with a crew of twenty-two officers and
men, was under my command; the latter, with a crew of
thirteen, was commanded by Mr Matthew Brisbane.'

His plan was to head for the South Orkneys, and if the
sealing was not good 'to prosecute a search beyond the
tracks of former navigators.' He could now sail through the

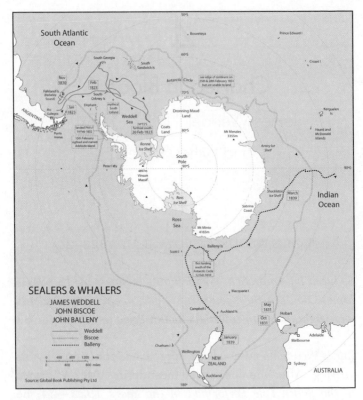

Map labels:

South Atlantic Ocean

South Georgia
South Sandwich Is
Bouvetøya
Prince Edward I
Crozet I
60°S
50°S
Antarctic Circle
70°S
Kerguelen Is
Nov 1830
Feb 1823
Falkland Is (Falklands) Sounds
Jan 1823
Elephant I
mythical South Iceland
ARGENTINA
Rio Gallegos
Punta Arenas
Landed Pitt's I 19 Feb 1832
15th February sighted and named Adelaide Island
Weddell Sea
74°15'S Furthest south 20 Feb 1823
Coats Land
Dronning Maud Land
see edge of continent on 25th & 28th February 1831 but are unable to land
Heard and McDonald Islands
80°S
Mt Menzies 3355m
Peter I Øy
Ronne Ice Shelf
South Pole 90°S
Amery Ice Shelf
4897m Vinson Massif
Ross Ice Shelf
Shackleton Ice Shelf
March 1839
Indian Ocean
90°E
Sabrina Coast
Ross Sea
Mt Minto 4165m
Scott I
Balleny Is
first landing south of the Antarctic Circle 12 Feb 1839
Macquarie I

SEALERS & WHALERS
JAMES WEDDELL
JOHN BISCOE
JOHN BALLENY
——— Weddell
········· Biscoe
·········· Balleny

0  400  800  1200 kms
0    400    800 miles
Source: Global Book Publishing Pty Ltd

Campbell I
Auckland Is
May 1831
Oct 1831
Hobart
Adelaide
Melbourne
Chatham I
Wellington
NEW ZEALAND
January 1839
Sydney
Auckland
AUSTRALIA
180°

area between South Georgia and the Falklands without fear
of wrecking himself on the Aurora Islands. They had been
recorded by the Spanish since 1762 when their ship *Aurora*
not only sighted them but sailed between them. For sixty
years everyone sailed carefully around them without seeing
them. In 1820, on his first voyage in the area, Weddell had
surveyed their supposed position in fine weather and
proved they did not exist. He then spent two months
navigating in the channels around Cape Horn. Everyone
who rounded the Horn did so as far out at sea as possible,
and next to nothing was known about the geography, or the

safe harbours and anchorages. He provided his own rough surveys and urged further work. It became the project that brought Robert Fitzroy and the *Beagle* here with a young graduate called Charles Darwin.

At daylight on 12 January 1823 they were in sight of the South Orkneys, and hoping to gain harbour. But the wind dropped and left them wallowing in a heavy swell surrounded by icebergs 'which made our navigation truly hazardous.' Weddell had briefly been to the islands the year before, heading home with a hold full of seal skins. They kept the ships out in the bay of Saddle Island, which lies off the centre of the north coast of Laurie Island, and sent in a boat from each vessel. He surveyed the sweep of the mountains that rise straight from the stark shoreline. 'This coast is,' he thought, 'if possible, more terrific' [terrifying] 'in appearance than South Shetland. The tops of the mountains, for the most part, terminate in craggy towering peaks, and look not unlike the mountains of a sunken land.'

After going ashore and having a fright when fog hid the ships from view, Weddell ordered his second mate ashore to take leopard seals. He 'captured' six, or as we usually say, shot them. Back in Edinburgh, they were the first leopard seals to be scientifically described. Weddell's own painting of them, inscribed 'drawn from nature' is carefully done, and does have the trademark ferocious teeth and unholy reptilian smile, but otherwise it is quite inaccurate. The tiny head at the end of a stretched neck makes it look more like a fossil plesiosaur than a seal.

He did not find fur seals in any numbers, so he continued as planned, 'beyond the tracks of former navigators' going south-south-east. At noon on 27 January they reached nearly 65°S. He was already south of the latitude of the South Shetland Islands, but on the other side of the Peninsula. The weather and ice conditions were good, but he saw the nights beginning to lengthen, and their darkness deepen: not the time for ice navigation in unknown waters. He decided to retreat north and explore east 'considering it probable that land might be found between the South Orkneys and Sandwich Land.' They immediately had a scare. At eleven o'clock that night a dark object appeared in the tricksy light of dusk, two ship-lengths away. It looked like rock. They stopped the ships, threw over the lead sounding line and found no bottom. As they cautiously edged closer, 'the chief mate ascertained it to be a dead whale very much swollen'; by such incidents are lands invented.

Alone in a sea of ice, winter darkness creeping north each day, they looked for Sandwich Land, not knowing Bellingshausen had already proved it to be islands, because the Russian had not published his findings. Weddell knew what motivated ordinary sailors: 'I had offered a gratuity of £10 to the man who should first discover land. This proved the cause of many a sore disappointment; for many of the seamen, of lively and sanguine imaginations, were never at a loss for an island.' All of them evaporated on approach. Showing his courage at sailing into the unknown, and generous to his precursors, Weddell 'carefully avoided the tracks of Captains Cook and Furneaux; and I may remark how narrowly Captain Furneaux in the *Adventure*, in December 1773 and January 1774, escaped seeing South Shetland and the South Orkneys. He passed within 45 miles of the east end of Shetland and 75 miles of South Orkneys.' But by 4 February they were back so close to Cook's course that Weddell was convinced no land connected Sandwich 'Land' to any southern continent: they were islands. But he 'conceived it probable that a large tract might be found a little farther south than we had been.'

Fogs and gales kept the decks soaked and the men suffered from colds and rheumatism. Weddell moved the ship's cooking stove near to their quarters and had fires lit to dry clothes. Added to the three glasses of rum per day, this removed, or at least took their mind off, the discomforts. At daylight on 10 February land was called, not by bonus-hungry seamen, but the first officer. Weddell came on deck and agreed. Here, at last, was the goal of mariners through the ages: the southern continent. By afternoon they could see it was just ice embedded with dirt. Weddell speculated whether many of the isolated rocks which were scattered over the charts of the Atlantic were similar casual observations of dirty bergs which might delay mariners for years to come if they were not investigated and deleted from the charts. However it was still 'a new disappointment, and seriously felt by several of our crew, whose hopes of having an immediate reward for their patience and perseverance were again frustrated.' It's easy to forget they were not explorers or scientists but common seamen being paid a share of profit: no seals meant no pay, no land meant no bonus.

Exceptionally for a sealer, Weddell had spent the huge sum of £240 on three chronometers for the trip. One by Murry of London proved exceptionally sound; even its slight rate of gain was extremely regular and could be allowed for precisely. He was therefore puzzled to find that his calculation of longitude by chronometer was very different from his dead reckoning using the ship's log. He reluctantly concluded that in difficult conditions, among the ice, his observations were not as good as he wished. In time he realised that observations made from the same spot, an hour apart came out differently, because near the magnetic poles, the earth's magnetic field dips downwards. The horizontal element of the force, which aligns the compass needle, becomes weaker, and the ship's iron equipment, such as anchors, began to influence the compass much more. Small movements around the deck could change the angle of north on the compass between three and five degrees. These confusing magnetic measurements were taken very seriously by the British Admiralty, and clarifying their variations would be the prime task of James Clark Ross's voyage of 1839–43. Meanwhile Weddell's calculations (estimates would be a better word) were being affected by the gyre or clockwise circular current that would later drag Shackleton's *Endurance* hundreds of miles while it was gripped in the ice. He correctly concurred with Cook that the great ice formations originated from land.

18 February became a historic day. They were more than 72° south, and by evening, with whales all around the ship, it was noted with capital letters on the log: NOT A PARTICLE OF ICE OF ANY DESCRIPTION WAS TO BE SEEN. They sailed on in hope. 'The evening was mild and serene, and had it not been for the reflection that probably we should have obstacles to contend with in our passage northwards through the ice, our situation might have been envied.' On 20 February at 74° 15′S they saw three bergs so big they called them ice islands; one was covered in penguins. Open water still beckoned them on, but the wind turned to the south, and February was almost out: 'taking into account the lateness of the season, and that we had to

pass homewards through 100 miles of sea strewed with ice islands, I could not determine otherwise than to take advantage of this favourable wind for returning.'

Weddell's open sea was to mislead generations of future navigators. He had been spectacularly lucky in arriving late in an unusually ice-free season. It breathed new life into the old story of open polar waters drawn by Gerhardt Mercator back in 1606. Many geographers had argued that in high latitudes, the long summer days would heat up the oceans and melt the ice. He wrote: 'the antarctic polar sea may be found less icy than is imagined, and a clear field of discovery, even to the South Pole, may therefore be anticipated.' However often his successors hit dense pack ice farther north, they pushed on, spurred by Weddell's experience.

He paid tribute to his crew. 'I expressed my approbation of their patient and orderly behaviour, and informed them that they were now to the southward of the latitude to which any former navigator had penetrated. Our colours were hoisted, and a gun was fired, and both crews gave three cheers. These indulgences, with an allowance of grog, dispelled their gloom, and infused a hope that fortune might yet be favourable.' Yet the crew still faced returning home with empty pockets to anxious wives, their credit run to the limit at every local store. They would be honoured and broke.

He was deep in the south-east corner of the sea he would name King George IV Sea, but would later be renamed for him: the Weddell Sea. As he sailed north he passed through 63°21´S and 45°22´W and looked at his South Atlantic chart, one in common use. It showed they were sailing through the mythical kingdom of South Iceland. Weddell had earned the right to be contemptuous: 'It is much to be regretted that any men should be so ill-advised as to propagate any hydrographical falsehoods; and I pity those who, when they meet with an appearance that is likely to throw some light on the state of the globe, are led through pusillanimity to forego the examination of it.'

They headed for South Georgia which they reached on 12 March 1823. He climbed a peak to measure the altitude of the sun; the weather was perfect: still, without a breath of wind. He set up the mercury dish which acted as an artificial horizon from which to measure the angle. He saw it trembling. This was the first record of seismic activity on South Georgia. He looked at the toll his own industry had taken on the wildlife of the island. The elephant seals were nearly extinct, twenty thousand tons tons of oil having been shipped to London alone; 1.2 million fur seal skins had been taken. Unlike the American sealers, the British sold their skins cheaply, despite Chapman having discovered how to dress them in 1799. Sealskin soon replaced the much more expensive beaver pelts for hats and other articles.

On 11 May he arrived at New Island in the Falklands, then frequented by whalers and sealers. Weddell moved to Quaker Harbour on Swan Island for the winter. While here, he was told that four years before quantities of ice seen had been seen at 50°S, but he admits he never saw it north of South Georgia. He also observed why, some time before, Commodore John Byron, grandfather of the future poet, had thought that fur seals could give birth to eighteen or more pups: he had mistaken the male's harem of much smaller females for a mother and her young. During his earlier stay in 1820 he was also caught up in a little piece of history that was to have a long fuse. He was visiting Port

San Salvador on the north shore of East Falkland when on 2 November he received a letter telling him of the claim made by the thirty-gun frigate *Heoind* of Buenos Aires. Colonel Jewett's commission, in the name of the United Provinces of South America, was to take possession of the islands. In deference to the colonel's commission and thirty-eight guns Weddell paid a social call without contesting possession. He left the Falklands on 7 October, bound once more for the South Shetlands.

On 16 October they saw their first tabular iceberg; the previous season's conditions had been so freakish they hadn't seen one. Later that day, still ninety-five miles from land, they met ice too dense to sail in. It wasn't until the next day that they found a channel leading into it. They probed the pack around a wild, high island for a week. On the 28th, a hurricane hit them. Everything movable on deck was washed away and replaced by so much ice that Weddell credited it with reinforcing the rigging and fixtures and reducing damage. There was a downside. The rudders became locked solid. Unable to steer, the vessels lost sight of each other.

Next day they regained contact but 'many of our crew were hurt in the early part of the gale, by being thrown down, and nearly all of them were frost bitten. They had been above a twelvemonth from home, and consequently their clothes were nearly worn out.'

They fought the ice with little success, Weddell and Brisbane's perseverance being all the braver since the bottoms of the ships had only 2½" thick planks. Their bow was damaged and temporary repairs made, nailing lead sheets and canvas over to slow the leaks. Weddell was familiar with navigation around Greenland, yet wrote 'sailing among ice in these southern latitudes is attended with a much greater risk.'

In 1820 James Weddell's had been the first vessel fitted out from England to anchor in the South Shetlands; William Smith had been trading out of South America. Weddell now singled out the island he thought the 'highest and most forbidding in aspect', the one they had fought round in the second half of October, and made the first landing on it, naming it for himself: James Island.

He began sealing. In the South Shetlands they killed two thousand elephant seals for oil, and noted the vast profusion of fur seals. His observations on elephant seals are highly professional. When the males first arrived, the fat from three or four of them would yield one ton of oil. If both males and females were taken, it required an average of seven animals to make a ton. The males might try to prevent a boat landing by swimming out and attacking it; the size and outline of a whaleboat's submerged hull would be comparable to an adult male, and they have mistaken boats for rival males. Descriptions of their death throes are tinged with whimsy: 'the sea-elephant, when lying on the shore, and threatened with death, will often make no effort to escape into the water, but will lie still and shed tears, merely raising the head to look at the assailant; and though very timid, will wait with composure the club or the lance which takes its life.' Their power was not doubted: 'in the agony of death, stones are ground to powder between its teeth.'

He realised the males were polygamous, and that Ross was wrong about multiple births, but he thought the harem was where males protected females throughout their gestation; he did not know how seasonal their visits to land were. He observed moulting, and the differing timings of seals' arrivals, dependent on age. He made fair guesses at the ages of maturity, and their longevity. He thought that after they had experienced hunting they began hauling out on rocks convenient to launch straight into sea. He mocked the myth that they would throw stones at pursuers with their tails when fleeing; it was just part of their clumsy flight. He tamed pups, hand-rearing them from a few weeks to two months until 'by some accident they were allowed to fall or walk overboard.' Until they escaped, we would say. In 1821–22, over 320,000 fur seals were taken. A sustainable yield was around a 100,000 a year. Before he left, on the western isles of the South Shetlands Weddell saw pieces of wreck and the scantling, or small timbers, of a seventy-four-gun ship; he thought it must be the *San Telmo*, the first ghostly discoverer.

Fifty years before, the Master, James Cook, had achieved a farthest south and written 'I can be bold to say that no man will ever venture farther than I have done.' He continued that if anyone did so, 'I shall not envy him the honour of the discovery.' Weddell had gone 214 miles farther south. He had done it as a sideline while doing his other job, sealing, and lost no one. He was a man who read all he could about where he went, but wore his learning lightly: with humour, without pretension.

After the voyage was over, the admirable Captain Brisbane, who had skippered a cutter the size of a Victorian racing yacht to the farthest south ever achieved, would go to the Falklands to manage a new livestock venture and be murdered by convicts left during the brief Argentine presence there. Weddell offered himself to lead or organise another expedition south but was rebuffed by John Barrow, effectively the Permanent Secretary at the Admiralty. Barrow, like Clements Markham at the RGS during the Heroic Era, could not believe that anyone but a naval officer could manage an exploring adventure. This was an interesting notion, for if excitement is the product of poor preparation, as William Speirs Bruce's men would later write, Naval expeditions were certainly exciting. Five years later, Weddell sailed from Buenos Aires in the ageing *Jane*, Gibraltar-bound. His part-share in her represented much of his wealth. Weakened by her battles in the Antarctic, she leaked so badly that he barely nursed her into the Azores, docking in the pretty harbour of Horta. A survey found her unseaworthy and beyond repair. He was forced to board another vessel to come home, but she in turn was wrecked off the neighbouring island of Pico. He had to take waged work as a captain on others' ships. In 1831 he was on the Derwent River, Hobart, Tasmania, as skipper of the sealer *Eliza*, helping the scurvy-rotted crew of the *Tula* ashore. Their captain was John Biscoe, making a circumnavigation on Antarctica described later in this chapter. It was Weddell's last voyage; he died in poverty in lodgings in London on 9 September 1834 and was buried at St Clement Danes on the Strand, Samuel Johnson's old parish church. Time and London air have eroded his headstone. Today, it cannot be found.

## THE SEALING FLEETS ARRIVE

*War in the South, and the first footprint is left on the continental mainland, but whose?*

The sealers were hot on the heels of the Royal Navy. Two months after Smith's first landing, the *Espirito Santo* under Captain Joseph Herring and financed by British businessmen in Buenos Aires landed at an unknown spot in the South Shetlands, looking for seals. Soon, a mob of sealers and whalers would follow. In 1821, Sherriff Cove in the north west of Livingston Island was the anchorage for the *Williams*, *John*, *Lady Frances* and *Mercury*, all of Liverpool, the *Dragon* of Valparaiso and two American ships. The four English crews alone took 95,000 seal skins from there.

In his memoir *Voyages*, the highly successful sealer Edmund Fanning from Stonington, Connecticut describes sealing around the globe. He had interesting comments about the Antarctic hunt. Elephant seals should be caught when they first came ashore and yielded three barrels of oil each; after a few weeks ashore, fighting and fasting, the yield halved. Young elephant seals could be clubbed, female and younger male adults could be lanced, but the biggest males had to be shot with muskets. They were provoked into bellowing open-mouthed then shot through the open mouth into the brain. Two musket balls were fired. They might not kill outright but would stun them so heavily they could be safely lanced. If they came across elephant seals sleeping they would hold the gun to the head and fire. The noise seldom woke the others.

The skin, with the fat, but not the meat beneath it, was cut into five- to ten-inch wide strips, washed, diced into two-inch cubes, and put in a kettle to render out the oil. The fire was fed by scraps of rendered-out skin. The tongue was a delicacy; Fanning thought it more delicious than ox tongue.

They also took 'sea leopards'. Sometimes it is hard to know whether they meant leopard seals or the other seal with a mottled coat, the Weddell seal, but Fanning specifies it was a species which would follow the boats and attack them. Weddell seals do not do that; leopard seals, as I know from experience, love biting boats. Leopards are now mostly solitary creatures, but the early Antarctic sealers saw sizeable rookeries, now unknown: 'on Palmer's Land, and the south part of Sandwich Land, they are found herded together in rookeries of many hundreds and furnish oil, as the elephant, in proportion to their size.'

Fur seals were killed like elephant seals; the females, known as clapmatches (the males were wigs), and the pups would let them approach within clubbing range. Only when they had become shy from what Fanning euphemistically calls disturbance, did the sealers have to shoot them, adding a cost. The killing was described by Captain Amaso Delano, a man immortalised by Herman Melville in his masterful but little-known story 'Benito Cereno', in which Delano appears in his own name as the weak-moralled master of a vessel which meets a slaver in which discipline has broken down. Delano had a descendant who shared his name: US President Franklin Delano Roosevelt. 'The method practised to take them was to get between them and the water, and make a lane of men, two abreast, forming three or four couples, and then drive the seal through this lane; each man furnished with a club, between five and six feet long and as they passed, he knocked down such of them as he chose, which are commonly the half-grown. When stunned, knives are taken to cut and rip them down on the breast from the under jaw, to the tail, giving a stab in the breast that will kill them. After this the hands got to skinning. I have seen men, one of whom would skin sixty in an hour.'

The skin was best cured by leaving half an inch of fat on it. They then washed it and, while it was still wet, rubbed salt well into the fat especially around the neck and the edges. It took about two kilos of salt per skin, usually picked up in the Cape Verde Islands on the way south. They then packed the skins flat, in tiers, or folded in books known as kenches. For the China market, all the fat was cut away, and the skins stretched on wooden pins to dry. An experienced man could dress thirty a day.

With few exceptions, the sealers did not explore inland Antarctica. Their prey stayed on the shore and so did they. But they competed to find new rookeries, going as far as the pack would allow. Despite the brutality of their business, running a mobile abattoir in a pristine wilderness, their ranks included men of science and curiosity. They made important discoveries and took risks with no promise of profit, to know more about this newfound world.

Two American fleets had historic impacts. One was Pendelton's Stonington fleet, the other was a group including the two hundred and fifty-ton ship *Huron* from New Haven, Connecticut and the eighty-ton schooner *Huntress*, a Nantucket schooner. But it was the *Cecilia*, a little schooner acting as tender to the larger vessels, which would make history. She was brought south 'knocked down', that is taken apart and stowed, on the *Huron*. There were two experienced seamen of forty-one and thirty, the average age of the rest was twenty-one.

When they arrived, the larger ships hove to, and the *Cecilia* went off to look for a safe harbour, quickly finding Yankee Harbour at the west end of Livingston Island, which was to be the main base for American sealing. You can still see their rusting iron try-pots on its shingle beach. The sheltered inner harbour is shallow. One captain I worked with, new to Antarctica, attempted to enter Yankee Harbour in the relatively deep-draughted ice-breaker *Polar Star*. The novices are always more cocksure than the veterans. I had been in on my Zodiac earlier in the season and dared to point to shallows I had seen on the inside of the bend. I still recall the patronising smile he gave me, a failed camouflage for anger. I retired to the top deck, from where, four minutes later, I photographed the yellow mud thrown up when we grounded. Cue astern. The fur seals had come back. When I returned to my Zodiac as the landing was wound up, a pup was leaning against it.

The *Cecilia* spent the following days ferrying men to the seal beaches where they cached their stores and pitched crude tents. It would return in a few days to pick up the men and the skins. On 19 December, Captain Burdick on the *Cecilia* made the first of three landings on the south shore of Livingston. At the next bay, 'it blowing a gale on Shore we Could neither Land nor they git off.' Burdick's spelling enlivens all the log entries. When he uses the expression 'wore off' (turning with the wind to stern); he adds an 'h' in the unluckiest place. The next day they made it, retrieving the men and 500 skins, and, at the third site, another 480.

Soon after the Stonington fleet arrived they used knowledge gained the previous season to head straight to the richest beaches and they creamed off the known rookeries. The other fleets had to discover new ones, or go without. Captain John Davis made a final pick up from the shore camps then left on 28 December to reconnoitre the other islands of the South Shetlands lying to the north and east. Despite going to the far end of King George Island and circumnavigating the principal islands over twelve days he 'found no Seal to speak of.' His only cargo had been the crew of an English sealer, possibly the *Lady Trowbridge*, sunk on 20 December, which he returned to their own fleet, before calling at their old shore-sites for 2470 skins which were in poor condition because they had waited two weeks without salt.

Captains Davis and Burdick sometimes sent a whaleboat to the west end of Yankee Sound to hunt for seals. On 24 January the *Huron's* bosun Charles Laing, twenty-one years old and five feet three, returned from a four-day cruise along the north shore of Livingston Island, to Shirreff's Cove. He had only fifty-two skins, and they had clashed with the English sealers. Another American whaleboat had taken a drubbing. Captain Burdick's log gives details in a brand of English which suggests his real schooling was the sea: 'a boat came in belonging to Captain Barnard brig *Charity* having ben robed of Eighty Skins by the English at Sheriff's Cape and Drove off the Beach 4 p.m. our Boat came in from a Cruce with 52 having Likewis ben Drove from the beach at Sheriff's Cape by the English where he said there was plenty of Seal.' A contemporary map of Livingston Island names one cove Robbery Beach.

The Yankees had not come so far to watch the British take the spoils. They would fight. They mustered 120 men: 'by the best information we can git the English have but about 80 men there.' One of them, Captain Barnard, would have been especially keen to get in a good fight. He had rescued a shipwrecked English party in the Falklands, who then seized his vessel and marooned him. A battle seemed inevitable: 'then we got under way and stood to the South & Westward in company for Sheriff's Cape at 11 p.m. Capt. Bruno came alongside in his boat and reported that he had examined the Beaches round Sheriffs Cape and Saw but a very few Seal nothing to make an object to stop for.' A few days later, John Davis sent his first mate Goddard to Shirreff's Cape and 'at 2 P.M. the Boat returned from Shore not being allowed to Land as the English had collected in numbers say from 65 to 70 men, all armed with Guns, Pistoles, & Swords and appeared in a hostile manner, Hoisted in the Boat and Proceeded on to the westward.'

The undeclared war ended as suddenly as it began because there was little left to fight over. The day before John Davis had admitted as much in his laconic log entry: 'Concluded to make the best of our way out for our people that is stationed on the South beach, and then to go on a cruise to find new Lands, as the Seal is done here.' I have never seen a log entry that wonders what they might do when they have killed their own livelihood. There would be other trades.

The American sealers returned to their vessels at Yankee Harbour. Captain Robert Johnson took the *Cecilia* and pushed as far south and west as he could, returning on 27 January after three weeks' absence. The log read 'he had ben to the Lat. 66° South and the Long. of 70° West and still found what appeared to be nothing but Sollid Islands of Ice and Snow.' Captain Davis decided to look for himself. On the morning of Tuesday 30 January 1821, he slipped the *Cecilia* south down the Morton Strait with Snow Island to starboard and Livingston to port. He visited his three shore camps, picking up a total of 902 skins, then steered south, into unknown waters beyond the South Shetland chain. Tracking their route now is hampered by the fact that they did not know their compass deviation was around 25°E. On occasion they locate their position relative to well-known landmarks, and we can pin down where they are. But when they give latitude and longitude, what you would really see from those co-ordinates is seldom what they describe. In fine weather, the clarity of the atmosphere deceived them, and here they often thought land was close when it might be forty miles off. On 1 February they reached the south shore of Smith Island, the westerly outpost of the South Shetlands. They closed on the shore and lowered a boat, hoping for seals. They were there, but so were seventeen British sealers on the beach killing them. John Davis pointed the *Cecilia's* bows south east to Low Island, a low shield of an isle compared with the pyramidal profile of Smith. This was new land to Davis when he landed on 2 February. The seals were there, the British were not. That day they took 200, and the next day 422. They stayed until 6 February, taking 109 skins on the final day. Twenty-two miles, and a little east of due south, lay Hoseason Island, named after James Hoseason, first mate on the *Sprightly*, an Enderby Brothers sealing ship which would operate in these waters in 1824–25. History was also in sight.

'Wednesday 7th February 1821 Commences with open Cloudy Weather and Light winds a standing for a Large Body of Land in that direction SE at 10 A.M. close in with it, out Boat and Sent her on Shore to look for Seal at 11 A.M.' The place is now called Graham Land on the

Antarctic Peninsula near Cape Sterneck, which forms the eastern arm of Hughes Bay. On 7 February 1821, at ten in the morning, the *Cecilia* dropped anchor. A boat was immediately lowered and made for the shore. The mate of the *Huron* Samuel Goddard was on board. At Low Island we know the second mates Smith and Philips went ashore, so they may have joined him. John Davis seems to have stayed on board. One or both of their black seamen might have been among them. Someone is in the bow, holding the painter (bow rope) watching for rocks. Like all the others, he is wearing seal-skin boots, warm and waterproof. He jumps into the shallows just before the keel scrapes the pebble beach, and steadies her in the surf. The other men step nimbly to the bow and jump for the dry shingle. Someone has left the first human footprints on continental Antarctica. We do not know the name of the man. In less than an hour they get back in the boat and return to ship. The land seems more extensive than other islands they had visited. It doesn't matter much. What does matter is there are no seals; they move on. The incoming tide washes away the lower tracks. The boot marks above high tide linger longer.

Unless a new document falls from unsorted archives or is found among forgotten papers in a New England attic, we will never know the name of the owner of those boots. I am fascinated by the possibility he might have been black. It's possible something will come to light; Davis's own papers were only discovered in 1952. The crew had no way of knowing if they had been on an island or on the mainland, but Davis had a gut feeling and got it right. His last log entry for the day reads: 'I think this Southern Land to be a Continent.'

At the end of the century, Dr Frederick Cook on the *Belgica* would describe the spot more lyrically: 'every projection seemed a continuous mass of impenetrable crystal solitude.' But the anonymous men of the *Cecilia*, who stayed long enough to confirm it was another disappointing landing in their bloodthirsty trade, were the first. There were now no other continents to discover.

## JOHN BISCOE'S (1794–1843) VOYAGE OF 1830–33

*Biscoe, working for a company so famous they are described in* Moby Dick *as whaling royalty, gains exploring fame through commercial madness.*

If John Biscoe's name is known today, it is by people who have visited Deception Island and asked why one of the British wooden huts is called Biscoe House. John Biscoe was a sealer for the great Enderby Brothers, so famous they were name-checked in *Moby Dick* when Captain Ahab meets the whaler *Samuel Enderby*, whose Captain Boomer has lost an arm to Moby Dick. Two of Samuel Enderby's grandsons were among the founding members of the RGS, and an Enderby sister was the mother of Gordon of Khartoum. Melville thought their family as noble as the Tudors and Bourbons. His life is illuminated only for the three years of one voyage. This is why.

Biscoe left Berkeley Sound in the Falklands on 27 November 1830 and sailed a little south of due east, passing to the north of South Georgia. Aged thirty-six, he was a former Navy officer recruited for his education and willingness to explore and take samples of plant and animals as he went. His ships were both slight; the brigantine *Tula* was just 157 tons, and the *Lively* much smaller, maybe less than 50 tons, a former Cowes pilot-boat.

Ice conditions were good and they turned south-east until they were pressing close to the Antarctic Circle. On 25 February 1831, Biscoe entered in the log, 'At 8pm saw an appearance of land to the southward.' In log entries, 'appearance of land' is the stock phrase for 'I think it's land but I'm not sure.' As they came closer it seemed Biscoe's caution was justified. 'At noon our latitude was 66°29´S, longitude 45°17´E; that which lately had the appearance of land' proved to be ice, and 'I could trace it in extent for at least 30 to 40 miles from the foretop with a good telescope; it was then lost in the general glow of the atmosphere.' It was ice, but although he did not know it, he was looking at cliffs of continental ice: the edge of the continent.

On 28 February 1831 Biscoe's luck turned: 'In the morning more regular sea. Tacked to the southward. Wind SE. Noon more clear. Latitude 65°57´S 047°20´30" E. pm, passed to the southward through much broken field-ice. 4pm saw several hummocks to the southward, which much resembled tops of mountains, and at 6pm clearly distinguished it to be land, and to considerable extent; to my great satisfaction what we had seen being the black tops of mountains showing themselves through the snow on the lower land, which, however, appeared to be a great distance off, and completely beset with close field-ice and icebergs. The body of the land bearing away SE.' He sensibly named it after his boss: Enderby Land. He ventured a boat into the dense ice but it was soon driven back, and he failed to land.

The weather soon turned on them, viciously, but first they were treated to a magnificent display of the *aurora australis*, playing the trick of seeming to be right above their heads, just out of arm's reach. It was 'without exception the grandest phenomenon of nature of its kind I ever witnessed.' On 5 March, a regulation gale force blizzard reduced visibility until the ships could not see each other or advancing icebergs. By midnight it was hurricane strength and the larger *Tula*, which even in normal conditions was cussed to handle, was almost beyond control. Ice and snow built up on the decks and in the rigging and spars, making her dangerously top-heavy. Seas broke over the deck and smashed one ship's boat and carried another away. The winds drove them 120 miles to the north. When the storm cleared, they could see the horizon, but no sign of the *Lively*. Biscoe doggedly turned back south with every hope that the southerly winds had dispersed the pack that had prevented him getting to shore. He fought his way to Cape Ann where they had been when the storm started. The pack was intact. Some men had been injured in the storm, three others were bedridden with scurvy, including the carpenter, who was vital in performing the running repairs needed to keep the ship working. By 16 March Biscoe concluded 'I feel myself absolutely obliged to give up all further pursuit.' Yet he could not quite let go. He persevered in probing the ice until 6 April but never achieved a landing. They headed for New Zealand but on 23 April the carpenter died, and soon after, another seaman. Only two mates, one seaman, one boy were fit for work. When night fell they hove to, drifting until dawn, under the pale green light of the dwindling *aurora* before dragging their exhausted bodies from their bunks to painfully haul on ropes, hoist sail, begin again. He encouraged his men but his diary reveals that I 'often had a smile on my face, with very different feelings within.'

In Hobart he began repairing the ship, waiting for the *Lively* to appear. Months passed; no incoming ship had seen her. He decided he had to continue. You can imagine his feelings sailing alone down the Derwent River watching the banks fall away to show him the sea that had claimed his companions. At the river mouth a familiar set of sails was coming towards them: the *Lively*. They turned and sailed back to port where Captain Avery described how disease and the hurricane had scythed through the crew until there was just one seaman and a boy left alive. The man was exhausted and the boy's hand was broken. They had arrived near Melbourne a month before the *Tula* had docked, and barely had the strength to go ashore for help. They returned to find the ship gone. It was two weeks before they found her grounded in an obscure inlet, her mooring lines having been broken or cut.

On 8 October 1831 the two ships joined company under sail again, making New Zealand, then the Chatham Islands, 450 nautical miles east of Christchurch. It was the second leg of Biscoe's circumnavigation. The seal colonies were there, but most had already been butchered. This didn't stop them killing the survivors. Twenty-three skins sailed with them south to the Bounty Islands, where there were no seals at all. They continued east, setting course for the archipelago marked as the Nimrod Islands on the chart, and finding the islands were as fugitive as the seals: another map-maker's myth. The last hope was the South Shetland; although all known seal rookeries had been wiped out by 1823, there were large areas of uncharted whiteness, on the map and on the ground. A few gravel beaches full of the stink and bark of fur seals would remedy all. He decided to head south of Cook's course in this same sea, hoping to find new land, not knowing Bellingshausen had sailed here eleven years before. They met fields of icebergs, and though short of water, Biscoe did not melt ice because he blamed it for past dysentery outbreaks.

On 15 February 1832, approaching the base of the Antarctic Peninsula from the west, they suffered 'strong gales from the southward. Water smooth. Latitude at noon 67°01´S, longitude 71°48´W. At 5pm saw land bearing ESE which appeared at a great distance – run for it all night with a light breeze from the SW. It has a most imposing and beautiful appearance, having on very high peak running up into the clouds, and occasionally appears both above and below them; about one-third of the mountains, which are about four miles in extent from north to south, have only a thin scattering of snow over their summits. Towards the base the other two-thirds are buried in a field of snow and ice of the most dazzling brightness. This bed of snow and ice is about 4 miles in extent, sloping gradually down to its termination; a cliff ten or twelve feet high, which is split in every direction for at least two or three hundred yards from its edge inwards, and which appears to form icebergs, only waiting for some severe gales or other cause to break them adrift.' Biscoe decided: 'This island being the farthest known land to the southward, I have honoured it with the name of Her Majesty Queen Adelaide.'

'February 19 – At 4pm I sent the boat to an island, which appeared to join the mainland, and some naked rocks lying off the mouth of a considerable entrance. I had great hopes of finding seal in them. At 10am the boat returned, not having found anything alive on the island, put having pulled quite round what Mr White informed me was an excellent harbour for shelter, although a rocky bottom. I have named this place Pitt's Island, from the likeness of an iceberg to that statesman in a sitting posture, and which for some time I took to be a rock.' Pitt Island is now the most northerly of the Biscoe Islands, which Charcot would later survey properly.

From naming an island after the Queen, there was only one more step to go. 'February 21 – On the 21st I again stood towards the mainland [actually islands] and at 8am went into the boat myself and pulled into a large inlet; the bottom appeared to be rocky in places where it could be seen, but I found no bottom with 20 fathoms, but as we found no seal nor indeed anything but penguins and a few birds, I did not sound with a deeper line. This being the mainland I took possession of it in the name of His Majesty King William the Fourth, the highest mountain I named Mount William on the same occasion.'

The ship, still all but empty, reached a harbour on the west end of Livingston Island called New Plymouth. Here Biscoe was looking for elephant seals: oil not skins. He met an English sealer, Adam Kellock, who enthused him with reports of rich pickings before sailing home. But after two weeks, Biscoe had found just a few pups. They prepared to sail north: the *Lively* returned to England, the *Tula* went whaling in a desperate attempt to salvage some profit. Before they could sail, a storm pinned them in the harbour, seventeen-foot waves driving the *Tula* with its deeper draught into shallows where its bottom scraped on the rocks and its safety hung on a single anchor chain. They evacuated to the *Lively* and watched the storm blow out.

The anchor held; they re-boarded and sailed to the Falklands. Having built a temporary furnace in Berkeley Sound to repair the *Tula's* rudder, damaged in the storm, they sailed west to New Island, a pretty island off West Falkland favoured by sealers and whalers. On the way the *Lively* went missing, but they had learned to be optimistic, she was a tough ship. There were no seals at New Island, and a month after leaving Berkeley Sound Biscoe began looking for his companion. Soon he heard that the *Lively* was sunk, but the men had got ashore. Slowly they made their way back to Biscoe. His orders were to wait where he was and pick up supplies shipped out from England, and complete another season's work beginning in the next southern summer. But the men began complaining about rations, and wouldn't be satisfied. Their real complaint was they had suffered enough, and their most effective argument was to desert, which they did, in numbers. Biscoe was forced to sail home.

Biscoe completed a circumnavigation of the continent, the third in all, that was at once fearless and unimaginative. He was a working skipper not much interested in geography, except as a business opening, but he discovered two areas of the continent that still bear the names he gave them. He did correctly deduce that all the land and ice he had seen was part of a whole. How much was land he could not say, but land and ice together made up a continent: 'I have not the least doubt that the whole spaces, from the latitudes I have visited to the Pole, are one solid mass'. It was a magnificent achievement for a small vessel at work in a now forgotten trade. The Enderby Brothers, one of whose ships had, in 1773, had its tea dumped in Boston Harbour by Revolutionaries dressed as

Indians, would continue to encourage exploration alongside commerce. It was admirable but it would cost them their business. Funding Biscoe's voyage cost the Enderbys £6,147, but he limped into London on 8 February 1833, with just thirty seal skins in his hold. Charles Enderby swallowed his disappointment, and invited Biscoe to speak at the new Royal Geographical Society, presenting the paper *Recent Discoveries in the Antarctic Ocean*. The Society gave Biscoe their second ever gold medal.

In 1838 he was in Tasmania, and destitute enough for a public subscription to be held to pay for his passage home. £109 12s 0d bought tickets for him and his wife and children. A contribution of ten guineas came from the Lieutenant Governor John Franklin. Yet poor Biscoe died on the voyage. His memory is preserved in the RRS *John Biscoe*, two BAS supply and research ships which carried that name between 1947 and 1991, when the RRS *James Clark Ross* replaced her. His name also survives on Biscoe House, Deception Island.

## JOHN BALLENY'S (?–1857) VOYAGE OF 1838–39

*The first footprints south of the Antarctic Circle.*

One final sealing voyage deserves mention, also sponsored by the Enderbys. They continued to direct voyages south and they continued to lose money. Two of the senior partners died in 1829 and young Charles Enderby was more interested in adventure than commerce. When they bought the *Eliza Scott* and the *Sabrina* in 1838–39 the bulk of the shares in it were immediately sold on. They had both been built as pleasure yachts and were poorly ballasted. They moved violently in bad weather, and the *Sabrina* was lost in a storm on the return journey. The Enderbys were evangelical in religion, as well as geography, and appointed masters with more regard for their piety than their competence. They had problems with officers and crew, and seem to have dragged John Balleny out of retirement at the last minute to skipper the *Eliza Scott*. He may have been in his late sixties, though details of his birth and upbringing are unknown. He was a very knowledgeable and capable navigator, but with no whaling or sealing experience. He was at least pious.

Most of his voyage is not relevant to the Peninsula area, but he did discover, 1250 miles south of New Zealand at nearly 67°S, a new group of islands which he named after himself. There they made the first landing south of the Antarctic Circle on 12 February 1839. They also sighted new continental coast which they named Sabrina Land, two remarkable firsts for a working sealer, but they returned with just 178 seal skins. Balleny slipped back into obscure retirement, enriched only by his name on an obscure corner of the map. There is no record of his death, no will. Charles Enderby blithely continued to suggest further money-losing ventures, and was for a while saved from himself as the RGS had already committed to supporting James Clark Ross on his voyage of 1839–43. In fact when Balleny sailed up the Thames he had passed Chatham Dockyard where the *Erebus* and *Terror* were being fitted out. When he departed twelve days later, Ross had copies of Balleny's chart and log, including a suggestion that from Balleny's observations of the ice, a drive farther south might be fruitful if made between 170° and 180°E. Those waters would soon be christened the Ross Sea.

# THE DRAKE PASSAGE

When he returned to England in September 1580, Drake was adamant. He had seen open ocean south of Cape Horn. The land they had reached on 24 October 1578 held the key. They had been blown south and fought their way back north to land on an island. They refreshed their water, collected wood and berries, there were 'herbs and trees flourishing.' He named it Elizabeth Island, and the harbour, Port Francis Drake. Fletcher drew the island as square, with a central lake, about thirty miles north to south. Later in life Drake yarned with Richard Hawkins, telling how he had gone 'seeking the part of the island, cast himself down on the uttermost point, grovelling, and so reached out his body over it. Presently he embarked, and then told his people that he had been on the southernmost known land in the world.'

They were there three or four days, and their descriptions should be accurate. The problem is, Cape Horn is not like that. The island is not square and has no central lake. There are no trees to offer wood, no sweet herbs or berries. Drake is known to have cooked the books and spread misinformation about his course to confuse the Spanish.

In 1908, in Mexico City an American named Zelia Nuttall was searching through the archives of the Inquisition into native witchcraft. On the floor, in a dark, dusty corner, lay a disposition to that Inquisition by Nuño da Silva. It included descriptions of his time with Drake.

In the General Archive of the Indias in Seville, a storehouse of documents on the exploration of the Americas. She arrived, chatting to friends, in a room banked high with documents which were only partly sorted. Still talking, she put out a hand at random to the label of a sheaf of documents. It was a bundle of papers about Francis Drake in the South Sea.

Her charmed search led to sixteen pages stitched roughly together. Da Silva's log is brief and factual: a navigator's record, not a narrative. 'October 24 Came to an anchor off an island in 57°S. October 25 This day we went ashore. October 26 We procured wood.' Not wanting to overdo the local detail, he continues 'October 27 Went ashore. October 28 We sailed.'

The log has no helpful description of Elizabeth Island but it did enable historians to track the wanderings of the *Golden Hinde* during the seven or more weeks of the storm, and solve the mystery of the supposed landing at Cape Horn. But when they plotted the course described by da Silva, the result was a location for Elizabeth Island which was well out to the south west of the Horn, in open ocean where there is no land.

Over the years, the original chart entries for Elizabeth Island began to be marked PD, position doubtful, then ED, existence doubtful.

In 1938, Felix Reisenberg calculated their movements and put Elizabeth Island back in the empty ocean in fifteen thousand feet feet of water. He added the W-E current to the equation and brought Elizabeth Island's supposed position back nearly a hundred miles east. But there was no island there either. He wrote to the US Navy Hydrographic Office who replied:

Captain W D Burnham reports that while running before a gale off Cape Horn in command of the

American ship *Pactolus*, at 4 o'clock in the morning of 6 November 1885, the wind lulled and the sea fell, and noticing very highly discoloured water, he hove the ship to and sounded three times, obtaining each time from 67 to 70 fathoms, black sand and small rocks. Then ran South for thirty miles before the water, which all the time was very thick and yellow, resumed its natural colour.

It is named after him, Burnham Bank. It was in the right place, thirty miles north to south, like Fletcher's Island, and for the *Golden Hinde*, with a northerly wind, two days sailing from Tierra del Fuego, as Nuño da Silva had said. A rock soaring from depths of fifteen thousand feet, to two hundred feet below the waves. Reisenberg had it. Small islands with a central lake are not common. They tend to be volcanoes with flooded craters.

# 5

## The Circumnavigators:
Jules Dumont D'Urville, Charles Wilkes
and James Clark Ross

*Adventurers from three of the great marine powers made circumnavigations of the Southern Ocean between 1837 and 1843. They were, in order of departure, the Frenchman Jules-Sébastien-César Dumont d'Urville, the American Charles Wilkes, and the Englishman James Clark Ross. Long stretches of their cruises were spent far from the Antarctic Peninsula but each contributed to the understanding of the continent, and to their own nation's claims to a stake in its future: one a handsome, sociable dandy; the other two solitary egoists.*

### THE FRENCH ARRIVE 1837–40
### JULES DUMONT D'URVILLE (1790–1842)

Jules-Sébastien-César Dumont d'Urville was born on 23 May 1790 at Condé-sur-Noireau near Caen, Normandy. Aged ten, he was told that no famous men had come from his town, and vowed 'I promised myself to work twice as hard to place my name on the wings of fame.' He joined the

French Navy in 1807, when it was licking its wounds after Trafalgar. He was twenty-five years old before he left harbour, as a botanist on board the *Chevrette* to the Mediterranean. On this voyage his career took off.

In April 1820, they lay off Milo in the Greek Islands. Dumont d'Urville went ashore to see the French representative on the island, a Monsieur Brest, who told them of some new statues discovered three weeks before by a local farmer. From the pose, d'Urville recognised Venus at the Judgement of Paris. It was extremely beautiful and finely made. They thought about buying it but the captain said he did not have room for it on board. In Constantinople d'Urville obtained permission to purchase the statue for France. But when he returned, it had been sold and loaded onto a Greek ship. Accounts of what happened next vary. It was either recovered by bribing the Greeks or they fought over it. Whichever it was, the arms were lost in the melee. It was taken to Court, then to the Louvre, and named after the place it was found: the Venus de Milo. A misunderstanding arose that d'Urville had discovered the statue personally; he never corrected it.

He added successful circumnavigations to his experience. With his friend Louis-Isidore Duperrey, he successfully promoted a trip to assess colonising parts of New Zealand and Australia, not yet secure as English colonies. It was led by Duperrey, who was more senior, with Dumont d'Urville as second-in-command. Relations between the two were soon strained. Dumont d'Urville was solitary and patronising; his coolness irked Duperrey. He often dressed scruffily, a colleague said he had 'the indifference of a tramp to his appearance.' He relished the misunderstandings when officers from other ships blinked at being addressed on familiar terms by someone without a uniform. An anonymous commentator observed that while he had 'the heart of an aristocrat, his outer husk was plebeian.'

On their return they anchored in Marseilles on 9 March 1825 after thirty-one months, 75,000 miles, and not a single fatality. Their work was praised by Cuvier and von Humboldt, but Dumont d'Urville thought Duperrey had been too timid and hampered the science. His remarks betray a paranoid strain that would be echoed by his American contemporary, Charles Wilkes: 'I was disgusted to see that officer get all the credit for an expedition that was almost wholly due to me.'

Comments from fellow officers are consistent, revealing both his competence, which was widely respected, and his character, which inspired no affection. In January 1837 he wrote to the Minister of Marine proposing a visit to the South Seas; D'Urville had become obsessed with equalling Cook's three Pacific cruises. The French King himself added a requirement to include Antarctica. It led to the first close circumnavigation of the Antarctic, nailing it as a sizeable landmass, and throwing a lasso around mapmaker's imaginations. From now on, they had to draw it in the latitudes south of his course. D'Urville took the *Astrolabe* which he had used on his previous voyage, and his old friend Charles Jacquinot captained the corvette *Zelée*. The crew were offered a one hundred Francs bonus for achieving 75°S and an additional twenty Francs for each extra degree attained. Dumont d'Urville was forty-seven, looked older, and his wife did not want him to go. When he boarded someone remarked, presumably very quietly, 'That old fellow isn't going to take us very far.' One additional scientist was recruited at the last minute when d'Urville met a Monsieur Dumoutier, who analysed character from the shape of the head using the fraudulent science of phrenology, and invited him along. He would, in the oddest way, be the only one to know his commander's body.

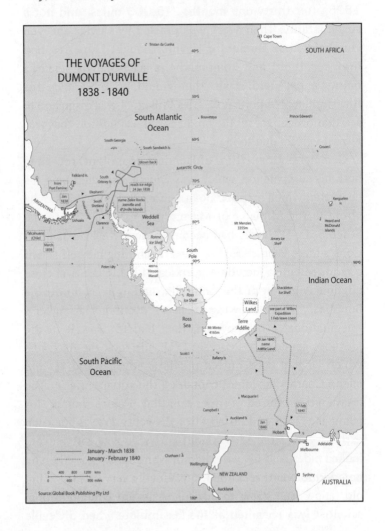

THE VOYAGES OF
DUMONT D'URVILLE
1838 - 1840

They left Staten Island, the last outpost of South America, on 10 January 1838, and within three days they saw their first ice. He quoted the inscription Dante gave to the gates of Hell: *Lasciate ogni speranza voi ch'entrate*: Abandon all hope you who enter. He wanted to chart the edge of the ice field, so they sailed east and south from Clarence Island, off the tip of the Peninsula, encountering the pack on 21 January and cruising along its edge for three days. Land glimpsed on 23 January proved an illusion. Illusions are big in Antarctic history. On 24 January they made a farthest south at 63°23′S and 045°17′W, and began to talk of reaching 80°S; after all, they were in the area where Weddell had reported open water. Like everyone who followed Weddell, they found ice. Fogs and gales drove them north to the South Orkneys hoping to kill birds and seals to augment their diet and strength.

When the winds eased on 2 February they decided to foray south once more. In two days they were again surrounded by massive bergs, and the other officers were alarmed when he decided to enter a narrow lead since the bergs were moving and soon menaced his exit. They were the first ship to sail into the pack and try to force a passage, just beating James Clark Ross, often wrongly credited with being the first. Despite taking such risks, d'Urville only just passed 62°S. He warped his way along on ice anchors: carrying anchors out in boats to distant bergs, securing them, then using the capstans to winch the ship forward. In ten hours they made one mile, and it was five days before they gained open water. At the time d'Urville could not decide whether to doubt Weddell's navigation or his honesty: 'Either Weddell struck an exceptionally favourable season, or he played on the credibility of his readers.' But when writing his formal account he later admitted, 'the recent success of Captain James Ross has altered my opinion.'

On Valentine's Day they headed west for the South Shetlands. Hopes for more open ice conditions were dashed; one berg measured eleven miles long and 120 feet high. Gales began to blow them back towards the South Orkneys, and they went with the weather. After failing to land at Saddle Island they made a landing at Weddell Island, where they took samples of rocks and penguins. On 22 February they made a second attempt to reach the South Shetlands. Bad weather and poor sketch-charts made d'Urville decide to name all the lands he saw around tip of peninsula and withdraw them later if they proved to have been previously named by Weddell. The first rocks seen were named Zelée, and the main island at the tip of the peninsula still bears name they gave them it: Joinville, named for King Louis-Phillipe's son, the Prince de Joinville. D'Urville Island next door was named for the leader by a later explorer.

This time they went down the Bransfield Strait and on 5 March reached 63° 27´S at a position west of Trinity Island, where Lt. Dubouzet on the *Zelée* wrote: 'The heavy north west swell forced us out to sea, the whole night we had freezing, penetrating rain which exhausted our sailors. Several of them were starting to get sore mouths, pain and fever, the early symptoms of scurvy, and this made a longer stay in these regions dangerous.'

That same day Dr Hombron informed d'Urville that scurvy risked becoming rampant on the *Zelée*; fourteen were bedridden, fourteen more showed early symptoms. D'Urville was shocked; despite two long voyages in his youth, this was the first time scurvy had broken out on any ship he was on. He banned even mentioning the word scurvy or referring to his plans to come south again the next Austral summer; such was the disease's power to undermine morale. They sailed for Chile on 20 March with a total of twenty-seven cases on the two ships. They were so short-handed that officers had to go aloft. When they disembarked at Talcahuano, some crewmen were so disfigured that their officers had to ask their names.

In port Dumont d'Urville received awful news. A letter from his wife was waiting. Their young son had died of cholera. He recorded, 'I no longer pray to God, I am cursed by him.' He could not replace his sick crew because other French seamen in port thought the expedition was disaster waiting to happen. During a spell in the Far East, the expedition picked up such virulent fevers that Dumont d'Urville made his will. They headed for Hobart then, once more, the purification of the ice.

D'Urville's task was to see where the edge of the pack lay in those longitudes south of Tasmania where no one had ever probed. At midnight on 18 January at 64°S they saw five huge tabular bergs, making them think land was close. Next morning there were more, even bigger. During one spell of fog, they suspected there was land to the west-south-west under the dark cloud oppressing that quarter, but as the sun rose higher the island vanished. At 18:00 Dumoulin went up the mast, and called land – new land! Others swarmed up and confirmed it, but Dumoulin had second thoughts and began doubting what he had seen. He ended up being the first to see it and the last to be convinced.

They crossed the Antarctic Circle on 21 January and the crew improvised a Crossing the Line ceremony, featuring Father Antarctic. An engraving of this is the most vivid image of the voyage. Many of the crew are in fancy dress, one is a stock carnival character slung about with animals skeletons, another is a giant penguin. The officers huddle above on the quarterdeck, hands jammed in pockets or armpits, looking glumly tolerant. Around them towered the icebergs: 'the spectacle they presented was both magnificent and terrifying. One could have believed oneself in the narrow streets of a city of giants.'

Nearing midnight the sun went behind a cloud and the glare dropped. Both ships were now becalmed, but the *Zelée* launched a boat which hailed the *Astrolabe*, saying they were sure it was land, but they could not see bare rock. The wind rose and huge bergs gathered about them, higher than their masts. At 22:30 d'Urville launched two boats which rowed towards the alleged shore until they were so far off only the masts of the ships were visible, knowing all the time that if the wind shifted, the ships would have to desert them and sail out to sea for their own safety. The boats reached small islands five hundred metres from the coast, and went ashore to raise the *tricolore* 'on this land that no human being before us had either seen or set foot on.'

They were struck by the extreme barrenness of their new realm; there were no shells or lichen, and just one piece of seaweed, dropped by a passing cormorant. The land lacked something else: a name. It is touching that d'Urville's wife, Adèle, was so much in his mind that he not only called this new coast after her, but he used his pet name for her: Adélie. With picks, the landing party prised out samples of a hard reddish granite or gneiss, and took penguins. They were a new species, and they were named Adélie penguins, a fine name for these chic, stylishly marked birds: the most Parisienne of penguins.

114

They made their way along 150 miles of coast, naming another section the Clarie Coast, for Captain Jacquinot's wife; Cape Pépin was named after his wife's family. Once the Pépins had not been good enough for him to marry, according to d'Urville's snobbish mother; now their name was written on the earth. D'Urville formally claimed Terre Adélie for France, and it became important as the foundation for France's future Antarctic claims. Ice conditions were difficult, and they were near enough to the South Magnetic Pole for the compass to be unreliable. Gales stacked so many icicles in the rigging that it was not safe to go aloft, and falling lumps and daggers of ice made simply being on deck dangerous. At one point the ships became separated and they were forced to fire cannons to locate each other.

On 29 January they saw the one thing that seemed impossible: another ship. More on that in the next chapter. On 1 February at 65°20′S 113°E they left the coast behind, the men exhausted. Their first port was Hobart, Tasmania where d'Urville compared notes with sealer John Biscoe. The French squadron did not anchor back home in Toulon until 6 November 1840, by which time twenty-five men had died, and all the living were worn down. He was visited by Captain Matterer, an old accomplice in the purchase of the Venus de Milo, who found 'he was no more than a ghost, a worn body that dragged itself painfully around, but his calm and austere features were still highly expressive, and his eagle eyes shone when he told me' of his voyage. Chronic gout had caused renal colic, and he complained: 'My friend I am finished, a being who is now worn out.'

Recognition for his suffering was everything to the small-town boy. When d'Urville was promoted to rear-admiral,

Matterer found him with letter 'against his heart and his eyes full of tears.' A Société de Géographie gold medal followed. The ten-year-old who had lamented the lack of heroes in Condé-sur-Noireau's cemetery had his fame at last. Dumont d'Urville published his account of the voyage in 1841 to great acclaim, but he was no longer fit for sea. He retired in 1842, aged only fifty-two. The official history of the voyage came out in 1846 in ten volumes, and the scientific results were published in twenty-three volumes and seven atlases completed in 1854. But d'Urville was already dead.

On 8 May 1842 d'Urville, his wife Adélie, and their son took the new railway out to Versailles on the Sunday of the King's official birthday. They returned on the 17:30 train, and the stationmaster locked the doors as the signal was given to depart. The train was crammed with 768 people in its seventeen carriages, and was too full to stop at any of the stations between Versailles and Paris. It departed three minutes late; the engineers were urged to go full speed to make up time. Just after Bellevue Station the axle of the lead engine shattered, the second engine and carriages piled up to the height of a house. Part caught fire. Dozens died, and the d'Urvilles were missing. Rear Admiral Jules-Sébastien-César Dumont d'Urville's skull was identified by the phrenologist Dumoutier. His wife was identified by the partly melted gold chain about her neck, their son only by his proximity to them.

# SCURVY

The first book you used to see as you walked into the Greenwich Observatory in London was a large ledger whose pages rippled with lines of browned hand-written ink. It was the log of HMS *Wager* under Commander George Anson on her voyage to attack Spanish treasure ships sailing from the west coast of South and Central America to the Far East. Financially it was Eldorado; they brought home treasure which filled thirty-two carts and paraded it round London. In human terms it was a massacre. They set out with 1972 men to actively engage with the enemy. They lost four men in combat and thirteen hundred to disease, many to scurvy. Such loss of life was intolerable even in a society where life was cheap. It triggered the first serious study by Edinburgh naval surgeon James Lind of a disease that killed more sailors than any human enemy.

We now know that the body needs vitamin C to make collagen, a protein which helps hold the body together. The vitamin is vital for the maintenance and repair of soft tissue, bones and teeth. It cannot be stored by the body; what isn't used leaves in urine. Humans are unusual among animals in not being able to make vitamin C; they must consume it in their food. If healthy people are put on a diet without vitamin C, their bodies start to run out of it after three months, so the disease was little known until men began to make long oceanic voyages, unable to take on fresh food. Without vitamin C, skin falls off, fingernails and toenails bleed, gums shrink, teeth loosen and drop out, long-healed bone fractures come apart, and the mind is afflicted with depression. Victims bruise easily and succumb more readily to infections.

The first detailed account of the symptoms comes from Sir Richard Hawkins on his voyage to the Pacific in 1593. He blamed it on the long time they had spent close to the equator and thought it could be remedied by eating the produce of the tropic zone. He recommended citrus fruit. Although his cure was exactly the right solution, subsequent voyages tried different fruits without success, and fresh food became just another recommendation, along with cleanliness.

James Lind's work concluded with a trial where he separated scurvy victims into groups and treated each one with a different contemporary cure. One was a cordial of lime and lemon juice. At the end of a week, all the men following that treatment were fit for work. All the other patients were dead. It still took the British Navy another fifty years to act. Finally, in 1795, lemon juice was issued on all naval vessels and by 1805 scurvy was virtually eliminated, although it later resurged because captains bought limes, which were cheaper than lemons. They did not know that levels of vitamin C in limes are half those of lemons. Lind saved the nation. Had health not improved in the Napoleonic Wars, Britain would have run out of sailors and lost.

# IT'S A CONTINENT!
## CHARLES WILKES AND THE EXPLORING EXPEDITION
## (1838–42)
## CHARLES WILKES (1798–1877)

In 1825 US President John Quincy Adams's inaugural address advocated exploring the Pacific North West; expansionism would make the United States. It was a sound idea; but the idea which launched Wilkes's Exploring Expedition was utterly mad. In 1818 John Cleves Symes, a thirty-eight-year-old retired army captain, had noted that some animals migrated north in summer and returned fat. He argued that the animals were going down through a hole at the pole to feed on richer pastures. The world was hollow with other worlds within, like Russian dolls. The curvature was gentle enough to allow you to sail over the rim and head into the interior without being aware of it. In March 1822, he petitioned Congress for money for a voyage north to demonstrate its truth. Jeremiah Reynolds, a talented public speaker, took it up, gathered support, but split with Symes when the author of the theory changed his plans to advocate a voyage south seeking the open water found by James Weddell. Symes died in 1829, before any voyage could be launched, and was buried with a hollow globe on his tombstone. Edgar Allan Poe's short story 'The Narrative of Arthur Gordon Pym of Nantucket' was inspired by Symes's theory. But the Exploring Expedition would take place, and a commander was needed.

That dryly witty stylist, Mark Twain, wrote that Charles Wilkes 'had gone wandering about the globe in his ships and had looked with his own eyes upon its furthest corners, its dreamlands – names and places which existed rather as shadows and rumours than as realities.' Wilkes led the last naval squadron to circumnavigate the world by sail without auxiliary steam. But when he died, his achievement as leader of the Exploring Expedition was already forgotten.

His officers on that trip began by loving and respecting him. The twenty-two-year-old Midshipman William Reynolds opened his journal declaring 'I like Captain Wilkes very much. He is a most wonderful man, possesses a vast deal of knowledge and has a talent for everything.' He was 'the most proper man who could have been found in the Navy to conduct this expedition.' In Polynesia Reynolds would revisit this entry and write over it: 'great mistake, did not at this time know him.'

Wilkes was born in New York City in 1798; his mother died when he was two. He was put in the care of his aunt Elizabeth Seton, who became an abbess and the USA's first native-born saint. His Welsh nanny had no objection to her own reputation as a witch, and predicted he would become an admiral although there was no such rank in the US Navy. After the end of the Napoleonic Wars in 1815, all navies cut back hard. You didn't need to lay off the men, they gladly walked, but the officers stayed on the books, inactive, on half pay, manoeuvring for positions. Wilkes's family contacts were good, but not good enough. Land-lubbered, he practised the scientific aspects of seamanship such as sextant work, and convinced himself that homework mattered more than experience. This caused problems when he went to sea with men who thought sailing provided the best experience. In desperation he eventually signed on as a midshipman. He did not like the fo'c'sle, it was chaotic, communal and familiar; he was aloof, scholarly and condescending.

After Wilkes returned from a voyage to the Pacific in 1823 he made a one-year trip to the Mediterranean. After that, he spent no significant time at sea for fifteen years until, through political manoeuvring and luck, he obtained command of the Exploring Expedition, though he had less sea time than many of the midshipmen. Private notes reveal his ambition outreached his confidence: 'It required all the hope I could muster to outweigh the intense feeling of responsibility that hung over me. I may compare it to that of one doomed to destruction.'

They sailed on 18 August 1838 with a varied fleet. The flagship was the 127-foot sloop *Vincennes*. The next largest was the *Peacock*, 118 feet, She had spent sixty hours on a reef earlier that year, and her captain, Hudson, was worried about her condition. The *Porpoise*, eighty-eight feet, was under Cadwallader Ringgold, two schooners, the *Flying Fish* and the *Sea Gull*, commanded by midshipmen were seventy-foot New York pilot cutters; with a crew of fifteen they were like yachts, they even had tillers instead of wheels.

Their orders, which Wilkes shared with no one, were to investigate reported mid-Atlantic shoals, go to Rio de Janeiro for provisions, survey the estuary of the Rio Negro, and establish a base in the islands north of Cape Horn. One vessel, the *Relief*, proved so slow she was ordered to sail straight to Rio.

Wilkes was scared of officers with real experience. He promoted two junior lieutenants from his coterie of favourites to skipper the cutters *Sea Gull* and *Flying Fish*, upsetting all his senior lieutenants. The resentful senior lieutenants were then despatched to other ships, to serve under officers who were also lieutenants. On 16 February they attained Cape Horn in sunny, warm weather and calm

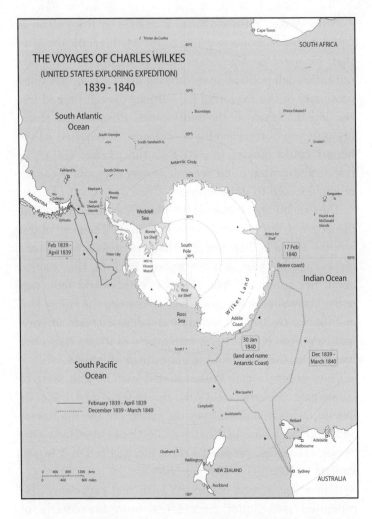

THE VOYAGES OF CHARLES WILKES
(UNITED STATES EXPLORING EXPEDITION)
1839 - 1840

South Atlantic
Ocean

South Pacific
Ocean

Indian Ocean

Feb 1839 -
April 1839

17 Feb
1840
(leave coast)

30 Jan
1840
(land and name
Antarctic Coast)

Dec 1839 -
March 1840

February 1839 - April 1839
December 1839 - March 1840

Cape Town
SOUTH AFRICA
Tristan da Cunha
40°S
50°S
Bouvetøya
Prince Edward I
South Georgia
60°S
South Sandwich Is
Crozet I
Antarctic Circle
Falkland Is
South Orkney Is
70°S
Kerguelen Is
ARGENTINA
Rio Gallegos
Elephant I
Moody Point
South Shetland Islands
Weddell Sea
80°S
Amery Ice Shelf
Heard and McDonald Islands
Ushuaia
Ronne Ice Shelf
South Pole
90°S
90°E
Peter I Øy
4897m Vinson Massif
Wilkes Land
Ross Ice Shelf
Adélie Coast
Ross Sea
Scott I
Macquarie I
Campbell I
Auckland Is
Hobart
Adelaide
Melbourne
Chatham I
Wellington
NEW ZEALAND
Sydney
AUSTRALIA
Auckland
180°

0   400   800   1200   km
0   400   800   miles

seas, and anchored in Orange Bay. The *Porpoise* and *Peacock* would go south with the schooners. Hudson in the *Peacock*, together with the *Flying Fish*, was ordered to head for the region around 106°W where Cook had made his farthest south, and try to beat it. This contrasted with the approach of previous leaders who shunned waters previously sailed in preference for new seas offering the prospect of discoveries.

Wilkes on the *Porpoise* would head, with the *Sea Gull*, for the South Shetlands, then to the Weddell Sea and the area where Weddell had found open sea. Possibly the lateness of the season could be converted into an advantage. In the ice, Wilkes found courage, or bravado. He wrote to his wife, Jane, of ice 'islands fifty times as large as the Capitol and much whiter.' When they arrived off the Peninsula they found the Government-issue cold-weather clothing was useless, which was especially hard on the crew of the little cutter *Sea Gull*, with waves breaking over her deck. Wilkes cut short her suffering, ordering her back to South America. He himself did not press farther south but went up the east side of the South Shetlands.

In the other party, a gale soon separated Hudson from the cutter *Flying Fish* and when she did not show up at the pre-planned rendezvous, he went on. If Wilkes got a buzz out of ice navigation, Hudson disliked it: 'This fancy kind of sailing is not all that it is cracked up to be.' On 23 March, Hudson stumbled across the *Flying Fish*. In storms she had lost her binnacle, and several seamen had broken ribs; the ship had leaked and all their clothes and bedding were wet. Five men were so hypothermic they could barely stand. Despite this they took time to be astonished at the rich wildlife. At one point a sleeping right whale had to be pushed out of the way with poles. In a comparison that reminds us that the world powers were now industrial countries, the spouts were likened to city chimneys. Size and distance befuddled them; they said that seeking ice for water they hove to against a berg 830 feet high. Including the invisible ice below the water, that would mean a piece of floating ice eight thousand feet high. There is none so large. But their sense of wonder was genuine, they felt like 'a mere skiff in the moat of a giant's castle'. Fog fell and a man called Palmer wrote that when they spoke: 'The voice had no resonance, words fell from the lip and seemed to freeze before they reached the ear.' The fog dispersed on 20 March, and they followed a lead through the ice between bergs like 'pale masses, like tombs in a vast cemetery.' On the 22 March they had reached 70°S 101°W, the farthest south for a US ship. Even James Cook had gone only ten miles farther. Two days later the sea began to freeze with an audible clicking like a death watch beetle.

Now came two incidents where officers coped well and Wilkes pilloried them. An officer called Dale was absurdly blamed for being trapped on a beach by a gale, and Midshipman Reynolds called it a 'turning point' in the feelings of the officers. In the Court Martial that followed back in the USA, one testimony proved most damning because it was temperate but acute. Asked if Wilkes's outbursts were due to provocation he responded 'No sir, in most cases directly the contrary; I have noticed that those most attentive to their duty would fall under his displeasure the soonest.'

Reynolds fumed: 'Here forward, there was no affection for his person, and consideration, humanity or justice was no longer hoped for at his hand.' That is chilling, though at this stage he was probably speaking more of himself and his intimates than the whole rank of officers. Reynolds developed a pathological hatred of Wilkes, and ultimately it blinded him to Wilkes's strengths, but his journal gives insight into the electric tensions between Wilkes's circle of favourites and the general run of his officers. Reynolds himself was a competent sailor and a popular man. He had little to learn from Wilkes, except, perhaps, how to hate.

When they sailed to South America, there was some drunkenness and desertion. The maximum number of lashes a captain could order without convening a Court Martial was twelve, a regulation often flouted. Wilkes gave punishments of between twenty-four and forty-one.

Rear Admiral Charles Wilkes

On 15 July 1839, one day out of Valparaiso, Wilkes appeared on deck in an 'immense pair of Epaulettes'. He had promoted himself to captain, commander, and commodore, and without authority flew a commodore's pennant from his masthead. 'It will give [Hudson and me] much more respect,' he wrote, as if respect were earned by tokens not action. His timing of this, as they entered the Pacific, meant that news of his presumption would be slow to reach home. It is fascinating to contrast two outward forms of the same arrogance: d'Urville, with a duke-like sense of superbia, dressing down; Wilkes collecting scrambled egg like a Latin dictator. You can imagine, if they had worn sunglasses, what size Wilkes would have bought.

On 13 August they reached the Tuamotus, north-east of Tahiti. The scientists chafed to explore. But science was permitted only as an afterthought, or not at all. Wilkes spitefully ordered that fraternising between ranks should be reduced, although he had begun by socialising with junior officers, before quarrelling with many of them. From this time forward there was war to the knife between Captain Wilkes and most of his officers. By mutual agreement, he and other officers now spoke only on business, and he was nicknamed Stormy Petrel because when he appeared there was bad weather ahead. Maybe compensating for his lack of general approval he drove himself very hard, seldom taking more than five hours sleep a night, some days none. Loss of sleep reduces emotional control, and makes it difficult to make complex social judgements. He recognised 'constant anxiety' in himself which he blamed on having to work with incompetents.

They went on to Sydney where Wilkes found it convenient to keep the US consul waiting two hours for an audience: 'I am now a great man, and others will wait patiently.' The scientists decided to stay in Australia. There, they would have leisure and freedom to conduct their investigations unhindered by Wilkes. They would also miss the cruise that proved Antarctica was a continent.

When the fleet next sailed towards the ice, south of New Zealand, Hudson's *Peacock* became detached from the other two large ships: the *Vincennes* and the *Porpoise*. The remaining two then lost contact with each other. Their continental sighting was handled shambolically. On 15 January the *Peacock* reached 65°25´ and no ice was visible ahead. Reynolds swaggered: 'Soon we would pass 70

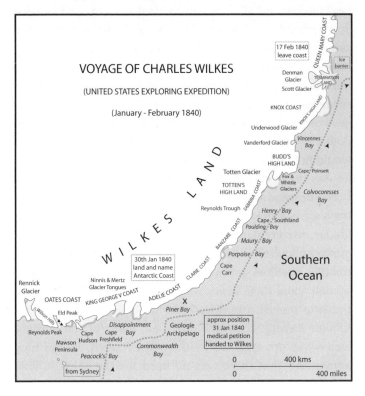

degrees – eclipse Cook & distance the pretender Weddell.' The ice soon taught them respect. They noted the compass dip was so steep that an iron button could deflect it 20°. The South Magnetic Pole was assuredly on this side of the continent. At 16:00 the *Peacock* simultaneously saw the *Porpoise* and the pack ice: welcome and unwelcome news in the same vista. The *Porpoise* had been cruising along its edge for several days. There would be no 70° here.

On 16 January, Reynolds and a colleague called Eld climbed to the masthead to enjoy the scene. He remarked on the entrancement of perpetual daylight: 'what a rooster would do here I cannot imagine.' Soon they saw three peaks at bearing 160°. They observed them for half an hour and fetched a telescope: 'We actually beheld the long sought for *Terra Firma* of the Antarctic continent.' They informed the deck officer Budd and Captain Hudson, but unbelievably neither would go aloft or send someone up to confirm. In fact Hudson would not leave his stove, and gave orders to tack away, adding contrarily that he had no doubt it was land but he would not enter it in the log. It would not be the only example of Hudson seeming to forget he was on an exploring expedition.

Fog descended to end any further arguments about what they were seeing. When vision is reduced, noises seem louder, the creaking of the rigging would have filled the misty hollow of their world. The sound of the small ice tinkling, the floes grating, and bergs grinding along the hull accompanied them every waking and sleeping hour. When the ship moved into deep clear water in the lee of a big tabular iceberg, the noise died, and many of the off-duty men woke up, spooked by the sudden hush. Wilkes now announced that there was no need for the ships to stay together, which promoted rivalry between crews to make new discoveries, but undermined safety. With a companion vessel, men can be removed from damaged ships to other vessels, but for a ship on its own, your only refuges are your open boats or possibly an iceberg.

On Sunday 19 January at 65°20′S and 154°30′E, Lt. James Alden on the deck of the *Vincennes* saw land, just as Wilkes was going below. Wilkes heard the call but went below anyway. He came out on deck later and, ignoring the officers, discussed with a gunner whether he thought it had been land. The gunner said if that wasn't land he'd never seen it. Still Wilkes did not enter it in the log.

On 23 January they sounded 350 fathoms, and killed an emperor penguin. The bird had stones in its belly. Having failed to prosecute enquiries when land was in sight, they now, on the basis of nothing more than shallow water and penguin ballast, celebrated with double grog rations the proximity of land.

On 28 January, in weather as 'clear as a bell', Lt. Alden made the first sighting of land that everyone could agree on. It was exciting, but islands had already been discovered in this sector by Balleny. On 30 January, still in beautiful weather, more land was seen, and a channel led through the ice towards it. This wasn't a group of small islands like the Ballenys; a chain of mountains ran east and west as far as the eye could see, sixty miles each way. It was a sizeable landmass, the length of Long Island or Wales. Wilkes named it the Antarctic Coast, and was desperate to land on it. In Piner Bay, named for their quartermaster, they lowered boats in a rising wind and got to half a mile from shore before the ice milling around made their position too precarious. Wilkes decided that any landing would have to be farther west. Before they could do so, Wilkes received a communication from one of the few groups of men he had yet to fall out with. The surgeons signed a letter on 31 January advising that the men were so weakened by cold and lack of sleep that any further reduction in the numbers able to report for work would place the ships in hazard. Wilkes's response was to warn they would sail west along the ice and shore 'until the ship should be totally disabled, or it should be evident that it was impossible to persist any longer.' Think about what he is saying: as many men as necessary will be sacrificed for his ambition.

On 2 February in fine weather there were twenty on the sick list. The next day blew a gale and thirty-six reported sick, many with ulcers and boils, a typical consequence of prolonged exposure to seawater and cold coupled with a poor diet. On 9 February darkness fell only to be relieved by a stunning display of the *aurora australis*. By day they cruised along the coast, Wilkes naming it after the officers he had not fallen out with: a dwindling choice. But he was still very fond of his young nephew, Henry Wilkes, who is always mentioned kindly in letters home to Jane. The boy must have found it trying to live in an atmosphere where his uncle was loathed by more and more men. He must also have dealt with it extraordinarily well; no one's private diary has anything but praise for him.

They landed on two large icebergs for magnetics and frolics. Magnetic measurements were more reliable taken safely away from the iron on the ship. The most memorable image of the trip is an informal painting of this day. It's a charming piece, showing the men at leisure. In the background, three men have planted a flag on hill. One man is tobogganing down on his belly, another tumbles over at its foot. Others swing pickaxes through a foot of ice to reach a pond of fresh water which their mates scoop into large leather flagons to take to ship. Young Midshipman Charles Erskine, good-looking with striking blue eyes, said: 'We had a jolly time, sliding and snowballing one another, and playing with penguins and seals.' In the foreground Wilkes's large Newfoundland dog, Sydney, lies watching his master slide decorously down a small bank in a sitting position, his large seal-skin boots braking his progress. Wilkes is taking his pleasure slowly, cautiously, alone. The painting is by Wilkes.

On 17 February the coast forced them north. Wilkes named it Termination Land. He had overridden the unanimous advice of his surgeons and forced his way along fifteen hundred miles of coast, while Dumont d'Urville had packed it in after a tenth as much, confessing: 'I very much doubt whether I could have stood it much longer.' Fifteen hundred  miles of coast does not belong to an island. Wilkes's cussedness had identified it as a continent. Meanwhile Ringgold, commanding the *Porpoise*, had sailed a conservative course north-west, largely remaining too far north to see land. What he did see, by a remarkable coincidence, were the ships of Dumont d'Urville, and they had seen him. The French vessels were slow, so d'Urville put up more sail to close the gap. Ringgold thought they were sailing away to avoid him, and veered off in a huff. The French saw this and blamed Ringgold; each felt rebuffed, so the Americans did not learn for some time that the French had sighted land on the 19 January: the precise day when a listless Wilkes refused to stay on deck and check Alden's sighting of land. Nor did he learn that on 21 January, the French had come to Piner Bay and done what they had failed to do and land, doubly pre-empting the Americans.

The Yankees headed for warmer water. Soon after landing at Sydney on 11 March, Wilkes heard the news of d'Urville's achievements. He now wanted to acknowledge Alden's sighting on 19 January and may have altered his own diary to say so; the entry looks suspicious. On the *Peacock*, Reynolds and Eld had seen land on 16 January, three days before the French, when the torpid Hudson had refused to abandon stove duty. Wilkes now conferred with Hudson who was in a dilemma. He could help Wilkes pip the French by endorsing Reynolds's and Eld's claims for prior discovery, but their claims also pre-dated Wilkes's discoveries, which would wound Wilkes's pride. It would also highlight Hudson's negligence in not checking for himself. In character, Hudson opted for the easy life, said nothing about Reynolds and Eld, and declared that Mr Wilkes had all the luck, and had beaten him once more. Wilkes now wrote in the *Sydney Herald* that he too had seen land on 19 January. When Wilkes later found out about Hudson's negligence on the 16 January, he wrote to Jane: 'for all we gained by the others they might as well been elsewhere employed'; one of his more justified gripes.

Wilkes wrote to James Clark Ross, who was soon expected in Tasmania, to tell him of the US discoveries. Wilkes included a chart of their discoveries, although divulging such details was completely against orders. His motive was vanity; the last time they had met Ross had been the senior navigator. Although Ross would not accept Wilkes's observations as conclusive, he took Wilkes's chart and later sailed though areas marked as land, generously observing that it was hard to distinguish ice from land without being much closer to shore than ships normally achieved.

Wilkes continued to Fiji then Sydney. Then tragedy struck close. Landings were resisted by the Aborigines; a party under the intelligent and well-educated Lt. Underwood was attacked on a beach and overwhelmed. Nephew Henry Wilkes was clubbed in the head and lay in the shallows while the fight continued. When it was over someone rushed to him, but he had drowned. By chance Wilkes arrived back at the ship at the same time as the boat carrying the bodies. When they pulled back the canvas he fainted. They returned to the island and in revenge for two deaths killed eighty natives.

Late in the cruise they received newspapers; Reynolds had been promoted, Wilkes had not. Hurt and frustration filled his letters home. Jane, whom he called his moderator, was supposed to placate him, but even she questioned the wisdom of his flying, without authority, a commodore's pennant. The homecoming was not to be an opportunity to recognise a team performance, it would be stage-managed to feed Wilkes's needy ego. The *Oregon* and *Porpoise* were diverted to Rio de Janeiro ostensibly for minor observations, but in reality so the *Vincennes* would enter New York harbour first and alone. Only a little over half the original crews remained, and two ships. The *Flying Fish* had been found to be unsound and was sold off in Singapore.

What he could not control was the politics at home.

They had departed under the Democrat President Jackson, but the Oval Office was now occupied by the Whig John Tyler, who was embroiled in delicate negotiations with Britain over the border between Canada and Maine. Tyler did not want attention drawn to the Pacific North West where Britain was fiercely jealous of the charter of her Hudson Bay Company. He imposed a news blackout. Wilkes fumed.

Several officers and scientists dismissed by Wilkes had arrived home long before and a tawdry exchange of accusations began. Wilkes was largely exonerated by a Court Martial, being found guilty only of unlawful flogging. But the whiff of bad eggs hung around his management. Having awarded himself captaincy years before and paraded in the costume, he was awarded only the lesser rank of commander, and not until the following year. He did not make captain until thirteen years later.

His character should not overshadow his achievement. His scientists had out-collected Cook's: 4000 ethnographic items, 10,000 species of plants, 2150 birds, 588 species of fish, 300 species of fossils and 400 species of corals. They had drawn 241 new charts, and surveyed fifteen hundred miles of Antarctic coast, confirming it as a continent. Dana's volume *Crustacea* identified over five hundred new species of crabs, lobsters, shrimps and barnacles. Charles Darwin read it with admiration, and wrote to him to say so: if Dana had 'done nothing else whatever, it would have been a *magnum opus* for life. I am really lost in astonishment at that which you have done in mental labour. And then, beside the labour, so much originality in all your works.' Being called original by Darwin is praise for life. Botanist Asa Gray worked on the botany specimens at Harvard. After corresponding with Darwin on similarities between geographically distant plants he became the USA's leading promoter of the theory of evolution. Humboldt called the expedition's results 'the most splendid contribution to science of the present day.'

They brought back so many objects and records that the US did not have the resources in its institutions to handle them. However four years before, in 1838, James Smithson had left the Government half a million dollars in gold for the 'increase and diffusion of knowledge.' Joel Poinsett created the National Institution for the Promotion of Science, as a vehicle to handle Wilkes's results. It became Washington's Smithsonian Museum.

Wilkes petitioned to have the copyright of both the official journal and his personal narrative, despite having heavily used his officers' accounts. Astonishingly this was granted. The volumes of the official account matched the leader's ego: vast and hide-bound. A limited edition of one hundred Morocco-covered sets of five principal volumes was produced: some of the most expensive books in the history of American publishing. Wilkes included much secondary material, the sign of an insecure writer. Charles Davies, writing for the *North American Review*, said it was 'crushed under the weight of irrelevant matter.'

The expedition had an impact on wider American policy and the creation of nationhood and policy. From 1840–60, Government-driven surveying and exploring expeditions, domestic and international, took between 25% and 33% of the federal budget. But Wilkes was not given another command until the Civil War, when he seized Confederate commissioners from a British vessel. He met President Lincoln, and was promoted to one of the new posts of rear admiral, just as his Welsh nanny had predicted. Persistent flouting of orders led to him being brought to Court Martial, and suspended for three years; he never again saw active service.

Charles Wilkes died at home on 8 February 1877, aged seventy-eight. Many obituaries made no reference to the

Wilkes Expedition. The Civil War had inflicted such a bloody trauma to the American psyche that a blind had been drawn across US history. Behind it, obscured, lay another country, and Wilkes's fame.


## DARING TO PIERCE THE PACK 1839–43
## JAMES CLARK ROSS (1800–1862)

Born in London in 1800, James Clark Ross was the nephew of Captain John Ross. James joined the Navy in 1812, and between 1819 and 1827 made four Arctic expeditions under William Parry, his uncle's Arctic rival. In 1825 James witnessed the loss of the *Fury* which made Parry conclude that 'a vessel of whatever magnitude, or whatever strength, is little better than a nutshell, when obliged to withstand the pressure of the unyielding ground on one side, and a moving body of ice on the other.' Young Ross would make his name hazarding his vessels to such risks.

He was back with his uncle from 1829–33, when he led the journey which claimed one of the great geographical prizes: the determination of the North Magnetic Pole, located on the Boothia Peninsula, Canada, in May 1831. In a delightful touch he planted the flagstaff of his boat to mark the position, so there was an actual pole at the Magnetic Pole. As overall commander, his uncle took the credit, the prize money and a knighthood; however, James was promoted. The actual magnetic pole is constantly shifting, so the flagstaff has been retrieved and is in the National Maritime Museum in Greenwich, London, a more convenient place to explore. They also have one of the numerous portraits of him; he was reputed to be the handsomest man in the Navy at a time when playing the peacock was one of the perks of working in uniform. He carried it off in grand style.

The eighth meeting of the British Association for the Advancement of Science at Newcastle, England, in 1838, noted of the earth's magnetism: 'That great and notorious deficiencies exist in our knowledge of the course of the variation lines generally, but especially in the antarctic seas, and that the true position of the southern magnetic pole or poles can scarcely even be conjectured with any probability from the data already known.' They resolved 'that the deficiency ... should be supplied by observations of the magnetic direction and intensity, especially in the high southern latitudes between the meridians of New Holland (Australia) and Cape Horn.' They recommended a naval expedition, and command was awarded to James Clark Ross. He must have thought this was his chance to bag a double: the North and South Magnetic Poles. The scheme was endorsed by the Royal Society, then the Government, and the Admiralty allocated the 370-ton *Erebus* and 340-ton *Terror*, both bomb ships: platforms to fire heavy mortars. Built to extremely strong specifications, they were considered suitable for demanding work in ice. Because of past problems with mixing military and civilian personnel, the civilian scientists necessary for the voyage were taken as 'surgeons'; the botanist J. D. Hooker was one, while on the *Erebus* was Robert McCormick, who had been with Darwin on HMS *Beagle* and with Parry on the *Hekla* in 1827. Each ship had a crew of sixty-four. Although much of Ross's trip took place far from the Peninsula, I describe it here because Ross's discoveries influenced all later explorers.

They left Cornwall, England on 5 October 1839, and sailed via St Helena, which they reached on 31 January 1840, pausing to establish the first observatory there. Their next passage, to the Kerguelen Islands via the Cape of Good Hope, took sixty-eight days, for forty-five of which they suffered gale force winds or worse. Two days after they left Kerguelen they were separated in a storm, and did not see each other until they sailed into their default rendezvous in Hobart on the 15 and 16 August 1840. Governor John Franklin was waiting with two hundred convicts who built a new observatory in nine days. In mordant irony, Franklin would later be given Ross's two ships in another effort to seek the North West Passage, and die a death that made him more famous than any deed in his life.

They left Hobart on 12 November and drove south via the Auckland Islands, then Campbell Island. On 27 December they saw whales and the first icebergs; fifteen were visible at one time during the evening. On 29 December 'a great many whales were seen, chiefly of the common black kind' (perhaps southern right whales, very profitable for oil and baleen); 'we might have killed any number we pleased: they appeared chiefly to be of unusually large size, and would doubtless yield a great quantity of oil, and were so tame that our ships sailing close past did not seem to disturb them.' This report became common knowledge at a time when Arctic and Pacific catches were declining, and it aroused fresh excitement over the possibility of a southern bonanza for whalers. On 30 December 'a beautiful white petrel was seen in the evening [a snow petrel] giving notice of our approach to a large body of ice.' These beautiful creatures feed on the zooplankton which graze beneath the ice, and are true ice-birds.

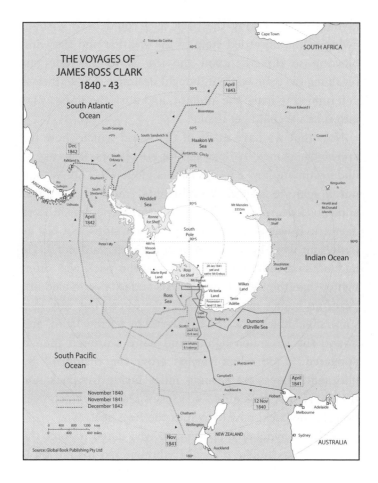

THE VOYAGES OF
JAMES ROSS CLARK
1840 - 43

South Atlantic
Ocean

SOUTH AFRICA

Indian Ocean

South Pacific
Ocean

AUSTRALIA

NEW ZEALAND

November 1840
November 1841
December 1842

Source: Global Book Publishing Pty Ltd

They crossed the Antarctic Circle on New Year's Day 1841, but 5 January was to prove a more historic date. Firstly, in the early hours, the number of large icebergs dwindled. At 08:00 they met the pack and sailed along its edge. 'From the mast-head it seemed sufficiently open to admit of our penetrating as far as we could see to the southward; and although other circumstances were not so favourable for taking the pack as I could have wished, owing to the unsettled state of the weather and the wind blowing so directly upon the ice as to preclude our regaining the open water if thought desirable, I nevertheless determined to make the attempt, and push the ships as far into it as we could get them.'

Now that we have maps of the world which show the knowledge gained by Ross and his successors, it is easy to underestimate how courageous his move was. Amundsen, not a man to scatter compliments, rated it the most audacious decision in all polar history. One reason Ross dared do it was the brute strength of his ships, but just as important were his ambition and his observant mind. He had noticed that the main body of the pack was often lighter than the ice at the edge. His audacity soon paid off. 'After an hour's hard thumping, we forced our way into some small holes of water, connected by narrow lanes' and 'found the ice much lighter and more scattered than it appeared to be when viewed from the distance.' By midnight, they were seventy miles inside the pack. On 8 January they took a new species of seal, one which lives deep in the pack, now known as the Ross seal.

Ross is remembered as the man who dared to force the pack because, unlike d'Urville who entered it first, on 9 January Ross forced through it and out of the other side. He discovered open water behind the ice, and called it the Ross Sea. For future explorers it was, like Weddell's farthest south in an open sea, an encouragement to push south regardless. It would often prove a siren call. On 10 January Ross wrote, 'We now shaped our course directly for the Magnetic Pole,' following the compass's arrow. Fog cleared during the morning and noon revealed that 'not a particle of ice could be seen in any direction from the mast-head.' Excited anticipation ran through the ship. They were sailing straight to the Pole! The very next day, he saw land blocking his path. His readings suggested that the Magnetic Pole was still two hundred miles away. He rightly guessed the South Magnetic Pole would not be found at sea, and it would be a land expedition, not a naval voyage that would claim it.

With Ross himself boarding a ship's boat, they threaded their way through hazardous ice travelling in a swift current, and leaped ashore on an island. On Possession Island the toasts and ceremonies of colonisation were conducted with relish. The new territory became Victoria Land on 12 January 1841, the first land to be claimed for the young queen, and the most southerly ever seen by man, surpassing Bellingshausen's discoveries. They tracked along the coast, still increasing their latitude, and on 22 January they passed Weddell's farthest south, a record which had stood for eighteen years.

Whales were everywhere, blue whales, humpbacks and sperm whales: 'here they have enjoyed a life of tranquillity and security; but will now, no doubt, be made to contribute to the wealth of our country, in exact proportion to the energy and perseverance of our merchants.' He could not have guessed such energy, allied with new technology, would almost wipe them from the seas.

On 28 January they saw a lofty peak which appeared to have snowdrift blowing far from its summit, 'but as we drew nearer, its true character became manifest.' It streamed flame and smoke, and was an active volcano, which they named Erebus. The eastern promontory at the foot of Mount Erebus was named after the commander of the *Terror*: Cape Crozier. It would feature as the base for Scott's attempts to reach the South Pole. Their sister ship *Terror* was remembered by a slightly smaller, inactive peak.

Their magnetic readings now suggested the Magnetic Pole was around 75°S and 174 miles away. On the same day as they discovered Mount Erebus they made another startling discovery, and one of the greatest sights in Antarctica: 'we perceived a low white line extending ... as far as the eye could see to the eastward. It presented an extraordinary appearance, gradually increasing in height, as we got nearer to it, and proving at length to be a perpendicular cliff of ice, between one hundred and fifty and two hundred feet above the level of the sea, perfectly flat and level at the top, and without any fissures or promontories on its even seaward face.' It was much higher than the tips of their masts, and formed a tantalising curtain closing off all views of the interior. He named it the Victoria Barrier, but it was later re-christened in his honour: the Ross Ice Shelf. It was often known simply as The Barrier, for as Ross wrote, damping down his disappointment, 'we might with equal chance of success try to sail through the Cliffs of Dover, as penetrate such a mass.' They tracked it for 250 miles, the edge of the continent, a vast bight filled with the outpourings of the world's largest glaciers. It was to be the base for all the early attempts on the pole.

On 15 February the sea began to freeze. The new ice was already four to five inches thick: 'had we not been favoured with a strong breeze of very precarious duration, which enabled me to force our ships through it, we should certainly have been frozen in.' In contrast to Wilkes's willingness to destroy men and bring ships to the brink of destruction, Ross thought their work did not justify such a terrible risk. As for work left undone, Ross devoutly wrote: 'we bowed in humble acquiescence to the will of Him who had so defined the boundaries of our researches.' They set a course northwards, but leaving the pack was much tougher work than entering it. They sailed through the line of Wilkes's mountains, drawn in the wrong place. When air sits in layers with denser air below, light is refracted downwards making visible objects normally below the horizon, and making them appear much closer to the American than he thought. Ross reached Hobart on 6 April 1841, with both crews healthy.

On 7 July 1841, with three years' more provisions stowed away, he set out once more to pick up his work where he had left it, sailing east towards the Antarctic Peninsula. By April 1842 he was back in the Falklands, with healthy men but tired and quarrelsome officers. There was one more sally south; on 17 December 1842 they sailed for the Antarctic Peninsula, and in the area now known as the Erebus and Terror Gulf, they picked their way around the north-west corner of the Weddell Sea, discovering, naming and taking possession. The island named after him dates from this venture. On 4 February 1843 they entered the pack at 64° south then tracked eastwards along its edge crossing the Antarctic Circle on 28 February 1843. On 5 March at 71°30′S Ross decided the season was over, and he headed home. His men were paid off in Woolwich, London on 23 September 1843, after an absence of four and a half years.

He was awarded the Founder's Medal of the RGS, the Gold Medal of the RGS of Paris; in 1844 he was knighted. When his account of the voyage was published he was elected to the Royal Society, but afterwards wrote very little. He married Ann Coulman and became a country gent near Aylesbury in Buckinghamshire. Ross refused command of a new expedition to find the North West Passage, having promised his bride's father he would make no more polar expeditions. Leadership passed to the governor who had shown them hospitality and friendship in Hobart: John Franklin. In 1848 Ross broke his promise by accepting command of the first expedition to discover Franklin's fate. He suffered terrible losses in the effort, but never found his friend.

# 6

## Deception Island

*There is one island I say goodbye to with poignancy at the end of each season in Antarctica. I know that one winter, vulcanologists' sensors planted in its dirt will tremble and satellites will spy plumes rising from its peaks. The first ships to break the spring ice will find the island changed, its harbour may be entirely closed, its anchorages sealed off from the sea by fresh lava, or uplifted land, the island almost unvisitable.*

The stone horseshoe of Deception Island is one of the most visited places in Antarctica, but don't hope for a sunny day or rich wildlife. Because its volcanic rocks are warm, it makes its own weather and prefers a lid of glowering cloud. Despite a harbour, Port Foster, that seems to shelter you for 350°, the winds can whistle over the surrounding mountains and come right down to sea level again, and rip through your clothing. Lieutenant Edward Kendall of the *Chanticleer* was on Sir John Franklin's second voyage and went through a particularly tough Arctic voyage on HMS *Griper*, but he complained of Deception: 'it was withal so

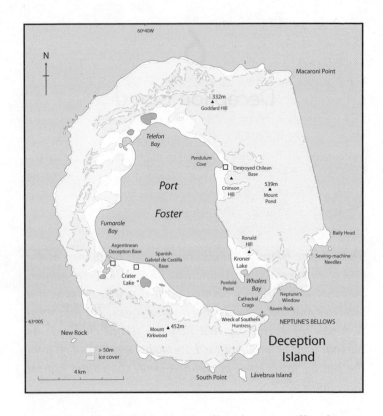

raw and cold, that I do not recollect having suffered more at any time.' In rapidly deteriorating weather I once shared the last Zodiac to ship with Peter Hillary, son of Sir Edmund Hillary of Everest, who has climbed many of the world's major peaks and skied to the South Pole. He pulled up his hood as we crossed Port Foster in a wind rising to full gale and remarked 'Feisty, isn't it?', which is as near as he gets to complaining about the weather. Although its waters are only slightly warmer than elsewhere, it's enough to make life tough for species of krill and fish that are extreme Antarctic specialists, so wildlife inside the harbour is scarce, and staff biologists on cruise ships usually loathe this visit. I love it.

First you squeeze through the narrow gap of Neptune's Bellows between the towering cliffs of Cathedral Crags and the barely submerged hazard of Raven Rock. To the left, red iron-rich rocks grip the last remains of the *Southern Huntress*, wrecked in 1957. Each spring the wreck is a little smaller, its carcase picked over by the winter gales. You may, if air pressure is low, smell the sulphur from the smoking fumaroles along that shore, for you are sailing into the flooded crater of an active volcano.

The key features of the shoreline are visible from on board as you turn starboard and see the arc of Whalers Bay before you. At the right hand end of the panorama, the bite out of the cliffs is Neptune's Window, famed from the Palmer story. Beneath it, and scattered all over the shore as you scan left, are the remains of whaling days. Many materials were abandoned in 1931 by men who left thinking business would soon recover, and never came back. The relics are all the more poignant for their smallness in the great and harsh landscape: staves still waiting to be made up into barrels, boat huts, and small, decked boats probably used to ferry fresh water to ships, a few whale-bones: a clavicle stabbing at the sky or a vertebra the size of a cable spool, but most bones now carpet the floor of the bay. Landings begin at a peculiar landmark: a huge U-shaped iron box. When flooded it could be slid under the hulls of catchers whose plates had been damaged by ice or rocks, then pumped with compressed air to raise the hull for repairs. In the centre of the bay is a mix of old huts from the days of Operation Tabarin, Falkland Islands Dependencies Survey (FIDS) and BAS, dominated by the rusting machinery and drunken storage tanks of the

Hektor whaling station. In the middle of them is a gap where the *lahar* triggered by the 1969 eruption cut a swath through the heart of the old settlement and flattened the cemetery where sealers, whalers and one BAS scientist were buried. The few crosses that now stand are 1970 re-interments of graves left partially exposed by the *lahar*. If you visit please ignore the fad of laying cairns around them. Such things were not part of the original cemetery. Away to the left the single large shed is a hangar, not from the pioneering days but from the post-war use by BAS.

Every human activity that has ever gone on in Antarctica has happened here: exploration, sealing, science, whaling, flying and spying. It's the continent in miniature. Initial exploration and sealing were dealt with in the chapter on Nathaniel Palmer, so we'll start with the first scientific visitors to Deception.

## THE PIT AND THE PENDULUM

In 1829 a small British Naval barque of 234 tons called the *Chanticleer*, commanded by Captain Henry Foster, sailed through Neptune's Bellows to the head of the harbour, and slipped into a creek lined with coarse black sand. He anchored securely in the manner of someone intending to stay. They began building strange structures, and erecting huts and tents. When these were completed to Captain Foster's satisfaction, unopened boxes were brought ashore under his strict supervision. They were handled like newborn babes. Under pain of severe punishment, no one, of whatever rank, was allowed to open or even touch one without Foster's express orders.

Foster was a rising star of the new breed of well-educated scientific Royal Naval officers, elected as a Fellow of the Royal Society aged twenty-seven. In 1827 he had won the Society's highest award, the Copley Medal, for magnetic and other observations in the Arctic on Sir William Parry's third voyage in search of the North West Passage. His current orders defined two main tasks: firstly, to make measurements of the power of the Earth's gravity here, in order to calculate the exact shape of the Earth in southern regions. Secondly he was to record the force and direction of its magnetic field. These might not seem priorities for military men, but the Navy had a life and death interest in both, because they affected navigation.

Magnetic research would make compass readings more reliable. A compass does not show true north and south, the geographic poles around which the earth rotates. Its needle points to the magnetic poles, and observations showed that they moved over time. Without an up-to-date map of the earth's magnetic field, you don't know where your compass is pointing.

The shape of the earth is important because distance travelled north or south over a curved surface like the earth is most conveniently measured using degrees, measured from the equator. If the earth were a perfect sphere, all these degrees would represent the same number of miles at the surface of the earth, but it isn't. Ninety years before, Newton's theory that the earth's rotation made it belly out at the equator had been proved by painstaking measurements on the ground. The circumference around the equator was shown to be eighty-five miles greater than that around the poles, so a degree of latitude at the equator is slightly larger than one at the poles. If you didn't correct for this, you would, as you approached the poles, always be nearer than you thought: a good recipe for sailing aground. Newton had also shown that the gravity of a large object like the earth behaves as if all its mass were located in a single point at its centre. Since gravity increases as objects get closer, gravity near the poles would be greater. As gravity influences the speed at which a pendulum swings, if you can measure the speed of a pendulum with fiendish accuracy, you can detect tiny differences in gravity and plot the earth's shape. Foster's forbidden boxes contained instruments that would allow him to do this. They were the best in the world: rare, expensive and delicate. He was one of the few men who knew how to use them with the necessary accuracy. The precision required to extract accurate results was exacting in a controlled laboratory. To do it in field conditions in Antarctica was a trial of science, skill, assiduousness, determination and perhaps sanity.

The spot where he worked is still named Pendulum Cove, but the creek has gone, and the beach is chiefly visited to find a pool of warm volcanic water for an Antarctic swim. The *Chanticleer* stayed two months and the men were heartily sick of it before they left. Midshipman Joseph Kay, only fourteen years old when the voyage began, heard the men muttering that Deception was 'the last place that Nature made.' When they were at last ready to leave, the shape-shifting island was not ready to release them. Contrary winds and icebergs blocking the Bellows kept them there another week.

They must have looked forward to reaching the turquoise anchorages of the Caribbean. In Panama, Foster made a canoe trip up the Chagres River to measure the longitude of the east and west coasts of Panama. That section of river is now the north end of the Panama Canal. Returning downstream Captain Foster was pitched overboard and drowned and the body not recovered for some time. He was thirty-four years old. Natives went through his pockets, and turkey vultures through his flesh. 'What a loss to England and to Science,' wrote Captain Fitzroy of the *Beagle*.

It was later found that the volcanic rocks of Deception Island were so full of iron that it had affected the pendulum's swing. All his painstaking measurements were worthless.

## PENDULUM SCIENTISTS: THE SULTANS OF SWING

The time it takes a pendulum to complete a swing depends on two things: the length of the pendulum (longer = slower) and the strength of gravity (stronger = faster). This was discovered by the French astronomer Jean Richer when in 1672, he left Paris, close to 49° north, and made measurements at Cayenne, French Guiana, at 5° north. To keep good time, he had to shorten his pendulum by 0.0226 cms. This means that you can measure gravity by timing the swing of a pendulum of known length. For example, a 40-inch pendulum (101.6 cms) has a one-second beat in Britain.

Foster had two models of pendulum to use in tandem. They worked best in buildings, so he first had to erect one: a wooden hut, double-skinned, and lined with blankets. The test pendulum was set up in front of a long-case clock with a marker on the pendulum of each. They swung at different rates and the simplest method of timing the swings was to time the interval between successive events where the swings coincided.

To correct for the expansion and contraction of the metals, parallel observations of air temperature were made from three thermometers at different heights in the room. He also measured the moisture of the air, the barometric pressure, the height above sea level, the state of the tide, and the line of swing of the pendulum. A telescope was used to make astronomical observations to determine the precise time of day. An average observation took 2 hours 40 minutes and he made 1017 of them. It was so time-consuming that he did not have time to calculate results from his own measurements, and the results were returned to Greenwich.

The magnetic results were still more complex. The lines of magnetic force were found to dip down into the earth as ships neared the poles. The horizontal part of the force became weak, and when a ship changed course the compass was sluggish in responding. The magnetic results were mostly passed to Woolwich Academy who made superficial remarks, published nothing, and filed them somewhere never since found.

# WHALING

In Antarctica's brief history, the only land-based activity to make much money was the brief slaughter carried out by the sealers. The oceans yielded more: the riches of whale oil. Until the middle of the nineteenth century, when coal gas and then mineral oil began to be heavily exploited, whales were the major source of high quality oils used in lighting, lubrication and various chemical industries. The last place on earth to be exploited was the Southern ocean round Antarctica, because it was far from the world's markets, dangerous to sail, and many of the whales were too powerful and fast to catch. By the late nineteenth century, technology had changed that.

Although whaling was a massive industry in Antarctica it was almost entirely ship-based. When the industry died and the ships sailed away they left few signs of their presence. In places like Neko Harbour where many people, including me, have taken their first steps on the continent, only the name remains of the whaler *Neko* which anchored here a few seasons. In other places, like Mikkelsen Harbour, there are bones and boat timbers, greying and crumbling, slowly becoming more like each other. Only at Deception are there significant remains.

In 1820, the year after the discovery of the South Shetlands, when Captain Edward Bransfield RN came down, there was a flotilla of sealers in his wake. Many whales were seen, but most were the massive rorqual species like blue, fin and sei whales. James Clark Ross found his wake was incessantly attended by whales. But although the whalers who followed him could and did take southern right whales, the great whales were too powerful for their harpoons and boats. Planting a hand-thrown harpoon in a rorqual was like throwing darning needles into a bull; it was barely enough to irritate it, never mind catch it. The industry wisdom was that even if you could catch whales, you were so far from the markets that most of your cruise would be inactive, sailing to and from the whaling grounds; the sums would never add up.

In 1870 a Norwegian named Svend Foyn perfected a small cannon which fired a explosive harpoon head that penetrated the whale's body deeply and detonated a few seconds later. Four fins would open up like an umbrella, and lock securely in the body. For the first time in whaling, securing a line and killing the whale had become a single operation. But they still did not have the boats to get close to the athletic whales. Steam-powered steel-hulled catcher ships of about 160 tons were being developed that could endure ice floes and keep pace with a sprinting whale. They brought a whole new way for whalers to operate, delivering the carcases to factory ships, then going straight out to hunt for more. In 1892 the first Norwegian whalers came down to Graham Land and the Weddell Sea. The steam factory ship *Admiralen* was in Antarctica in 1905, but lost money that season because of the coaling costs. Slowly they learned how to make it pay. While the catchers were purpose-built, the factory ships were mostly converted old freighters and passenger vessels of some three thousand to five thousand tons, bought cheaply for £6000 to £9000 in the years before the First World War, and lodged in safe harbours to await the catch. They soon realised that ageing sailing vessels were even cheaper to buy and didn't burn coal. The beautiful old Cape Horn clipper *Pisagua* was one such ship. In early photographs of Whalers Bay its graceful lines stand above the ugly shoeboxes of the steamers.

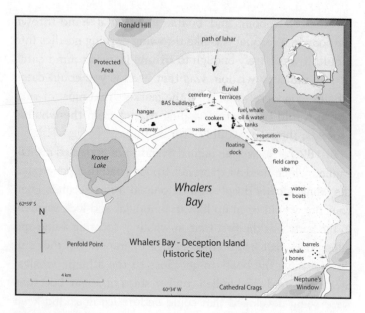

The men usually slept on board ship though some bunkhouses were built ashore.

The British recognised the terrible wastefulness of the industry. Even though the southern whales were much bigger than those now caught in northern waters, the oil yield per whale was only three-quarters. In part, this was deliberate. Whales were so abundant it was more profitable to take only the oil-rich blubber, then push the rest of the carcase out into the bay, with the meat and bones untouched. There were plenty more whales in the sea. Company balance sheets tell the story. 1911 was the last year the Hektor Company relied solely on ship-based processing with their single factory ship, the *Ronald*, and three catchers. They paid a dividend of 32%.

A flensed carcase (one stripped of blubber) might sink, drift away, or be blown back on shore. When there was an onshore wind at Whalers Bay, it was sometimes so deep in rotting carcases that men attempting to land waded through a swamp of rotting flesh being pillaged by clouds of scolding gulls and terns, blizzards of pintado petrels, and bloated southern giant petrels, their lumpen heads scarlet with gore. The shore station was encouraged by the British, who wanted an industry that had a chance of surviving the Klondike days of wanton killing, and they granted The Hektor Company a twenty-one-year lease. Their steam pressure cookers used far more of each whale, including the sawn bones which held up to 30% of the oil. They were also granted the rights to process any carcases discarded by other stations. The seas administered by FIDS, including Antarctica and South Georgia, contributed 65% of world production in 1913–14. The following year Hektor's shore-based operation, the rusting remains you see today in the centre of the bay, became operational. The improved efficiency showed in profits; by 1915 Hektor had taken over two other companies, and paid a dividend of 50%.

The Great War provided respite for the whales as ships were requisitioned for other uses and the seas became too dangerous to sail. But two inventions changed the industry. One was the stern slipway, rising through the stern of the factory ship, to haul whales smoothly and quickly onto deck. The other was the perfection of reverse osmosis to make freshwater from seawater. By the late 1920s the industry was independent of the shore and free of regulation. The industry overfished so savagely in 1930–31 that the price collapsed. Next year Hektor's twenty-one-year lease expired, and soon the Great Depression was on everyone. No land station ever operated again in Antarctica.

# AVIATION AT DECEPTION ISLAND

The first ever flight in Antarctica was made from just above the beach on a bumpy 600 yard (550 metre) ash track enlivened by two dog-legs, three ditches and two mounds. The pilot was Alaskan Carl Eielson but the imaginative force and directing genius was Hubert Wilkins. He was born on 31 October 1888 into a family forging a living on marginal land 100 miles (160 kilometres) north of Adelaide, South Australia, where unpredictable droughts wiped out the profit and stock painstakingly accumulated in the good times. In one three-year drought his father lost ninety thousand sheep. Cattle died, families starved. Wilkins wondered: 'Why should it not be possible to learn of the laws which govern the movements of the atmosphere, the conditions that bring about the seasonal rains and droughts? I determined to devote my life to that work.' He vowed to spend twenty years familiarising himself with polar regions, then twenty more promoting international co-operation in weather and climate studies. He did just that, and in doing so Hubert Wilkins advanced polar aviation beyond recognition and became one of the most famous people in the world.

He first came to Antarctica as one of the four members of the British Imperial Antarctic Expedition of 1920 under Dr John Lackland Cope. He returned in 1928 after making the first aircraft flight over the North Pole, pioneering the circumpolar routes flown by modern airliners, despite Roald Amundsen warning him: 'What you are trying to do is beyond the possibility of human endeavour.' He had done it in a new plane, the Vega, manufactured by a then unknown company called Lockheed. The company was so impressed with Wilkins they sold him the third one ever made at cost price. It was a wooden monoplane with a monocoque fuselage, that is, it needed no internal frame. Wilkins began making various adaptations for cold-weather flying. While he did so, Vega number one vanished in a race to Hawaii, and Vega number two crash-landed while he watched.

Lockheed were keen to help him because he was already one of the groundbreaking aviators of the day. Less successfully Wilkins would nearly drown in a low-budget failure to take an ageing submarine to the North Pole.

With Wilkins's public profile, funding his Antarctic trip was easy. He intended to make the first Antarctic flight, to see if he could confirm the existence, reported by several land and sea expeditions, of channels crossing the Peninsula from the Bransfield Strait to the Weddell Sea. The climax was a possible continental crossing of some three thousand kilometres to the Ross Sea. His principal backer was the radio and newspaper magnate William Randolph Hearst, the man Orson Welles parodied in *Citizen Kane*. Hearst offered $40,000 for exclusive press rights plus a $10,000 bonus should Wilkins land at the South Pole, something Wilkins said he didn't want to do. But Wilkins was allowed to create just the kind of no-fuss small team he craved: two planes, five men, and a lift south on the Norwegian whaler *Hektoria*. He stuck with the plane that had proved itself, but in honour of new sponsors, he renamed his existing Vega *Los Angeles* and a new one *San Francisco*.

When Wilkins called at the Falkland Islands on his passage south, he met the British Governor who had secret instructions to ask him to drop the Union Jack on any newly discovered territory. Britain was concerned that a parallel attempt to fly over the continent by American

Naval Officer Richard Byrd was a covert means of mounting a bid for US sovereignty, and wanted to stay one step ahead, piggy-backing financially on Wilkins. Despite having American backers, he quietly agreed, because of his loyalty as an Australian to the Mother Country.

He had done all the homework he could about local conditions but Antarctica makes its own rules. At Deception Island, after fourteen consecutive years of solid spring ice holding fast in the harbour until Christmas, Wilkins found that this year the ice was too thin to land on and too thick to allow float landings on the water. In the end, the *Los Angeles* was fitted with a pontoon undercarriage and lowered directly from the ship onto a patch of open water. They were reluctant to use the sea as their main method of take-off and landing as pontoons are liable to damage by small, hard-to-see pieces of ice, and in flight, their drag reduces a plane's range. On 16 November 1928 Carl Eielson and Wilkins lifted off from the water of Port Foster in the first ever Antarctic flight. Their reserve pilot, Joe Crosson, Eielson's best friend from Alaska, took up the *San Francisco* soon after. The first task was to look for a better site for a landing strip, but they found nowhere more promising than where they'd come from: the small hummocky land at Whalers Bay, a mix of volcanic material ranging from coarse sand to fine gravel.

They now prepared to reconnoitre the Peninsula. A picture taken on 20 December 1928 shows Wilkins and Eielson boarding the *Los Angeles* carrying two large, angular backpacks and long snow-shoes. They had two months' food and some survival gear, but no one really expected to survive a crash. If they did not return, their support pilot, Crosson, had orders not to search for them.

Wilkins had found no new lands on his North Pole flight, but now, for the first time in history, he could be sure that new lands would be seen by man for the first time from the air. He had fuel for more than 1250 miles (2000 kilometres) of flying, and set course down the Bransfield Strait, past Trinity Island and the Danco Coast, then over Waterboat Point where Wilkins' two young companions Bagshawe and Lester had overwintered during the John Cope Expedition. They crossed the west side of the Peninsula at Forbidden Plateau, then turned south to follow the east coast of Graham Land. Reading unfamiliar landscapes from the air is tricky, and they now made a mistake which gave ammunition to Wilkins's detractors. They included rival aviators like the American egotist Byrd and, sadly, fellow Aussie hero Douglas Mawson, as well as conservatives of all nations who thought ship and sledge journeys were the only manly road to achievement. Wilkins and Eielson saw valleys cutting across the Peninsula and recorded that some of them were chasmic channels, big enough to swallow skyscrapers. These channels would, they reported to the world, block any expeditions attempting to exploring the south overland. There were no such features. They were an illusion.

Near the end of their range they saw the weather behind was deteriorating. Before turning around at 71°20′S 64°15′W they saw a new plateau and named it Hearst, while quietly dropping a British flag with a note claiming sovereignty. Needless to say, these have not been seen since. A full storm was brewing and they could not take a second look at the channels. Wilkins instead plotted a course taking the shortest route north, into darkening skies. The wind shifted to blow on the nose and reduce their range further. It was a race against time. After a flight lasting 9 hours 25 minutes, covering 1200 miles (1920 kilometres) of which 625 miles (1000 kilometres) were over new territory, their Vega bumped down into the soft dirt of Deception Island, and the history of exploration had taken a new direction.

Today you cannot see much evidence of the two ash runways which once crossed like open scissors outside the later hangar of the British Antarctic Survey. Until a few years ago, one of BAS's tiny orange De Havilland Otter planes still stood outside the rear of the hangar, looking halfway in size between a big toy and a real plane. Its wings stood against the wall inside, steeped in the snow which drifted through the partly open doors each winter. The plane has now been brought back to England to be restored and exhibited at an aviation museum. Outside, heavy girders lie in the dirt. They were brought to enlarge the hangar, but when the volcano erupted again in 1970, expansion plans were put on a high shelf and never taken down. It's hard to justify investment when a blow from a side vent of Deception could melt five years' work in an afternoon.

Wilkins contracted a long series of articles about the expedition and meditated on the nature of exploring. He was candid about its unfulfilling nature; a feeling no other explorer I know has voiced so plainly. The next time he was down here it was without his old comrade Carl Eielson who had chosen to pioneer commercial flying in Alaska, and been immediately been killed by a storm coming in from Russia. The Russians had known about it but were not sharing information with America. Wilkins's dream of international co-operation improving understanding of weather and climate seemed more urgent and personal than ever.

Wilkins was the organiser of one more historic polar flight. It was funded by Lincoln Ellsworth, a playboy heir who contributed nothing to the planning, except letting his obsession with the Wild West frontier life dictate the name of the plane: the *Wyatt Earp*. Wilkins organised the first trans-polar flight, taking off at 10:00 on 23 November 1935. It was planned to last fourteen hours and took twenty-two days because they came down twenty kilometres short of the Bay of Whales, at the gates of the Ross Sea, and had to walk the rest.

After a lifetime of adventure, Wilkins died in November 1958, suffering a heart attack alone in the cheap hotel room where he preferred to work when in America. He still had one last dramatic journey to make. His ashes were scattered at the North Pole by Captain James Calvert when the nuclear-powered submarine USS *Skate* surfaced there on 17 March 1959. A new generation had not forgotten his worth.

## VOLCANOES

Deception is a relatively new island, and is a form of collapsed volcano called a *caldera*, a Spanish word for a pot or cauldron. When liquid rock, or magma, forces its way up from around twenty-five miles (forty kilometres) below the surface of the earth, and erupts onto the surface as a volcano, it creates huge stresses which are often relieved by ring-faults: cracks in the rocks which are circular when seen from above. The central area often has the most pressure under it and is driven up by the terrific pressure of the rising lava. When a major eruption dies down, it has, through lava flows and explosions, relieved the pressure, causing the centre to collapse downwards. When this happens on continental land, rain may fill it, creating a lake. In a few rare instances, where the volcano is a small island, the sea may flood in. At Deception this happened through a small gap in a nearly complete crater rim: Neptune's Bellows. Visitors often look around the island and ask where the volcano was. The answer is: You are in it.

The first sailors knew it was active, and Wilkes, who saw it in 1842, saw 'the entire south rim of the crater on fire.' In 1820 sealer Robert Fildes surveyed the harbour and found a depth in the centre of the harbour of 1080 feet (329 metres). Lieutenant Edward Kendall of the *Chanticleer* resurveyed it in 1829 but was unable to sound more than 582 feet (177 metres). Both were trustworthy surveyors, it was the harbour bottom which had moved in an intervening eruption. It currently has a maximum depth of 630 feet (190 metres).

Foster's Pendulum Cove later became the site of a Chilean research base which was damaged by the eruption of 1967 and then destroyed by the 1969 eruption. Only the stumps of concrete bases and tangles of steel reinforcing rods remain. Each time all the personnel in the island's three bases (the other two were Argentinian and British) escaped, though it was a close thing, as molten lava bombs fell side by side with ice blown out of the ice-cap.

Since 1948 the Argentines have maintained their small Base Deception at the head of Port Foster, and the Spanish Gabriel de Castilla Base is nearby. Both monitor the levels of vulcanism. If you see remote sensors around the island it's rude to jump up and down near them, as it panics the staff. No one now overwinters after a third eruption in 1970 highlighted the risks that rescuers would run attempting to pick up researchers during winter.

## OPERATION TABARIN

A snazzy Second World War poster hangs above the partition between the bunks and the kitchen in the living quarters at the restored historic base of Port Lockroy. It shows a cabaret girl at the Tabarin Club, Paris. In its smoky atmosphere British servicemen hatched a smoke and mirrors scheme. By 1944, under the guidance of a man called Moxon, it emerged from the Admiralty as a plan for a top secret operation in Antarctica. Winston Churchill's officials waited for one of the handful of occasions during the war when the Prime Minister left the country, to rubber-stamp the initiative in his absence. In 1943, fourteen men were taken from different parts of the British Armed Forces to join Operation Tabarin. They were sworn to secrecy. Their leader, 'Jimmy ' J. W. S. Marr, then in Ceylon, was a geologist who had been one of the two boy scouts chosen in a competition run by the *Daily Mail* to accompany Shackleton on what turned out to be his final expedition in the *Quest* in 1922. They were to form bases in Antarctica. To convey them there, they were allocated a Norwegian sealer renamed HMS *Ramsey*. They were given little information but one piece of advice proved very true: 'She may leak.' She did little else. At frequent intervals in the painfully sluggish Atlantic passage Marr would call the men together and lecture them on the need for total secrecy: 'Don't let anyone, family friends or sweethearts, know what you are doing.'

After a while one man protested: 'But sir, we don't *know* what we're doing!'

They first made for Deception where, since the war had begun, some Argentines had painted their flag. The British promptly painted out the blue and white and painted in the red, white and blue. They set up at a comfortable wooden hut, code-named Base B, and another at Port Lockroy, Base A. A projected third at Hope Bay, on the tip of the Peninsula, proved impractical due to ice conditions. Further bases were added later.

At last they learned their top secret task: monitoring German naval communications. In 1916 during the First World War, a British squadron had won a major naval battle in Falkland Sound, between East and West Falkland. Perhaps the theatre of war might move even farther south; German warships might hide in Antarctica and take coal from British bases and whaling stations. The first thing that strikes you looking at the location of these bases is how poorly located they are to monitor anything, being tucked away in nice sheltered bays. Deception's Base B, for instance, was built inside the island at sea level not outside on the mountain, commanding the Bransfield Strait. A few years ago the records of Operation Tabarin were made public. The daily report sheets were all bare. Not one enemy communication had ever been intercepted. The specialist teams, pulled from all over the world and sworn to secrecy, had returned blank forms day after a day. There was no radio activity of any sort. Was it a foolish mistake or something more subtle?

A coding machine known as Chiffriermaschine E was invented by the Dutch in 1919 and was on general sale until 1929. It had, for the first time, solved a fundamental problem of all coding: that in any language some letters occur more often than others, in a known pattern. Any code that substitutes one symbol for a letter of the alphabet repeats that pattern and is easily cracked. Chiffriermaschine E had mechanical rotors and electrical switches that made seven changes to every typed letter. Each one was routed in a continually changing way to the next rotor, hiding the frequency at which individual letters appeared. The rotors of the machine were changed each day and codes let the receiver know how they had changed. The final letter was given to a Morse code man and transmitted separately from the main coding transmission. It seemed foolproof.

In 1932, Polish mathematical cipher-crackers, fearing it might make an extremely tough code to crack in any future war, set a team of mathematicians to break the code. They found they could crack it, but too slowly to defeat the daily change of rotors. In 1938 the German state added two more rotors to increase to the complexity. The German Navy added three, and was convinced it was now far too complex to break. They reserved it for top secret strategic communications. When war got under way, the British knew such a code was being used, but could not devise a way of decoding the complex transformations before they changed again. They christened it the Enigma Code. In February 1944, Alan Turing, working at Britain's Bletchley Park intelligence centre, built a machine called Colossus I to extract and analyse patterns for further analysis. Ten were made. They were capable of sifting through unheard-of amounts of data, and extracting patterns before the rotors were re-positioned the next day. The enigma was solved. Today we have these machines in our homes and workplaces; we call them computers.

Cracking the enemy code required agonising decisions from those conducting the war. If they acted on all the new knowledge it would quickly become obvious the code had been broken. It would be changed and the advantage lost. Some information must be ignored, and decisions taken that appear to be made in ignorance of the actual plans. Sometimes, lives would be sacrificed to maintain the illusion. More kindly, men will be sent to the other end of the world to carry out surveillance on operations that the enemy never intended to perform: like occupying Antarctica. There is clear evidence that British officers in Antarctica occasionally broke normal security by sending parcels through Uruguay, which was sympathetic to Germany, knowing they were likely to be intercepted and betray a British presence in Antarctica.

It seems that Operation Tabarin was a smoke screen designed to cover up the fact that Britain had cracked the Enigma Code. In French dialect *tabarin* means a cloak, and one of the islands chosen for a base was called Deception. Just because there is a war, there's no reason to lose your British sense of humour.

## THE CHEEK OF MR BORCHGREVINK

In 1894, schoolmaster Carsten Borchgrevink, living in Melbourne, was desperate for polar experience. He persuaded expedition leader Henrik Johan Bull and Captain Leonard Christiansen to take him on board the whaler *Antarctic*, bound for Ross Sea, as an unpaid Ordinary Seaman. Although he had an English mother and wife, he was born in Norway and, as a boy, played with Roald Amundsen.

It was a primarily a whaling expedition, sponsored by Svend Foyn, the inventor of the exploding harpoon. On 24 January 1895 at one in the morning, they lowered a boat off Cape Adare in the Ross Sea. They knew this was the mainland and thought landing would make them the first men to set foot on the continent; knowledge of the sealers' landing on the peninsula had been lost. Its crew included Capt Kristensen, Bull, Borchgrevink and four others. Conditions were calm, with little swell. For an hour they rowed through loose ice, the water swarmed with vast red jellyfish trailing yard-long tendrils. As leader, Bull expected to be given the honour of landing first, but the captain prepared to go first. As the boat ran into the pebbly beach, Borchgrevink slipped over the bows before either of them, and turned to hold the boat. Bull and Christiansen were furious at his insolence. Bull would later claim he was the first to land, and Borchgrevink had only stood in the shallows: playground boasts. It is a blessing that the sealers had long pre-empted them, and the quarrel does not need to be resolved. They were there less than ninety minutes, but as Bull recognised 'Mr Foyn would no doubt have preferred to exchange this pleasing sensation on our part for a Right whale even of small dimensions.' It was a commercial failure.

In 1898 Borchgrevink secured £40,000 from British publisher George Newnes and led his own expedition back to Cape Adare in the *Southern Cross*. Most of the men were Norwegian or Finnish, but Newnes's money bought the right to fly the British flag. Historians have sometimes damned their efforts with faint praise, but they successfully executed their plan to set up Camp Ridley and be the first people to overwinter on the continent. They also pioneered the used of sled dogs, climbed onto the Ross Ice Shelf, and saw it extended as far as the eye could see. This would become the route by which Amundsen and Scott attained the Pole. Borchgrevink's farthest south here: 78°50′ was a new record. Their magnetic measurements showed the South Magnetic Pole must be much farther north and west than had been assumed. It would be discovered on Shackleton's 1907–09 *Nimrod* expedition by the sled party of David, Mawson and Mackay.

# 7

# The First Antarctic Night 1897–99:
## Adrien de Gerlache

*A surgeon who will soon go mad takes a book of Edgar Allan Poe's stories to the Antarctic. Their expedition is locked into the ice and their own story begins to outdo in horror anything in the author's dark imagination. Black doubts walk the ship like spectres: were they trapped by accident, or design?*

The 250-ton barquentine *Belgica* sailed out of Ushuaia, then just twenty-five sheet metal houses at the foot of Argentina. Before they reached open sea they ran aground and had to be rescued by a farmer. 'Early in the morning of New Year's Day, 1898,' wrote Lucas Bridges, in his father's remote mission farm on the north shore of the Beagle Channel, 'I looked out of a window of the Cambaceres house. Across the outer harbour to the southward, about half a mile away, lay a little vessel on a shoal.' They were hooked on a rock which was sawing through their hull as they swung about, helpless and out of control. The captain was in his cabin and crying his eyes out with frustration. They had run aground trying to enter an uncharted, unfamiliar harbour in near-darkness

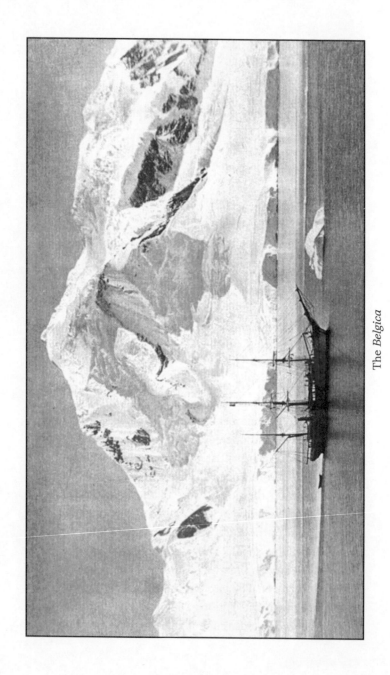

*The Belgica*

during a storm. Mariners have a technical term for this manoeuvre. It's called being stupid.

The expedition commander, Lt. Adrien Victor Joseph de Gerlache y Gomery, had taken special leave from the Belgian Navy to gain sailing experience off East Greenland in the sealer *Castor*. The physician, Dr Frederick Cook, although a last minute replacement, was a veteran who had travelled with Peary in the Arctic. The only other man with polar experience was the second officer, who had sailed on the famous sealer *Jason*, a veteran of both Antarctic and Arctic seas: Roald Amundsen. When they returned in triumph, Amundsen declared: 'Modern scientific exploration has now been initiated and de Gerlache has won his place.' The voyage was de Gerlache's idea. He secured private, public, then government support in Belgium against the tenor of the times, as King Leopold was trying to focus Belgium's colonial ambition on his personal scheme: the murderous exploitation of the Congo that inspired Joseph Conrad's *Heart of Darkness*, and later the film *Apocalypse Now*.

Novices sometimes innovate where experts stick to a formula. Harland and Wolff, who made the *Titanic*, were professionals; Noah was an amateur. With Otto Nordenskjöld, William Speirs Bruce and Jean-Baptiste Charcot, de Gerlache was one of four men who, at the turn of the century, mounted compact expeditions that put science to the fore and jingoism to the rear. The money de Gerlache raised was barely adequate. His crew was the minimum needed to sail the vessel, just fourteen plus scientists who would have to double as officers. Only two seamen, the bosun Adam Tollefsen and Johansen, were able to lead a watch. It was only possible to sail at all because

173

they had Cunningham's patent furling topsails which could be handled from deck without sending men aloft. He was not short of supplies. In fact they seemed to have more than they might ever use. When they left, the deck was just fifty centimetres above water. The few seamen they had were so ill-disciplined that when they bunkered coal in Punta Arenas on the Straits of Magellan, he had to call the local police to regain control of them. They sailed without signing the formal articles of discipline. De Gerlache remarked that the only disciplinary power he had was to put men ashore, but that's quite persuasive when you are going to Antarctica. The scientists were to be unpaid simply because there was no money to pay them, but he recruited talented men because he was offering a rare chance to carry out extended scientific research in a virtually unknown environment. Despite the Belgian flag, they were a multi-national crew. Many of the other seamen were Norwegian and the *lingua franca* of the trip was going to be French until the arrival of Cook, who had no French. English and Norwegian were spoken as necessary to communicate orders. The international mix was in large part a gesture to defy the nationalistic expeditions of the great powers.

The oldest man on board, at thirty-four, was the Chief Engineer; de Gerlache was thirty-one. The zoologist cum botanist was Emile-Georges Racovitza, a twenty-nine-year-old Romanian. The Pole Henryk Arctowski, after whom the modern Polish Base is named, was geologist, meteorologist and oceanographer. The assistant meteorologist was the Pole Antoine Dobrowolski, twenty-five and the other scientist was a man known to de Gerlache's family: the Belgian magnetist, Emile Danco. De Gerlache harboured reservations about accepting Danco's application. Young Emile had a weak chest and a strict father who frowned on frivolity. In protective isolation Emile grew into a man full of juvenile opinions and naïve enthusiasms. When his father died, he was left with an independent income but no close family. He had had enough of being cosseted; he wanted adventure, and believed fresh cold air would restore his chest. De Gerlache relented only when he heard that if he was not accepted Danco's back-up plan was to go to the Congo which was so unhealthy that most men arriving were expected to die of disease somewhere between passport control and customs. De Gerlache sent him to Vienna, Paris, Jena, and Berlin to buy instruments, and be trained directly by the manufacturers or expert local academics.

De Gerlache had prepared thoroughly for many aspects of the trip, including consulting the Norwegian explorer Fridtjof Nansen and Nansen's captain Otto Sverdrup, a giant of polar navigation who shunned the limelight. The plan, which would alter frequently, was to reconnoitre the Weddell Sea then sail the long route east to Victoria Land and overwinter with three other men while the ship retreated to Melbourne. Their last call before leaving South America was at Staten Island, the desolate slab of rock east off the tip of Tierra del Fuego. For the Argentine official administering the island, it was the posting from hell. Most of its occupants were convicts, the sweepings of Argentina's jails. Its Sub-Prefect was the cultivated Nicanor Fernández, who served dinner to the adventurers on fine china marked *Esmeralda*, the name of a ship wrecked there a month before. The visitors brought ashore a machine called a *Coelophone* that played music from a punched paper roll. Deprived of music since his arrival, Fernández listened, remembering what polite society had been like, and burst into helpless tears. They sailed on 14 January 1897, already so late that their original plan was reined in. They would remain in the Peninsula area for the rest of the southern summer, study the area around Hughes Bay in Graham Land, and leave a trip to Victoria Land for the next summer. Come winter, they would return to Ushuaia in the Beagle Channel to study zoology and the ethnography of the Ona Indians. The latter was deeply ironic as de Gerlache was spiteful to the Bridges family in his memoir, implying they were more interested in trade than saving souls: 'He will nevertheless be leaving his sons in an enviable situation when eventually the last of the Yaghans dies of consumption on the threshold of the mission.' In fact Bridges senior, with a wife and six children and no income, had resigned from his missionary society because he insisted evangelism on its own was useless to natives without skills for the modern world. Meanwhile de Gerlache attended a most agreeable picnic with a millionaire whose 100,000 sheep were being harassed and killed by mad dogs. He always called them mad dogs, and he paid a £1 a head for each one shot. The 'mad dogs' were the Ona Indians.

Their work began, lowering the oceanographic gear donated by the Danish Navy, netting samples of sea-life and measuring depth. Off Staten Island they found 296 metres, but late the same afternoon the bottom plunged to 1564 metres. The next day they saw three ships, all Europe-bound, and thought how those sails were spread for home, whereas theirs would take them to two months of solitude. They could not know it was their last sight of the outside world for well over a year. Or perhaps one person could. That day they sounded at 4040 metres. Though mariners

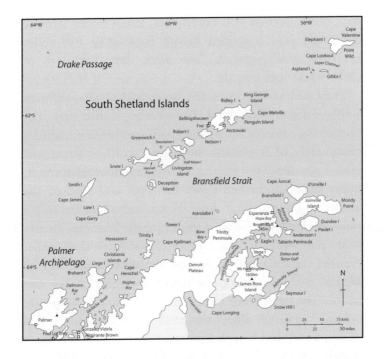

had sailed these water regularly for nearly three hundred years, no one had hung around to take measurements. Before they even saw Antarctica, they had made an important discovery: the Drake Passage was a basin, deepest in the middle.

On 20 January 1898 at 16:00 they saw land at 63°11′S 061°37′W. No one forgets their first sight of Antarctica. They were awe-struck. The next day, before they could even plan a landing they lost steerage among icebergs and rocks with steam pressure too low to pull them clear. Through luck, they gained steerage before they hit anything. De Gerlache claimed he told the engineer that the boiler pressure was low fifteen minutes before this happened. Even if you credit this, you wonder why he continued into a hazard before confirming the boiler pressure was restored. The next day, the cost of carelessness was tragedy.

They had sailed down the Bransfield Strait and were south of Deception Island. The weather turned ugly. The underlying cause of the accident was overloading: the fifty centimetres of freeboard. In stormy weather, some coal stored on deck, because there was nowhere else for it, burst loose. It crashed down the deck and blocked the scuppers, the gaps that drain deck water under the ship's rails. On the undermanned ship, Auguste Wiencke, twenty years old, with the invincibility of youth, worked alone. Against standing orders, he tied himself to a line and let himself over the side to help free the coals. A cry was heard. The details are lost in the confusion of desperate action. The watch officer was studying an iceberg lying in their course, and it took him some time to see Wiencke's danger. Dr Cook saw Wiencke had come free of his line and, in water only a degree above freezing, the seaman's hands would only work for four or five minutes. Cook threw the ship's log line to him: a slender rope with a flat piece of wood at its end, ideal to grasp. Wiencke caught and held it. Cook began to haul him in, desperate to bring Wiencke close before his grip failed, but fearful of ripping the wood from his grasp. Feeling drained from Wiencke's numbed hands. The wood slid from his grasp. He began to drift away. One man showed true heroism. First Officer Lecointe tied a line about his waist, and leapt overboard. He swam to Wiencke and was within arm's length of grasping him when a vicious gust within the storm tore them apart. Wiencke was borne into the night, and suffered for brief minutes before solitary resignation overcame him, and unconsciousness relieved him from experiencing the iciness of mortality. The watch officer felt he should have been more aware of the problem with the deck cargo; he had focused on the iceberg to the exclusion of other matters. No one else blamed him, but the officer's standards were high. He was Roald Amundsen.

De Gerlache's account of the incident may reflect his anxiety at losing a member of a slender crew so soon after reaching Antarctica. He was young and it was his first command. 'On the afternoon of the 22nd ... our young sailor August Karl Wiencke paid with his life for a minor act of disobedience ... heedless of the danger and believing he was doing his duty Wiencke went over the side on a rope.' This puts pride before compassion. Maybe he felt responsible for the fifty centimetres freeboard that made any blockage potentially fatal. De Gerlache added: 'Wiencke was popular with his shipmates, and his superior officers recognised an unusual intelligence, an excellent character, and a devotion to duty. His loss was keenly felt by all.' Wiencke Island on which I have twice camped, enjoying spectacular views of the highest peak in the region, Mount Français, is named for him.

Their first landing, on 23 January 1898 at 19:00, was on an island named Auguste Island after de Gerlache's father. Cook's reactions are fascinating because he had previously seen the Canadian Arctic and Greenland. He said there was nothing in the landscape that reminded him of anywhere. Antarctica, above all else, is itself, like nowhere else.

Henryk Arctowski observed the sense of disconnection, both with past experience and with the artificiality of his expectations, with the sketchy records that were all that was known of a whole continent. 'At 7pm we passed close to a headland, which very probably was Cape Cockburn, but as we went on the charts became valueless; what we saw corresponded to nothing that they represented ... '

He was first ashore, followed by Racowitza; de Gerlache and Cook had to scramble back on board to stop the surf throwing the boat onto the rocks. Cook, itching to spend a few moments ashore, was forced into observing the lucky pair, walking where no one had ever walked. 'We tried to

Adrien de Gerlache in furs

Author, John at Neko Harbour

Barrels abandoned at Whalers Bay, Deception Island around 1930 when whale oil prices slumped

The factory whaling ship Guvernøren caught fire and was beached without loss of life in January 1915

Stromness, South Georgia, from the Shackleton Walk; the *Polar Star* waits for us in the harbour

View from Neko Harbour on a perfect day

The Detaille Base, abandoned in 1959, is a time capsule from my youth

The shell of an Argentine base at Mikkelsen Harbour, Trinity Island is typical of small old bases unsuited for modern needs

Thermal pools are for wimps,
the author after a swim at Deception Island

Nordenskjöld expedition, the homemade overwintering
hut of the Hope Bay three today,
with the Argentine Esperanza Base behind

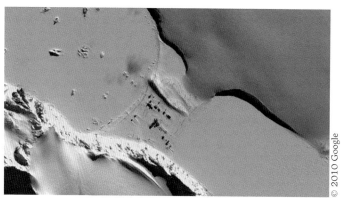

Founded by Scotsman Bruce, run by Argentina: Orcadas Base
in winter, between two frozen bays, satellite image

William Smith died in Whitechapel in Trinity House
almshouses like these

A blizzard sweeps over the site of Hubert Wilkins's
runway on Deception Island;
the old Hektor whaling factory in the distance

Adélie penguins look particularly mad when moulting

James Clark Ross, brave, humane and handsome with it.
Portrait by John R. Wildman.

follow them with our glasses as we rocked about in our boat, but soon lost sight of their movements in the darkness. We were able to locate Arctowski by the dull echo of his hammer, and we were able to trace Racowitza by the chorus of penguins which greeted him from rock to rock. The alternate interchange of the music of the hammer and the war song of the penguins was an entertainment which to Gerlache and myself, will be a long and weird remembrance.'

The landing lasted only thirty minutes. Danco brought back souvenirs: two live penguin chicks which he looked after, said Lecointe, with maternal care. Many photos of other early expeditions show them playing with penguins as if they were toys. Racowitza was a rare, kind observer, withdrawing when the birds seemed stressed. He was especially intrigued by the sociable and noisy chinstraps. 'From a distance they resembled nothing as much as two fishwives discussing the freshness of their respective wares.' He characterised them well, and though he anthropomorphises them shamelessly, he has clearly observed them with patience, empathy and humour:

Imagine a small, upright gentleman, with two paddle-like flippers in place of his arms imagine him dressed in a dark coloured coat with blue patches, ending in a pointed tail dragging along the ground ... now put him in motion on his two feet and give him an odd waddling gait and a constant movement of his head, and you have before your eyes something both irresistibly attractive and comic ... We began to think in our surprise that we had come across a political meeting in the middle of an election, and I was taken ashore to find out what was happening. ... The moment I set foot ashore I was received with a violent outcry and shrieks of vehement indignation which left me in doubt of the opinion these birds had of me. I thought I would in time become acceptable to them, and sat down on a rock a little distance away. But my patience and friendly demeanour were a waste of time. All the birds turned to face me, drawn up to their full height, with the feather on their heads raised in anger and beaks agape, and assaulted me in language which I judged from the tone to be decidedly insulting.

When you first see Antarctica you cannot tear yourself away from it. Seamless light does not encourage sleep. Cook is always better than de Gerlache at the detail that stirs the heart. 'Though the sun was sliding eastward just under the high mountains to the south-west it seemed perfectly dark. Nevertheless, on the water, as we paddled over it, there was a curious luminous gray light, by which it was possible to read coarse print, even at midnight. The sky, however, continued black, made so by the sooty clouds which ceaselessly rose out of the Pacific to drop their white cargoes of snow on the neighbouring lands.'

In February 2008, I worked on an expedition taking a party headed by the grandson of de Gerlache along his ancestor's route. The present baron is a man who enjoys his family's obsession with the Antarctic (each generation has followed Adrien down there). We flew the same Belgian flag that Adrien de Gerlache had flown. The problem with following de Gerlache's route was that he landed where he could, and that is not the most interesting itinerary. After a few days of squeezing onto ribbons of shingle and paving stones of rock, some of the less obsessed travellers wanted to know why there was nothing to see. We began to slip in landings unrelated to Gerlache's route, but with lots of penguins. Morale soared. That trip cured me of another problem. I am sometimes asked if I have ever trodden on land which no one had ever walked before. The honest answer is I really don't care, but saying so sounds churlish. On 29 January 2007 we made the first recorded landing on Ghent Island. The organisers had asked that the baron be the first ashore. We asked if they realised this would mean him leaping out of the bow of the boat and holding it in the surf. When the day came, the staff landed first to check out the site, walking in different directions. I walked on new land.

The films and documentaries that form our images of Antarctica only paint a one-dimensional view of the weather: killing cold. In fact, Scottish visitors to the Peninsula often receive emails telling them it's colder at home. Visitors from the Mid West and north-east of the USA, never mind Canada, have certainly left colder weather behind. A sunny calm day can take the thermometer well into double figures, centigrade. On 25 January Arctowski noted it was 'fine and calm, the air perfectly transparent, the sky cloudless, and the heat of the sun intense.' When they landed at Harry Island, de Gerlache observed: 'the radiant sun showed nature "grandiose" and savage. It was so hot one of us caught sun stroke.' The day before on Moreno Island, Arctowski had recorded: 'I had the pleasure of discovering the first Antarctic insect, almost microscopic in its dimensions.' This was christened *Belgica antarctica*. It's a nice bar-room question on an Antarctic cruise to ask what is the largest land-predator on the continent. Leopard seals are usually mentioned, but they and all the other big beasts hunt in the sea; on land, the top predator is a wingless midge. On Louise Island Dr Cook remarked on something else that startles many Antarctic visitors. 'Our greatest surprise here was the discovery of large quantities of moss and lichens, which gave the spot an appearance of life that to us, after having seen nothing but ice and rocks for so many days, made it a true oasis.' The mosses can be as green as in any oak wood and the lichens the same brilliant orange as those on the rocks of temperate seashores.

At the end of the month, they landed with ease on snow reaching down to the shore at d'Ursel Point on Brabant Island, and made the first ever Antarctic sled journey. They aimed to survey the island and obtain a view far into the west from the Solvay Mountains above them. The team comprised de Gerlache, Cook, Arctowski, Danco and the first man to master Antarctic sled travel: Amundsen. They had two Nansen sleds, the lightweight wooden models developed by Fridtjof Nansen after he crossed Greenland successfully in 1888. The Inuit sled was lashed together rather than jointed or screwed, and designed to flex with the stresses; all rigid structures broke eventually. The last dog sleds used in Antarctica were the direct heirs of his design. Arctowski was not impressed: 'The sledges were horribly heavy' and 'there was far too much luggage.' He helped haul them up a snow slope of 40° for four hours until they found level ground to camp at 1100 feet. Cook described a night of stormy discomfort in their silk tent: 'A wind came out of the bed of a glacier above us, against which we could hardly stand.' It is strange to read in Amundsen's journal: 'The doctor, an experienced polar explorer, went first and I followed.' Little more than a decade after this trip ended, he would never need to defer to any living explorer, except his mentor: Nansen. That night they were very warm in their reindeer bags. Next day they began walking but soon camped again, because of fog. At 13:00 they tried again, aiming for high land, but after four hours of heavy labour were frustrated by a huge crevasse, and had to retreat to the plateau. On 1 February it was snowing. De Gerlache and Danco were roped together hauling the same sled. 'Suddenly,' wrote de Gerlache, 'my friend vanished as if a trapdoor had opened under his feet.' De Gerlache was pulled towards the yawning crevasse, trying to dig his feet into the snow, unable to hold the weight. He was approaching the lip of the chasm when Danco's skis wedged tight in the crevasse and stopped him falling further. He emerged unhurt. There were many narrow crevasses, and they were hard to see. The following day they got to the summit of the nunatak at 315 metres but frustratingly the visibility closed in before the theodolite could be set up. Next morning revealed vast panoramas of Danco Land, a clear light illuminating the snow plains of the interior. Cook wrote, 'The view before us was even more beautiful, if possible, than anything we had seen since our first entrance into this new white world. To the south-west there was an opening through a new land and into a new sea, which remained for us to explore later.' Below them icebergs split with 'mysterious explosions' like 'a thousand cannons.' On 4 February Cook and Amundsen cut their way across a very steep ice face which fifty feet below ended in crevasse they estimated as over a hundred feet deep. Above, overhanging ice-masses prevented them climbing away from danger. They gingerly went forward, Amundsen trusting to Cook's judgement and experience. If

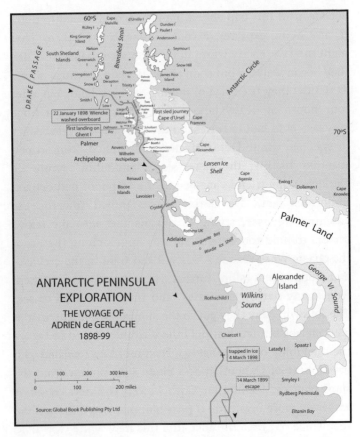

**ANTARCTIC PENINSULA EXPLORATION**

THE VOYAGE OF
ADRIEN de GERLACHE
1898-99

Labels on map:

60°S

Cape Melville
Ridley I
King George Island
Nelson I
South Shetland Islands
Greenwich I
Livingston I
Snow I
Deception I
Smith I
Low I
Ghent I

Bransfield Strait

DRAKE PASSAGE

Tower I
Trinity I
Liège I
Brabant I
Spong
Melchior Mts
Hoseason I

d'Urville I
Dundee I
Paulet I
Anderssen I
Seymour I
Snow Hill I
Detroit Plateau
James Ross Island
Robertson I

Antarctic Circle

Cape Renard
Two Hummock I
Higher Key

22 January 1898 Wiencke washed overboard

first landing on Ghent I

Palmer Archipelago

first sled journey
Cape d'Ursel

Cape Framnes

70°S

Anvers I
Wilhelm Archipelago
Port Charcot
Booth I
Port Circumcision
Peterman I

Dalmann Bay
Schollaert Channel

Cape Alexander

Larsen Ice Shelf

Cape Agassiz
Ewing I
Doileman I
Cape Knowles

Renaud I
Biscoe Islands
Lavoisier I
Crystal Sound

Palmer Land

Rothera UK
Adelaide I
Marguerite Bay
Wordie Ice Shelf

Alexander Island

George VI Sound

Rothschild I
Wilkins Sound

Charcot I

trapped in ice
4 March 1898

Latady I
Spaatz I

14 March 1899 escape

Smyley I

Rydberg Peninsula

Eltanin Bay

| 0 | 100 | 200 | 300 kms |
| 0 | 100 | 200 miles | |

Source: Global Book Publishing Pty Ltd

Cook slipped, Amundsen remembered thinking, it was 'doubtful if I could have hung on to him.' Then they crossed the crevasse by crawling over a bridge of thin ice. Crevasses cut off access to all the higher peaks; a glimpse of unknown territory was quickly obscured by fog and snow. Descending what has seemed from above to be a more appealing return route, they found it much more heavily fissured. Without trees or buildings or any object to give scale, the Antarctic landscape fools you into seeing what you want. Amundsen: 'Until you are standing in the middle of it, so you can touch and feel everything, you know nothing with certainty.'

At the time Amundsen was thrilled with Antarctic life: 'I hope that there are more of these wonderful trips to come.' But when he looked back at his first experience of man-hauling sledges, lasting just one week, he damned it. It wasn't heroic but 'unpleasant, sweaty, toilsome and stupid.' Fifteen years later Scott was still measuring manliness by the yardstick of misery endured, and extolling its virtues. Amundsen's men would return from the Pole heavier than when they began while Scott's men suffered death by scurvy and starvation.

From the top of Brabant Island, Danco and de Gerlache thought they recognised Two Hummock Island which would join their present survey areas to their previous ones, uniting the known geography. Sailing to Hughes Bay, on the mainland opposite Two Hummock Island, confirmed their guess. On 8 February de Gerlache navigated 'a series of the most picturesque locations we were ever privileged to see.' This is now the Neumayer Channel. Many seasoned Antarctic travellers prefer it to the much-hyped Lemaire Channel, which has become such a must-see item for some cruise passengers that they feel swindled if they don't make a passage of it. Frederick Cook wrote of the Neumayer: 'It was a photographic day. As the ship steamed rapidly along, spreading out one panorama after another of this new world, the noise of the camera was as regular as the tap of a stock ticker.' Three hundred photographs were taken that day. He continued: 'Everybody was on deck with pencil and paper, some making nautical and geographical notes, other geological and topographical notes, and all recording the strange, other-world scenic effects. Even the sailors, the cabin-boy, and the cooks were out with paper and note-books, taking long looks and then bending over their paper.'

Despite this Arctowski was frustrated. He recorded privately on 10 February:

> Since we were always in sight of the coast, I never ceased to ask for more landings; I urged Lecointe, de Gerlache, and the others again and again, but not with so much effect as I could wish. For this eighteenth landing he conducted me himself, but for ten minutes only. A few strokes of his oars brought us to the beach amid cries of 'Hurry up, Arctowski.' I gave a hammer to Tollefsen, with orders to chip here and there down by the shore, while I hurriedly climbed the moraine, picking up specimens as I ran, took the direction with my compass, glances to the left and right, and hurried down again full speed to get a look at the rock in situ; meanwhile Cook had taken a photograph of the place from the ship – and this is the way geological surveys had to be conducted out in the antarctic.

On the evening of 11 February, a message to the engineer was misunderstood and they crashed into an iceberg losing their figurehead: a loss often regarded as bringing bad luck. On 12 February they made their twentieth and last landing, at Cape Renard, then sailed south through the Lemaire Channel without commenting on the scenery: just another channel. The next day the expedition landed at Wiencke Island and later on the Wauwermans group, Arctowski described them as 'like great whale-backs appearing above the sea.' The water was as calm as glass.

Around 1873 the German Edouard Dallman had been sealing in the *Grönland* in this area and attained 65°S, going beyond Anvers Island, and discovering Kaiser Wilhelm I Islands. To the south he could see only sea leading east from between himself and Booth Island (the island that forms the seaward side of the Lemaire Channel). He called it the Bismarck Strait, and believed it to be the western end of a strait Carl Larsen thought he had seen looking westward from the other side of the peninsula. From 8 February to 11 February the *Belgica's* probings proved Dallman had seen nothing more than a large bay, now called Flandres Bay. De Gerlache sailed out to the open ocean via the Argentine Islands area, where the Ukrainian Vernadsky Station now stands, and saw another large opening which he thought might have been the Bismarck Strait. Phantasmal sightings of this non-existent strait would continue until the British Graham Land Expedition finally banished it in 1937.

On 15 February they guessed, without being able to confirm by observation, that they were crossing the Antarctic Circle. In other sectors of Antarctica it is possible to sail much further south. In recent years it has become possible for vessels with only moderate ice-strengthening to cross it in February and early March before winter returns, but the line still has a magic to it. De Gerlache moved on, threading his way among heavy ice on 17 February to 67°58′S 069°53′W, into a sea where no vessel had sailed for seventy-six years since Bellingshausen had named the shore Alexander Land, and the wild neighbouring islands, Alexander Islands. Chances to take navigational sightings were rare, now they had one at 69°06′S 078°28′W and everyone reminisced of home, where it was breakfast time, 9989 miles away. Cook, always subtly watchful of the psychological state of his charges, likened it to a starving man finding comfort that, somewhere, food exists. He reflected on the reality: 'we are as hopelessly isolated as if we were on the surface of Mars, and we are plunging deeper into the white antarctic silence.' A decision would soon be taken in secret that would plunge him into the mad heart of that silence, and turn him, for a time, into the head of a small and very exclusive lunatic asylum.

As de Gerlache approaches this decision, his account, the *Voyage of the Belgica*, is revealing in a way he does not intend. They probe the ice edge trying to edge further south. He recalls Ross forcing his way through the pack and finding open water beyond, discovering the ice shelf, and achieving a new furthest south. He notes that Ross and later Larsen in the sealer *Antarctic* both escaped the pack 'in a few days'. But they had done it earlier in the season. A week before, the *Belgica* had three times become surrounded by ice and only escaped, at de Gerlache's own admission, 'with some difficulty'.

There is no doubt he was tempted by the prospect of entering unchartered waters, philosophising that there were two types of sailor, one for whom uncharted means 'Avoid!' and another for which it means 'Come!'. He had three scientists on hand to consult. They all opposed delving into the pack because they had valuable specimens which they wanted to get safely home. That didn't carry any weight with de Gerlache who concluded that 'it was our duty, it seemed to me, at least to try' to force a route deeper into the pack. He chatted to Lecointe on the bridge; they agreed and shook hands. Amundsen was informed but not consulted. Everyone else would find out the hard way. It was 09:00 on 28 February, 'a date that will forever be remembered in the history of the expedition.' They proceeded south under sail with occasional assistance from the engine. The wind, 'already strong' at noon, reached 60mph by 18:00: an inauspicious start. De Gerlache's account doesn't mention one fact that probably trumped any scientific argument: money. They only had £640 remaining, quite inadequate for their plans; returning to a port, and creditors, would end the expedition.

Entering the ice greatly reduces your room to navigate and manoeuvre. When it is tight, you are a prisoner in its grip. They soon saw the perils of trusting to luck. On 3 March a massive tabular iceberg passed one hundred metres away when they were helplessly trapped in dense ice. The sea was also beginning to freeze. The next day the pack was too dense to allow them further south and when they turned north, the leads they had used already had fresh ice closing over them.

Even the familiar became strange. On 4 March they saw an odd light moving low over the horizon and changing shape. Whispers spread through the ship and all hands gathered at the rail. The light grew higher and clearer and began changing shape. When it settled on one shape they saw it was the moon. That day Cook admits they are stuck fast, at 71°22′S: 'To be caught in the ice is ... a life of certain dangers and uncertain rewards.'

The following day the ice thickened; they made no progress. The day after they made some headway until the lead became blocked. The promise of hope was withdrawn almost before they could start to believe. Morale was subtly dented on 7 March when Bébé, the last survivor of three gentoo penguins taken on 9 February, died of convulsions.

To lighten the mood, ski practice was organised for 10 March, and a one-mile run was marked out. One diary suggests this was still a novelty for many, the writer feeling the need to explain that skis were 'long flat pieces of wood, tapered and turned up at each end.' It suggests Belgian's Alpine industry was in its infancy.

By 12 March winter had arrived, the thermometer dipping to −18.6°C. The men had been set to cut and break a channel but it was now done with apathy as they felt de Gerlache had intended they should be trapped and did not want to succeed in freeing them from the ice's terrible grasp. The first aurorae on 14 March did little to lift the crew, though Dr Cook was so entranced he decided, without telling anyone, to sleep out on the ice to enjoy them. The temperature fell to −20°C. He found out his hair had frozen to his hood when he turned round to face away from wind, and tore out a clump. In the grey morning light he was woken by a tapping: penguins were pecking at him. He returned to ship to find Lecointe putting away a rifle. He had been waiting for better light to shoot a 'seal' when it got up and turned into Dr Cook. The physician wrote that Antarctica reminded him of 'a period of the earth in its infancy, long before the advent of man. Everything about it is new yet old; every sight is simple yet clothed in mystery.' He mused that one of the lures of the polar areas was seeing the earth in its youth: a grand extension of an individual's nostalgia for his youth.

De Gerlache was ready with a quote from Nansen: 'The winter is approaching in great strides.' It is, in turn, an echo from Coleridge's *The Rime of the Ancient Mariner*: 'At one stride comes the night.' A show of trying to escape is maintained. On 16 March 'we again entertained the hope for a few hours that it would be possible to escape the clutches of the ice' when a gale from the ENE sent swells that cracked the ice. A great fissure snaked towards them, they fired the boilers, but the wind soon veered to east and fell. The ice closed. 'Without doubt a winter station had become inevitable.' Lecointe wrote, 'It is certain that we *honestly* tried to return northwards, but it is also certain that de Gerlache and myself were happy at the failure of our attempt.' His use of *italics* for honestly undermines every syllable of the sentence.

They were drifting three miles a day to the south-west, and calculated they could easily survive a five-month passage over the pole and out into the Ross Sea. Edgar Allan Poe had anticipated them in 'Manuscript Found in a Bottle': 'a curiosity to penetrate the mystery of these awful regions predominates even over my despair, and will reconcile me to the most hideous aspect of death. It is evident we are hurrying onward to some exciting knowledge – some never-to-be-imparted secret, whose attainment is destruction. Perhaps the current leads us to the Southern Pole itself. It must be confessed that a supposition apparently so wild has every probability in its favour.'

In fact, de Gerlache admitted he had two years' provisions on board, an extraordinary excess for an expedition short on cash. His father Colonel de Gerlache was interviewed by the *Geographical Journal* when the *Belgica* did not show up as first planned in Melbourne, Australia. He said his son had three years' provisions on board. It looked like they were trapped accidentally on purpose.

On long expeditions, men always stayed healthier when

rations were augmented by fresh local game. They soon realised there were fewer seals and penguins around. Early explorers generally assumed that Antarctica's animals stayed there all year. In fact nearly all of them come only in summer to breed and feed. When they leave, they go quickly. Men like Shackleton, Larsen and Nordenskjöld who were forced by circumstance to overwinter were caught out by this and did not lay in sufficient food to augment their stores.

For the time being, de Gerlache was still caught up in the romance of their predicament. Even his prose bucks up. In a single paragraph of *Voyage of the Belgica* one can read: 'The future seemed full of menace and mystery. We were about to spend a winter in the pack, and this fact alone promised plenty of data to collect and phenomena to study. Was that not what we had asked for and for which we had been looking?' It wasn't what one group of men had been looking for. None of them wonders how the sailors might take it: the wage-men who had not been told that a three-month voyage would become the first experience of a full Antarctic night, if they ever got out at all. Most of their usual duties would cease. They had no reason to be there, no science to pursue, no motive to get up at all in the months of darkness that would be relieved only by moonlight and the supernatural glow of the aurorae.

Perhaps the gentlemen now took out the expensive, inscribed editions of books gifted by the sponsors for Christmas. Each was chosen specially for that officer or scientist. The bear-like Arctowski received Balzac, de Gerlache had chosen for himself the *Uilenspiegel* of Charles de Coster, a romance about Ancient Flanders, and the delicate Danco received Flaubert's slender masterpiece

*Trois Contes*. With what feelings did Dr Cook take out that masterpiece of American Gothic: Edgar Allan Poe's *Tales of Mystery and Imagination*? When would he feel ready to read 'Manuscript Found in a Bottle', a story of a man rescued from the ocean by a ghost ship, propelled south to disaster with men who cannot see him?

Overwintering initially creates a lot of work, and keeps hands and minds busy. They banked snow against the sides to reduce the heat lost from radiation, and put an awning over part of the deck, using materials intended for accommodation ashore when overwintering. On deck they built a shed finished with waterproof canvas and tar paper. A forge, water distillation plant and changing area were set up. Provisions had to be sorted to leave only frost-proof materials in the hold. The scientists erected observation huts on the pack and maintained a hole in the ice on the starboard side for soundings, fishing and a ready supply of water in case of fire. On 26 March an act of lasting symbolism was carried out; the boiler fires were left to die out. When you live on a powered vessel the background noise of the engine is always with you. When it is turned off, it feels as if the ship's heart has been stilled. They had left seventy tons of coal and forty of anthracite. Most sails were stowed, but the topsails, one staysail and the spinnaker were kept to hand in case a sudden break up of ice left them without power or steerage. To save coal, only blubber was used from now on to fuel their water distiller.

De Gerlache recognised the importance of discipline and a structured day to keep men healthy and sane. He abandoned the ship's watches and decreed everyone's day should consist of eight hours' work, eight hours' sleep and eight hours of leisure. For safety there was a ban on going out of sight of masts. They had noticed that seemingly fixed landmarks like distinctively shaped icebergs could move about, making navigation across the ice treacherous.

Food was vital not just for nutrition but for morale. When there is not much to do, meals give shape to the day and are something to look forward to. Ideally, de Gerlache only manages memorable humour when writing of the cook: 'If the provisions were not wanting, the same could not be said for the cook.' Michotte had been an Algerian missionary 'unwilling to tell me he was not possessed of a genius for cooking ... imagination was not lacking, in so far as he was capable of putting together the most disparate of ingredients.' The only thing consistently good was the tomato soup because he could think of nothing to add to it. De Gerlache took charge and drew up a cycle of twenty-eight daily menus but the meals didn't quite arrive as planned. Dinner was seldom the item on the menu, but a mélange of last two days' leftovers. However Michotte's enthusiasm bought forgiveness, especially since no one else thought they could do better.

The menus looked varied but most tinned meats and foods tasted the same, whatever it said on the label. The men first fantasised on what animals might be in the tin and then what they would do to the manufacturers. Tinned meat and fish with cream were the most despised and, top of the hate-list was Fiskabolla: Norwegian tinned fish balls. They were used in bets; the loser had to eat them. There was little fibre in their diet, and de Gerlache obliquely referred to the consequences: 'Our organs of secretion functioned with difficulty.' Sugar and milk were running out, and sorely missed. Living off the land did not enthuse anyone. Dr Cook diagnosed the problem: 'We have tried penguin and cormorants, but the majority have voted them unpalatable.' In fact de Gerlache had another, rather peculiar motive for not serving fresh meat. On 26 March they had shot many seals and caught penguins for food, but they did not appear on de Gerlache's menus. Five weeks later Lecointe asked where they were and de Gerlache replied he was worried what the press back home would say about killing and eating seals.

They concluded the sea was 'too deep' to fish, and penguins and seals were 'more plentiful than tasty.' They learned with relief that numbers of emperor and Adélie penguins would stay in the area all winter, the poor Adélies often tobogganing towards the hunter out of curiosity. Seal and penguin meats were both 'black and hard, very fat and oily but without the least taste of fish, as is commonly supposed.' It was just bad cooking. I have eaten seal which was as tender as fine beef, and richer. Grog was served only on Sunday nights and celebrations; otherwise spirits were banned. Every Sunday a 15cl glass of wine was drawn for each man.

Scientific work could continue. They trawled with filter nets for fine organisms; their catches were the first at this latitude. After each trawl, Racowitza would spend two to three days in the laboratory examining, drawing and describing those specimens which were hard to conserve, and making notes for future watercolours. They found beautifully coloured corals and sponges. Arctowski and Dobrowolski led the meteorological observations, assisted by Lecointe, Amundsen and de Gerlache. Danco, whose health during the coming winter was of special concern to Dr Cook, kept busy making three sets of magnetic observations per day.

Cook began to monitor the men's health. They were fortunate in being able to keep the living quarters around 10°C which meant there was little condensation, the bane of polar accommodation. All the men were encouraged to bathe often, and at least once a week. In May, Cook gave everyone a check including temperature, pulse and weight. That month saw a thaw and their observation hut first settled drunkenly in the ice, then broke off on a floe and had to be recaptured. When it grew cold again head-sized lumps of ice began crashing to deck. By mid-May the sun showed for only a few moments each day. Then 'the Polar night descended on us.' They would live 1600 hours before seeing it again.

In the dim light new distortions taunted them. Scale and distance became confused. De Gerlache himself set off to see why packing cases had been left on the ice some hundred metres away and after a few strides reached what he had seen: a newspaper blown onto the ice. He lamented: 'How much more, therefore did we value the fine clear nights too rare alas! – in spite of their atmosphere of intense melancholy, above the few daily hours of nebulous light.' He considered the ship their only hope of salvation. It was 'the dead star lighting up a dead world.' Being suspended above the ocean made them muse on the vast unknown of the waters beneath and how all creatures perishing at the surface 'fall down into the abyssal depths to feed other mysterious and shadowy beings.' Once the ice silenced the water they learned the subtle new sounds 'indecipherable and almost imperceptible, like the gentle and regular breathing of a world asleep.' Animal companions were now few. The seals went to sea, among the birds, only a few snow petrels remained. Of all the flighted birds, it is the true ice bird.

Exercise days were organised. The dress for recreation was Icelandic wool jerseys, a balaclava, a leather cap with ear-flaps like the Norwegian sealers wore, a canvas anorak, and Inuit-style finnesko boots lined with sennegras insulation. In cold weather they added canvas pants or Siberian wolfskin outfits.

Once they were reconciled to overwintering, morale began at a good level. Each night Racowitza posted a cartoon of something topical that day. One revealed that after Arctowski had carefully planted a measuring stick to measure new snowfall, Danco had sneaked out and hammered it deeper into the ground. Danco was still in good spirits and told everyone that all this fresh air would help his chest.

But as the darkness continued, in varying degrees for different people, optimism was steadily eroded. Cook caught the disintegration of daily routine: 'In the first days of our life in the pack, we ate when we were hungry, slept when we were tired, and worked when the spirit moved us. But later we were never hungry, always tired, and the spirit never moved us.' Even de Gerlache, who felt bound to both justify his decision and lead by positive example, reflected that 'for the time being we were no longer navigators, but rather a little colony of convicts serving out time.'

Lecointe thought he was going mad on the morning of 17 May when at 07:00 he report seeing a light, like a lantern being waved as a signal. Everyone congregated half-dressed on deck, peering into the gloom, getting colder. After ten minutes they all saw it, a pale glow slowly waving to and fro. Amundsen was one of the best skiers, and more fully dressed than most. He skied alone across the ice and found a piece of ice had popped out of the pack and was bobbing up and down. Its underside was coated with luminous algae.

One man felt the winter first, the man they all feared for: tall, kindly Emile Danco. As soon as sun went he became short of breath very easily and withdrew from exercise. Normally extremely conscientious, on 20 May he gave up all work. His spirits shone as his health declined. He alone believed he'd survive or he affected to believe; it was nothing, he insisted, and would pass when sun returned. He smiled always and the men used their leisure time to play whist with him.

Up until May, Dr Cook had not been anxious about the general health of his charges, but his fears began to grow.

The truth is, that we are at this moment as tired of each other's company as we are of the cold monotony of the black night and of the unpalatable sameness of the food. Now and then we experience affectionate moody spells and then we try to inspire each other with a sort of superficial effervescence of good cheer, but such moods are short lived. Physically, mentally and perhaps morally, then, we are depressed, and from my past experience in the arctic, I know that this depression will increase with the advance of the night, and far into the increasing dawn of next summer. Physically we are losing strength, though our weight remains nearly the same, with a slight increase in some. All seem puffy about the eyes and ankles, and the muscles, which were hard earlier, are now soft, though not reduced in size. We are pale and the skin is unusually oily. The hair grows rapidly and the skin about the nails has a tendency to creep over them seemingly to protect them from the cold.

There was one widespread symptom which threatened to reduce them to helplessness.

The heart action is failing in force and is decidedly irregular. Indeed, this organ responds to the slightest stimulation in an alarming manner. The observers, going only one hundred yards to the observatories come in almost breathless after their short run. The usual pulse, too, is extremely changeable from day to day, in one case it was yesterday 43, today it is 98, but the man complains of nothing and does his regular work. The sun seems to supply an indescribable something which controls and steadies the heart. In its absence it goes like an engine without a governor.

About half the men complain of headaches and insomnia; many are dizzy and uncomfortable about the head, and others are sleepy at all times, though they sleep nine hours. Acid dyspepsia and frequent gastric discomforts are often mentioned, there are also rheumatic and neuralgic pains, muscular twitchings and an indefinite number of small complaints, but there is but one serious case on hand.

This is Danco:

He has an old heart lesion, a leak of one of the valves, which has been followed by an enlargement of the heart and a thickening of its walls. In ordinary conditions, when there was no need for unusual physical or mental strain, and when liberal fresh food and bright sunshine were at hand, he felt no defect. The hypertrophied muscular tissue is beginning to weaken. If it continues at the present rate it will prove fatal within a month.

At intervals, the ice attacked. From 28 to 31 May they were squeezed tightly in the pack. In a premature rehearsal of Shackleton's later dilemma, when the *Endurance* sank in the Weddell Sea, they looked at various options should they lose their ship. They proposed to haul the ship's boats over the ice, and sail to the South Shetlands, then on to South America. De Gerlache candidly assessed their chances of success at 1 in 100.

On 5 June Dr Cook came to de Gerlache, who recalled: 'His expression was disordered and his voice trembled as he said, "Commander, today is the day." He meant the day Danco would die. Danco was installed on stateroom sofa and the officers ate in captain's cabin, then later gathered round his bed. He said, "I can breathe lighter and will soon get strength."' They were his last words.

They improvised a memorial. Rysselberghe produced flowers, given to him fresh by his mother as he left Belgium, now withered and dried. They were sewn into Danco's canvas burial bag. He was buried on 7 June on a day so bitter the ice was hard to cut. At 11:00 they followed the sled bearing Danco to the ice hole, and bared their heads. When the service for the burial of the dead was concluded, they tipped the bag into the ring of dark water. The bag did not slide below, but stood upright before sinking, making the sailors recoil in horror. Dr Cook was rightly worried about the impact of kindly Danco's death on a group he thought was already approaching dissolution. He had urged de Gerlache to order the playing of the *Coelophone* music machine at the funeral, but de Gerlache thought happy music might trivialise the ceremony, and instead sent grog to the men. Cook was right. Death changed the atmosphere; it became profoundly demoralised. It was hard to tell whether men's constitutions were slipping into ruin, or they were hiding in psychosomatic illnesses.

De Gerlache himself was sicker than he would admit. Dr Cook confided to his diary: 'At present I have the captain in the baking treatment.' [Giving patients a dry sauna.] 'He is pale and yellowish, with a feeble almost imperceptible pulse of 100–140 – his recovery, while hopeful, is uncertain.' Lecointe was in such a poor state he sorted out his affairs and made a will. Cook suspected anaemia was exhibiting itself in confusing symptoms and prescribed a diet to remedy this, including eating lightly cooked seal and penguin meat. It is fortunate that this would also cure scurvy, which is what they were actually suffering from. Danco had been asked to follow this regime and had replied he would rather die. Lecointe's initial response to the doctor's request to serve more fresh meat was to be offended, taking it as criticism of his issuing of the stores. As he got sicker he changed his mind, saying he would sit on the stove for two hours a day and eat penguin for the rest of his life if that would help. He followed the prescription and in two weeks he was back at work.

In these months Cook earned the admiration of all. Amundsen, not hasty to scatter praise, described 'Cook, the calm and imperturbable never losing his temper. He gives advice on everything. He gives it in a likeable and tactful manner; not with fuss and noise.' In his later career, Cook made absurd and soon disproven claims about reaching the North Pole and climbing the USA's highest peak, Mount McKinley, then spent seven years in jail for fraudulent promotion of oil shares. But Amundsen could not be persuaded to change his opinion of the character of the man he considered had, more than anyone else, held the *Belgica* expedition together. It was 'during these thirteen long months in which almost the certainty of death stared us in the face, that I came to know Dr Cook intimately and to form the affection for him and the gratitude for him which nothing in his later career could ever cause me to alter. He, of all the ship's company, was the one man of unfaltering courage, unfailing hope, endless cheerfulness, and unwearied kindness.'

Van Rysselberghe complained of heart pain, Arctowski and Racowitza suffered persistent stomach pain without diagnosed physical cause. For a while Lecointe was described as 'in danger' and, wrote de Gerlache, 'for some days I too was severely ill.' Cook told de Gerlache it was scurvy, and the symptoms were seldom mistaken. De Gerlache, who had ordered the stores and devised the menus would not have it. He complained that 'seal and penguin literally had to be burned to a cinder to get rid of the excess fat.' Fresh meat would cure scurvy if undercooked, but nearly raw meat was nauseous to most of the men. Cook also prescribed exercise. In poor weather they tramped round the ship on skis, muffled to the eyeballs like the damned.

Compare the image with Poe's 'Manuscript Found in a Bottle': 'It is a long time since I first trod the deck of this terrible ship, and the rays of my destiny are, I think, gathering to a focus. Incomprehensible men! Wrapped up in meditations of a kind which I cannot define, they pass me by unnoticed.'

In good weather they escaped to an iceberg two miles off. Nevertheless Cook was alarmed to observe a high pulse of 130/140 in many men after just thirty minutes walking. More had vertigo while still on the ground. Prolonged intellectual work became impossible, complaints multiplied to embrace insomnia, nightmares and constipation. Cook soon found symptoms of cardiac and cerebral malfunction.

One man on the *Belgica* went deaf and dumb for days, apparently without physical cause. The Norwegian bosun Adam Tollefsen had been trained up to help prepare animals for the microscope and the specimen jar, but he suddenly went on strike saying it was unworthy of him, and that colleagues were out to kill him. He abandoned his bunk and moved to a corner of between-decks, living like an animal in a den, where he was clandestinely watched for fear of aggression to himself or others.

There were moments when nature provided the relief of beauty. On 21 June their midwinter night was filled with aurorae so bright one could read a book. Finally, on 21 July, a Sunday, they climbed to the top of a berg and saw a long-missed friend: the sun. The few seconds were treasured but fleeting. They all looked bloated and yellow, older and tired, with sad grey hair which they grew long for warmth. De Gerlache thought Racowitza looked like a Turk's Head brush for cleaning ceilings. On 2 August de Gerlache celebrated his thirty-second birthday.

Before any spring ice melts the animals return: the whales and seals. Birds lifted their heavy souls, but the return of the light brought no other relief, and the warmth brought an infestation of rats, which must have boarded

de Gerlache officers' mess

when they were bunkering at Punta Arenas. Winters which come early often linger late, and sometimes they do not let go. A second winter would destroy them; that was the unspoken wisdom of the senior officers and Dr Cook. Did Dr Cook re-read his Poe?: 'But I could not help feeling the utter hopelessness of hope itself' and 'my very soul has become a ruin.'

On 8 September they experienced the lowest temperature of the whole trip: −43.1°C. They experimented with the Tonite explosive brought to break ice, and found it useless. The penguins heard the explosions without alarm, but when some imp prompted Van Mirlo to play his cornet to them, they fled in terror. On 20 September they enjoyed a thaw and ice began to fall off the rigging. The leaders' thoughts were not about getting out and going home. The expedition would continue. On 21 September, officers met to discuss the coming summer programme. They planned to break out of the ice and conduct oceanographic studies off Graham Land, then explore the Dirck Gherritz Archipelago (a mythical group). Their key objectives: firstly, not to get iced in again, secondly to connect their surveys to d'Urville's. In anticipation of spring they dismantled their deck awning, but October came and went without the sea ice weakening its grip. November should have brought early summer weather, but blizzards dropped so much snow it was hard to open the doors to go out on deck. By 21 November, almost the whole stern was buried.

They counted that in the year from March 1898 to March 1899 they had 257 days of snow. The midnight sun began on 27 November and thawing progressed. Before the month ended, Amundsen made a discovery about de Gerlache's instructions for the transfer of command in the event of his death. He found the spirit of international co-operation did not extend to the transfer of power, which would pass not to the next most senior officer, but to the next most senior Belgian. Amundsen found both the instruction and its concealment from him unacceptable, and resigned on the spot, though continuing to perform his duties as before.

By mid-December, Cook, Amundsen and Tollefsen, whose mind had rallied, got to a distant berg thirty-five metres high and saw small movements in another berg nearer the open sea. On 20 December, a day short of midsummer, the engineers began preparing the engines, and on 23 December they were able to free the rudder with boiling water. But the sea ice was still an unbreakable eight metres thick. On 31 December, the year's end found them at 70°03´S and 82°20´W. They had drifted thirteen hundred miles in the ice and come back to where they had first been frozen in. They had not drifted deep into the pack where they might never escape. This gave hope that if this area had been ice-free last year, it would thaw again. In the next days a tantalising crack appeared before and behind the *Belgica*. On 7 January, at Dr Cook's urging, the men set to work to saw ice and set explosives. A penguin stood watching the explosions. It had little effect. They tried reversing along the fault risking damage to their rudder and propeller. A returning storm petrel flew over. Did that mean there was open water nearby? They worked in three eight-hour shifts, twenty-four hours a day. A bottle-nosed whale surfaced in their new channel, offering encouragement. Tollefsen suffered a relapse but denied anything was wrong.

On 31 January, after sitting in their lead for three weeks, a crack opened up ahead. They now lay at the centre of a crescent-shaped lead with a lagoon between the two tips.

But the ice was teasing them, and the channel astern, which they had laboriously sawn and blasted, began to fill with ice. The officers were nearly resigned to spending another winter in the pack. Cook assessed their prospects, and concluded at least four would not be strong enough to survive it. De Gerlache reduced their meagre butter and sugar rations immediately, and reviewed food stocks to devise how they could be made to last until April 1900. On 1 February the temperature fell and so did the snow. The pack tightened and de Gerlache became fully resigned to another Antarctic night. They also prepared to be able to evacuate if the ship became damaged, going as far as bagging up a spare set of clothes ready for emergency evacuation.

Then, on 4 February, the ship began to gently rock. A sliver of hope crystallised. In the morning all was once again still and there was new ice in the channel thick enough to be walked on. On 11 February it loosened again, and at 17:30 the crack and their channel re-opened. In the early hours of 15 February they slipped the *Belgica* into the small lagoon. The sea between them and the long-unseen open ocean loosened then closed, but on 20 February a dark line was seen from crow's nest. It was open sea at the edge of pack, and appeared about ten miles off. By early March it was less than a mile away, and surf breaking at the limit of the pack was visible from the deck. It had to break soon, as they were reminded every minute, by the flocks of moulting penguins surrounding them on the ice; summer was nearly over.

On 14 March a new threat appeared. Two large bergs began to move towards the ship in a pincer movement. The sickening prospect loomed of being crushed to pieces when escape was in the fingertips of their grasp. The swell rose and helped break up the ice around ship. At 02:00 de Gerlache ordered the engines to be fired up, and at 04:00 they began to delicately work a passage through the channels, evading the bergs. By noon, they were clear.

They broke out of the ice 335 miles from their position when they had entered it on 2 March 1898. The ice had taken them on a journey of 1700 miles. In their absence from the world, they had missed Marconi's invention of radio. It would, in time, transform exploration of all types, by removing the dread of isolation. They sailed home via Punta Arenas, from where Racowitza, Cook and Arctowski went ahead on steamers to prepare their return. Amundsen stuck by his resignation and refused to accompany them. He booked himself, Tollefsen and two other men who had gone mad onto a regular passenger vessel and escorted them safely home.

As well as being the first people to experience an Antarctic winter, the expedition made the first Antarctic sled journey and added hugely to the systematic knowledge of the Peninsula and its islands. Before de Gerlache, the cartography of the Peninsula had been constructed partly working by speculative theories and partly through reconciling observations which either did not join up or did not tally with each other when they did. De Gerlache re-drew the chart of the area. Arctowski added greatly to geological knowledge, zoological specimens were taken from new parts of the ocean, and animal behaviour had been observed over time. They more than doubled the number of plant species recorded from the last continent. Under the direction of the *Belgica* Commission, the records and samples they collected kept seventy-eight international scientists busy for many years. Frederick Cook's highly readable *Through the First Antarctic Night* became a best-seller.

# 8

## A Permanent Foothold:
### William Speirs Bruce (1867–1921)

*A tale of self-effacing scientific achievement, quiet and noble self-sacrifice, and the first confirmed sighting of bagpipes in the south.*

In the photo-portrait he gives nothing away. He does not look at the camera, and the drooping lids he inherited from his father half cover his eyes. A heavy beard hides his mouth, though you can see the folds of his cheeks above the corners of the mouth are raised slightly as though he has been asked to look cheery but the effort is all too much. His editor wrote: 'He was seldom seen to smile; life for him was earnest and demanding.' The man is William Speirs Bruce, leader of the Scottish National Antarctic Expedition of 1902–04.

Bruce was not part of what would be styled the Heroic Age of polar exploration. Peary, Amundsen, Scott and Shackleton would have chosen whatever form of public endeavour was most likely to bring them advancement and acclaim; in their era, it was being a polar hero. Bruce was a scientist with work to do; he did not care if he came back to crowds and medals so long as he came back with specimens and measurements. He was as self-effacing as that portrait. Only the sleepy eyes deceive. He was a man in whom sense and judgement were energised by great drive and courage.

He read medicine at Edinburgh, where a friendship with William Burn Murdoch persuaded him that science was part of the romantic Scots-Celtic revival being promoted by Professor Patrick Geddes's circle. With Otto Nordenskjöld, Adrien de Gerlache, and Jean-Baptiste Charcot, Bruce went on to pioneer small, agile expeditions that were conceived and led by private individuals, even if they received public funding and government endorsement. Aged thirty-five when he headed his own expedition, he had already been to the Arctic four times and Antarctica once. His first Antarctic voyage had been an imaginative innovation. In 1874 the brothers David and John Gray, whalers from Peterhead, Scotland, had published a pamphlet entitled *A Report on New Whaling Grounds in the Southern Seas*, including Ross's reports of bountiful whales during his voyages from 1839–43. The Grays urged whalers to look south, stressing: 'We think it is established beyond doubt that whales of a species similar to the right or Greenland whale found in northern high latitudes exist in great numbers in the Antarctic seas, and that the establishment of a whale fishery within that area would be attended with successful and profitable results.' In 1892, faced with declining Arctic catches, Robert Kinnes of Dundee sent four steam whalers south: the *Balaena* under Captain Alexander Fairweather, the *Diana*, the *Active*, and the *Polar Star*.

The whalers would transport scientists south to conduct research; in return, the ships would receive doctors on each vessel and superior instruments, including chronometers, compasses and meteorological kit. The captains would assist by allowing their routes to be closely charted, and by stopping as often as was feasible for observations of the weather and magnetics. Bruce was appointed surgeon for *Balaena* despite having no training in surgery. It's hard to know whether to feel reassured or scared by reports that he embraced his new role with enthusiasm and confidence. The captains were equally nonchalant about the spirit and word of the agreement. On the *Balaena*, Bruce soon found the old Arctic hand Captain Fairweather interpreted 'stopping whenever feasible' as 'never', but Bruce's choice had been an unsatisfactory voyage or no voyage at all, so he persevered and did what he could. In the Erebus and Terror Gulf, they saw the whaler *Jason*, and went on board on 24 January to meet the veteran skipper Captain Larsen who would later establish the Grytviken whaling station on South Georgia. 'He is a frank and very pleasant man, and one who seemed to take an enthusiastic interest in everything connected with the expedition.' He would have been a perfect captain for Bruce. From the last week in December to the end of January the Dundee men hunted whales without success.

Publicly Bruce complained diplomatically: 'commerce was the dominating note. A great deal more might have been done for the geology and the biology of these Antarctic regions if some opportunity for landing had been afforded me.' His assistant surgeon Murdoch expressed how they really felt: 'Perhaps it seems incredible that gentle, loving, law-abiding Bruce and the writer, if possible more so, could have lain swinging in our hammocks abiding under an inverted whale-boat watching the blue lace-lined seas slipping past and planning how to tip the old man overboard or slit his throat.'

On 26 December Bruce made himself more miserable by dropping and losing his only bucket for sampling surface water. Unable to land, they sampled rocks recovered from ice or retrieved from penguin stomachs. Even this modest haul was sabotaged by a vindictive sailor heaving some of the biggest specimen boxes overboard. The captains gave up on whales and began sealing for skins and oil; the scientists were made to help with skinning. Donald, on the *Active*, put his finger on the flaw in the scheme: 'It is useless to trust sealers for exploring purposes, for as long as they can fill their ships with blubber in latitude 64° they will never penetrate to 65°.'

But despite the aggravations the boffins made the first full description of salps, which are tunicates, or sea-squirts; they look and feel like a pulpy yellow sock. The whalers took seals and even penguins for blubber. Penguins proved deceptively difficult to kill. One walked off after being pronounced dead on the reasonable grounds that it had an ice pick through its head. The whalers turned home on 18 February, without whales, but with enough seal oil and skins to cover their costs.

Bruce settled down for a while. He was director of the Ben Nevis meteorological station from 1894 – 96 and, unusually for a British polar explorer, became a competent skier, and the first president of the Scottish Ski Club. He worked as a naturalist on the Jackson-Harmsworth expedition of 1896 – 97 to Franz-Josef Land in the Arctic. In 1900 he was eager to go south once more. Bruce had unwittingly offended Sir Clements Markham, easily done, the influential President of the RGS, when, after the

Jackson-Harmsworth Arctic Expedition, Bruce had presented his paper first to the Royal Scottish Geographical Society, not the London RGS. Markham was now putting together the team for what became the *Discovery* Expedition of 1901–04. With a predilection for handsome young naval officers, he wanted his protégé Scott to lead the team, and Bruce was dangerous in having the qualifications and experience Scott lacked. Markham first excluded Bruce from the *Discovery* team then, when he proposed a Scottish venture, challenged him in writing to dissociate himself from any rival venture, an impertinence bordering on the delusional. Bruce made peace by undertaking to stay clear of the *Discovery's* route and not to fund-raise outside Scotland, which hampered him severely.

While Bruce was driven by science, there was a broad streak of jingoism running through his project, and it was not British, but Scottish. So although Bruce contributed fewer than twenty lines as a preface to his colleagues' popular account of the voyage, he found space to say: 'While "Science" was the talisman of the Expedition, "Scotland" was emblazoned on its flag.' First they needed a ship. Late in 1901 Bruce went to Norway to purchase the four hundred-ton whaler *Hekla* and bring her to Troon, West Scotland for a refit under yacht and naval architect G. L. Watson who worked without fee. Designed for polar waters, she was barque-rigged with an auxiliary steam-powered screw; 140 feet long, she drew 15 feet. The refit was so thorough that 'very little of the old *Hekla* was left.' She now had a nine-foot depth of timber in the bow, and her main hull was twenty-five inches thick and sheathed with greenheart. She was renamed *Scotia*, the Roman name for Scotland.

The refurbished quarters provided a well-lit deck-house for scientific work, comfortably warm next to the galley, and a second lab beneath it. Her stores and equipment included a thousand gallons of methylated spirits for preserving samples, and 36,000 feet of cable for trawling. They were the first expedition to record sound, on a phonograph, and to use a cine camera, although it jammed most times it was used.

Their captain was Thomas Robertson from the *Active*, who had been one of the more helpful skippers on the 1892 – 93 Antarctic trip. The staff included Robert Rudmose Brown, a botanist who had worked at Kew, J. H. Harvey Pirie who came as geologist, bacteriologist and Medical Officer, while R. C. Mossman was both meteorologist and magnetist. Those three would write the popular account of the trip *The Voyage of the Scotia*. Assisting Bruce was Wilton, a second zoologist, who had lived in north Russia and was an experienced skier and sledder. Their major sponsors were textile tycoons, the Coats brothers, James, Andrew and Thomas, who donated £30,000 of the trip's slim budget of £35,000. The next largest donation was £250.

Like most expeditions, the last days were chaotic. When they sailed on 2 November 1902 'the ship was like a midshipman's bag, everything on top and nothing handy.' Pirie wrote: 'we got away fairly quietly, – a proceeding much to our taste.' One reason was that it was Sunday, prompting the local newspaper to muse: 'Stands Scotland where she did, when a ship can sail on the Sabbath with pipes playing and people singing, not psalms, but profane songs, such as "Auld Lang's Syne".'

Pirie is one of the livelier chroniclers and is soon putting on his medical officer's hat and defining the second stage of seasickness: it was characterised by deep fear, the fear that ship is never going to sink and put you out of your misery. En route they measured the sea temperature and salinity, vital to track currents. The first sight of southern land was the bare slopes of the Falklands. They leaned on the rails, warmed by their Fair Isle woollen knitwear. Some of their socks were a macabre but very warm mix of goat and human hair. Workmen were still finishing the squat tower of Stanley cathedral, but the city immediately endeared itself to them; the smell of burning peat from the chimneys was the scent of rural Scotland.

Continuing south, on 28 January they saw their first tabular icebergs: the spectacular calvings from the great ice-shelves. On 2 February 1903, at 01:00 they approached the pack; at 60°28′S 043°40′W they had met it much further north than d'Urville (63°30′S) or Ross (65°S). The wind and swell were driving directly onto the ice edge throwing up surf and agitating the floes deep into the pack. Men who had not sailed in ice before, including the ship's carpenter, James Rice, who had worked on the refit, could not believe a ship could survive being driven into that fury. He went to the bow to watch. Twelve miles in they laid up snug in the ice on a fine calm night, and the contented carpenter went below.

The next day the South Orkneys were visible about twenty-five miles off to the WSW, but they had to run north to escape dense pack ice closing in on them. On 4 February they tried again and made their first landing, getting ashore at Saddle Island, only the third ever visit there after its discovery by the sealer John Powell in the *Dove* in 1821, and then d'Urville in 1838. They landed on the north side, and took penguins, including two live ones, and eggs, as both specimens and

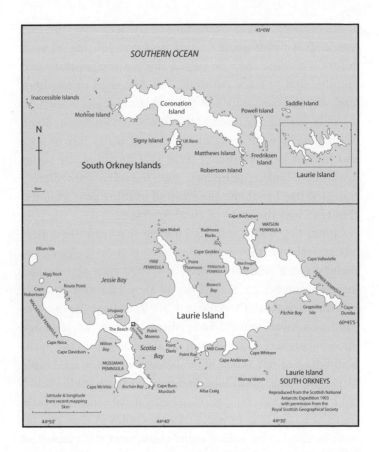

food. The penguins were loosed on deck to be tormented by men and dogs playing with them, but soon proved smarter than they looked by escaping overboard.

The season was growing late, and they were anxious to push south, leaving Laurie Island at noon to steam south west; by 21:00 they were laid to, in heavy ice. Next day it was so dense at 07:00 that further progress would only be possible by burning precious coal. Captain Robertson turned north-west, the only direction in which there was still loose ice; even so, some of it was fifteen to twenty feet thick. They followed the pack roughly along the line of latitude 60°S but by mid-month they had inched their way back into the pack as far as 62°S and now sailed between the wakes of Ross and Weddell.

On 18 February they crossed the Antarctic Circle in open sea; at times no ice was visible. It was eighty years ago to the day that a little west of there James Weddell had made his famous farthest south in an ice-less sea, at 74°15´S. They hoped to go beyond Weddell's farthest south by Sunday, but progress immediately slowed: 'We made little southing next day, owing to the increasing tightness of the pack, which Captain Robertson did not consider expedient to negotiate.' It was five years since de Gerlache had been trapped, and it was at the forefront of their minds: 'Any mistake now would finish our work for the season, and we had no wish to repeat the experiences of the *Belgica* and drift helplessly about all winter, frozen up in a sea of shifting ice.'

Reading early accounts it is interesting what attracts their interest. Those who journey to the interior soon quit the ocean and wildlife, so accounts of attempts on the pole are all about snow and ice conditions, weather, navigation, logistics and the health of men and animals. For them, sea voyages are just the parentheses around the real business of the trip. But *The Voyage of the Scotia* is written by three ship-based scientists and they are very good at describing the sea ice that controls their movement and safety. Because they observe closely, the writing is vivid. The following passage tells you sea-water freezes in a way you would never imagine:

The formation of 'young ice,' as met with in the polar seas, is an interesting process. The first stage, which takes place when the cold is very intense, is the ascent of large clouds of vapour from the sea, so dense it looks as if a veil had been spread over the surface of the ocean. If there are spaces of water and portions covered with ice, the water spaces look like boiling cauldrons, so dense are the masses of vapour that ascend. ... Soon a thickening is observed on the surface of the water, and threads like the web of a spider radiate in all directions. ... The salt-water ice is now a pasty mass, so elastic that every movement of the water on which it floats is clearly discernible. The ice, however, is quite different from that formed on fresh water; for although it becomes tougher with very intense cold, it will not support a man with safety until after thirty or thirty-six hours. Even after twenty-four hours, with a temperature of 40° below zero, the new ice is still so soft that, in spite of its thickness, a stick can still be easily pushed through it. After three days it is still in no way brittle, and bends under the weight of a man without breaking. The impression it gives is as if one were walking on well-stretched leather; and this characteristic it retains for a considerable time. After a fortnight, when over a foot and a half thick, the young ice looks as if the water had been surprised by the cold and every wave turned suddenly into ice.

Antarctica's rare fine days are sweet. The afternoon of 21 February brought the cheeriest conditions since Stanley: bright, clear and calm. They passed 70°S, a feat achieved in this sector only by Weddell and Ross, and by no one for sixty years. The sea was a blue sheet mirroring the sky until their wake creased the reflections and rocked the ice; the ripples softly shushed along the ice edge, and the plates of sea ice grated against each other. Sometimes a crack would snake across a large floe watched by the permanently alarmed white-ringed eyes of the Adélies. Today there were many emperors, stately and slow. Mossman tore himself away to go back to work; good weather or bad, it was time to take another barometer reading. Bracing his eyes for the sudden blackness inside, he entered the deck laboratory and found he could see perfectly well because the stove was one sheet of flame, and in a second remembered he was surrounded by bottles of alcohol and benzene, and in the deck immediately below, were a thousand gallons of methylated spirits. Someone, the account is generous in leaving them unnamed, had put a pan of sealing wax to melt on the stove, left the lab, and forgotten all about it. As Mossman entered, the pan had just burnt through and caught fire. He put it out; two minutes more, and it might have been uncontrollable. They narrowly avoided climbing into open lifeboats, warmed only by the blaze of their sinking ship.

Normal weather returned, bringing with it tricks and mirages. The next day they met ice, newly formed after the coldest February frost then recorded in the Weddell Sea, and only breakable under steam. At 03:00 there was a bank of fog in front of which was a thin bluish vapour. Here and there through the fog could be seen castellated towers and battlements rising above it. At 08:00 on 22 February they reached their farthest south at 70°25′S and 017°12′W surrounded by new ice cementing together the old. The captain decided to retreat north, then go east and

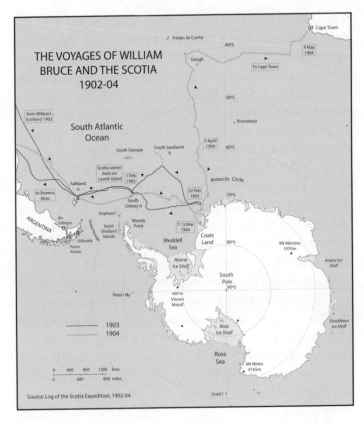

THE VOYAGES OF WILLIAM
BRUCE AND THE SCOTIA
1902-04

Source: Log of the Scotia Expedition, 1902-04

try to probe south again where Ross and Weddell had reported meeting freer seas. The ice had other ideas. They made only half a degree north, where they found the line of least resistance lay to the west. Deferring to Nature, they followed.

Sometimes bad weather elsewhere helped them: a storm to the north brought in strong swells which loosened the pack on 27 February, but the next day the ice repeatedly threatened to grip them. On 1 March they crossed Weddell's path again, but he had been in open sea and they

224

were clamped in tight pack. Once you enter March on the Peninsula you are on borrowed time. Bruce had to decide where to winter. Seas were being kept open only by ocean swell, and would soon freeze over; the nights were growing long and dark. The Chief decided to winter the ship at the South Orkneys, where it was expected that the spring ice melt would arrive in October. There would be no de Gerlache moment, succumbing to the temptation of a final push, no impulsive gamble. On 8 March the *Scotia* was shaken to her keel as a following gale drove her hard onto ice, but the old whaler's hull showed its mettle, emerging undamaged. In three more days they crossed the Antarctic Circle going north. The nights were dark once again, so unless there was moonlight, dense ice forced them to find a pool of open water each night to spend the night. On 20 March they reached open sea but any celebrations were brief since, in the shelter of the ice, most men had lost their sea-legs. By 20:00 all the officers and scientists except the captain and Bruce were seasick. They got little rest. By 23:00 a gale had blown up, and all hands were called to deck when icebergs were seen. Early next day they spied the South Orkneys, near Cape Dundas at the east end of the group. The islands strike a wild profile with sharp peaks rising straight from the sea. The wind carves the snow into grand sweeps, and the surrounding reefs and rocks snare massive oceanic bergs. What followed shows how Antarctica can make you suffer very hard for small gains.

The southern shores were ice-choked, so in a 'tremendous swell' they looked for a place known to them only from Powell's chart and a passing glimpse on their way south: Spence Harbour. On 22 March they steamed past

Saddle Island and at 09:00 suffered heavy squalls from the land which blinded everyone on deck with sharp snow. Round noon, the wind and sea fell, but visibility was bad, the lookouts suddenly shouting 'Full astern!' to avoid bergs looming out of the murk. Preoccupied by bergs, they narrowly missed rocks that appeared out of the snow-choked air just yards from the ship. At dusk, frustrated at being so close to shore but not being able to land and feel earth under their feet, they were forced to move out to sea.

Next day they saw Spence Harbour in good weather for the first time and felt misled enough by previous accounts to call it a 'fraud.' It was very deep, which is bad because it requires a lot of anchor chain to be let out, allowing the ship to make large swings when wind and tide change. It was also exposed. A second choice, Ellison Harbour, proved too small, and Bruce and his captain began to feel their charts were not to be trusted. Not wanting to denigrate the two fine navigators who had preceded them, they speculated whether, in the eighty years since Powell and Weddell had mapped the Orkneys, receding glaciers might have altered the shape and size of harbours, making them less suitable. Still unable to land, but still uncomplaining, they put out to sea at dusk, where snow squalls and poor visibility made life 'unpleasant': a very Scottish under-statement. On 24 March around 18:00, the wind moved to the west and built to a full gale, but they enjoyed good protection in the lee of the island, and 'but for the proximity of bergs [we] would have felt in clover.' Then, at 04:15, they were woken by a horrible noise: they'd drifted out beyond the lee and into ice which had torn the rudder until it hung by one pintle. They fixed it up as best they could, which wasn't much. The jury rig reduced their manoeuvrability, and hence their ability to miss big bergs and meet the wind and waves on their best quarter. They suffered a beating until they made open water at 10:00.

On 25 March they thought it had improved enough to close in on the land again which they did by 13:00, finding, south of Laurie Island, a good anchorage in sixty feet. Four days had passed between arriving and landing, but Bruce's account has no word of complaint or self-pity. It still bears their name: Scotia Bay. At a little over 60°S, it seemed a kind latitude to overwinter, equivalent to Bergen in Norway or Anchorage, Alaska. Their shortest winter day would still have five hours of light. Bruce's would be the first study of the islands. Because the group was on the border of the Antarctic and sub-Antarctic regions they anticipated interesting and new results in biology and meteorology. The beach on which they started to make camp is the only extensive area of flat land. Although extensive, it is exposed: a storm beach 350 metres wide connecting two islands, and making a bay each side. In a flash of inspiration they named it The Beach. What the sea builds, it can also destroy.

Brown noted that Weddell had referred to the island's 'terrific appearance', meaning terrifying, but as Brown sensibly observed, Weddell might have been influenced by the poor weather he endured. In sun, Brown wrote, 'I can imagine nothing more beautiful', but gloom made it 'a weary and depressing landscape', 'one that made me often long for some colour – any colour – to rest my eyes on; then the black hull of the ship was a delightful relief, or better still, the bright red of Copeland Observatory.' Brown looked in the dusk light at the deep violets of the ice-floe: 'There is, I feel sure, no region of the world more grand in its scenery than the Antarctic, and no place more transcendent in its beauty. Its very vastness, no less than its beauty, while it quickens the traveller's daily wonder and deepens his reverence, forces him to feel that it is a world that he can never conquer, a world in which the forces of nature are too tremendous to overcome, and which must resignedly be bowed before in the hope that they will suffer him to come and pass again unscathed.' It is a return to an earlier world where nature was feared and had to be propitiated. He declines to use the military language of conquest, and talks of reverence and respect: a modern sensibility.

Reflecting on their winter realm, they were pleased it belonged to no country, and they were its only human inhabitants. Less idealistically, Second Officer Fitchie thought it would make a fine penal settlement with convicts house building in summer and shovelling snow off glaciers in winter. Brown agreed: 'It is an excellent plan, with much to recommend it.'

The *Scotia* was anchored a quarter mile off, her stern to shore. The bay was relatively shallow: good, because large bergs could not be driven in. They had expected to take the ship out of the harbour, now called Scotia Bay, to trawl for specimens, but three days after their arrival, the ice blown into the bay froze together. Soon snow papered over the cracks between the ice, and for a week they fell through the gaps when relaying stores and equipment ashore. The first week in April saw them securely frozen in, and the ship was prepared for overwintering. Down came the top-gallant yards, the furnaces were allowed to go cold, and the boiler emptied. The sailors banked snow to the *Scotia's* sides and on the decks as insulation to limit the damage

Building Omond House

severe frosts inflict on the surface of the wood. They cut a fire-hole in ice to maintain a supply of water in emergencies.

As they tramped from ship to shore it was hard to see where the land actually began. The tidal range is about six feet and they took the last of several fissures parallel to the shore to be the high tide mark. They chose a site for their hut a little above it, and fifty yards from the cliffs running inland from the left hand side of the beach, as you come ashore. Although the ship was overwintering, they immediately began constructing shore accommodation for when the *Scotia* returned to the Falklands for repairs in the spring. It would also provide a base to continue work in future years after the expedition, an aim already central to Bruce's plans for continuing scientific study. Britain had declined to take it over (Markham's malevolent finger might have been in that pie) but Argentina had expressed interest. They had a prefabricated wooden hut, which they could surround with stone walls. Ironically, they had assumed they would winter in Antarctica proper where the weather would not allow them to build in stone, so they had no masonry tools or cement. As a result, they could only build clumsy dry stone walls five feet thick, buttressed at the corners.

A yard-arm sawn in half formed the gable pole, from which they suspended a roof of doubled canvas with insulating felt between, and the outside coated in oil and grease. The interior was canvas-lined, and the captain sacrificed his tween-deck hatches for flooring. Inside it was fourteen feet square, with six to eight feet headroom. When the ship's spare cooking range was installed, to the left of the door, it was snug and warm in all but the fiercest blizzards. To the west, they built a coal store and store-room whose walls were made of boxes of ship's biscuits, many sailors over the centuries having noted their masonry-like qualities. It was roofed with their thirty-year-old Arctic whaleboat. On the oak door lintel salvaged from the whaleboat, Brown carved Professor Geddes's educational motto *vivendo discimus* (by living we learn), and they christened it Omond House after R. T. Omond, the meteor-ologist who promoted the Ben Nevis observatory at which Bruce had learned his cold weather meteorology, and who had been a major supporter of the expedition.

They soon found their choice of site had been both unlucky and careless. The unlucky part was that snow drifted deeply in this corner of The Beach. A hard winter's shovelling lay ahead. Spring would show how they had been careless. Building continued with a cairn for surveying and a magnetic hut beyond that, located clear of distorting iron and jostling humans. This Copeland Observatory was named for Professor Ralph Copeland, an Edinburgh astronomer and a supporter. Next to the ship they preserved two holes in the ice and maintained a six hundred-foot whale line in the water between them to pull a trawl through. This raised *isopods*, the group of *crustacea* which includes woodlice, and they found a new ten-legged kind of *pycnogon* (sea-spider). They employed patent traps like lobster pots to tempt bottom-living creatures to donate themselves to science. When the skeletons of larger specimens needed a final clean, they lowered the bones in cages to the sea floor where the *amphipods* (shrimp-like crustacea) nibbled them spotlessly clean in a week. They would discover that the seas were startlingly rich and diverse. A BAS survey of the South Orkneys carried out in

2008 recorded 1224 species, more than in the Galapagos islands.

Thousands of penguins walked through The Beach, mostly gentoos and Adélies, which they took for food and specimens. Although they professed themselves uncomfortable at killing animals with no fear of man, they often saved ammunition by knifing seals to death, a brutal business which Brown observed with awed insensitivity. 'I have seen a Weddell seal, with a six-inch blade and the hilt of the knife as well, buried right in its side, live for forty minutes.'

Although the islands were largely volcanic, Pirie found fossils in a small deposit of sedimentary rocks near Cape Dundas. There was sufficient work to keep everyone busy; sometimes they were even competing for labour. The solitude of the night watch, when it came round on the rota, could be a welcome refuge from the daily bustle. In their leisure time they had use of a good library including the account of the *Belgica's* forced overwintering, which it was wise to save for an optimistic mood. There were few men with musical talent, their harmonium had not sounded the same since it had been deluged by a wave, and only Chief Engineer Ramsay played it properly. There were fifty records, and a major attraction was simply hearing a voice that was from the outside world. Talk often gravitated to fantasies of their favourite foods, feasts they would eat when they got home. The cook Florence made a hit with seal heart stuffed with sage and onion, and mastered penguin cooking, browning then stewing the breasts to stop it being too fatty. Adélies were judged the best; two birds' breasts would feed twelve to fifteen men.

In September, still winter, they grew impatient, and tried to saw and blast their way free, but the weather turned colder and they abandoned their efforts. On 1 November, with the impending departure of the *Scotia* in mind, they transferred the meteorological observations from ship to shore. Their results quantified the gloom: the mean cloud cover was 82% and there were 180 sunless days a year. They were growing tired; on a grey day, thought Brown, snow was a blessing 'since it obscures the monotony of a wider view.'

Spring spirits were lifted by preparations for sled journeys to survey farther afield. The first six penguins to arrive made a mistake as the men were pining for fresh meat. When the penguins began to lay eggs each man ate an average of fifteen a day. This was not science with a light ecological touch. When the weather was slow to improve, the whalers blamed it on a 'jinker', an unlucky presence. A mannequin of the person believed responsible was made and revealed in a dramatic flourish: Brown was obliged to burn an effigy of himself. The weather remained cold. Winds are often more important than temperature in loosening the pack, and over the days of 22–23 November, north and north east winds broke the pack in twenty-four hours. They were itching to get away; the *Scotia* sailed on 27 November.

The South Orkney party's agenda was prompted by recalling their dangerous search for a harbour, which had shown the inaccuracy of the charts. Sled journeys would now allow accurate surveying from a stable platform. They didn't have many dogs; there were two Siberian Samoyeds and six collies. In the winter, one Samoyed and three collies died from accidents, and one collie of old age. Pirie, Wilton and able seaman William Martin made an eight-day trial trip to Delta Island in the mouth of the bay. They ate a light lunch on the ice, but waited to get back to the tents for the highlight of the day: a mug of tea. 'How the thought of that hot tea kept us going all day! The recollection of it is the strongest I have of our camping-out experiences, – how both hands having clasped the cup so as not to lose any heat, the warm glow gradually spread and spread, till at last even the toes felt warm ere the cup was drained. Truly it was a cup that cheered.'

On Midwinter's Day the sun could no longer be seen from the ship, and just forty-five minutes was enjoyed on the highest part of the beach. They broke open one of the barrels of porter donated by Guinness. The first sailors to sample it quickly became drunk, then it ran out far too soon for the size of the barrel. They found all the water in the drink had frozen and only the alcohol remained liquid.

The three authors of the official account are silent on one man's suffering, until the consequences force them to mention him. Alan Ramsay, the Chief Engineer, had been ill with heart disease since March; on 27 June Bruce records that 'he is not at all well.' A month later he suffered an evening where he could scarcely breathe. Bruce charts his decline with tender sensitivity. *Mitral stenosis* was diagnosed: a malfunction of a heart valve, reducing blood supply to the body. He had felt twinges in his chest before they reached Stanley but said nothing because he realised they would find it very hard to find an engineer to replace him. He did not want to let anyone down. On 6 August Bruce recorded Ramsay had a bad night.

He thanked me for my kindness to him, and asked me to stay with him to the last. I held his head for several hours, as he wanted me to – for which he was most grateful. He had many terrible paroxysms of pain, in each of which he prayed and hoped to die. Ramsay held out his hand feebly, and said, 'Good-bye, I'm dying,' and in another two minutes or less all was over. Pirie had his hand on his heart, and 'Hands off' were the last words he said. He never said much but he always did his duty. This morning he opened up his heart to me more than he ever did before: 'I came here with the intention of doing my best, and making a name out of this job.' He said to me 'I've not been very good, but I haven't led a bad life.'

Two days later he was buried away from Omond House in Uruguay Bay. 'We placed Ramsay's head to the southward, his face looking to the sun, northward and homeward.' Three Adélie penguins came to them and stood with them by the grave. There was little they could do to raise a monument, but they collected boat-loads of green moss to lay on Ramsay's grave, signifying the new life of the Resurrection. His grave is still on the beach, looking north with other servants of the base. The doctor, Pirie, wrote, 'That scene we can never forget: one of those perfect days we sometimes had – crisp, clear, and cold, but absolutely calm; the melancholy little procession to the shore, headed by the piper playing *The Flowers of the Forest* and *The Old Hundredth*. He gave his life for others, and gave it uncomplainingly. There are those, I know, who envy him his last resting place beneath the shadow of the ice-capped hill that is named after him, where throughout the ages the seabirds wheel in their restless flight, and the waves crash upon the shore save when frost holds them in its mighty grip, and there is stillness deep as death.' They named the most imposing peak Mount Ramsay.

They mounted a second expedition to the west. It was hard progress, covering six miles in three hours. Wilton said: 'If this is Science, she's a hard mistress; give me Art.' They were rewarded with fossils: Silurian *graptolites* (an extinct colonial form of plankton) and a crustacean. The geology prompted them to guess, quite correctly, that the South Orkneys were part of the Andean chain, and they even asked why the Drake Passage had opened up across it: a question which would, in time, be answered by the theory of plate tectonics. Wilton and Martin became snow-blind after two weeks of bad weather. Cocaine eye drops eased the pain. Pirie, still unaffected, climbed a nunatak from which he was able to survey a wide area. Then he decided to walk Wilton back and on the way he lost sight in one of his own eyes for several days. It didn't blind him to the beauty: 'But what a delightful sensation it was to breast such a hill with the feeling that you were the first human being whose foot had trodden its summit, and whose vision had drunk in the beauty of the scene that lay spread out below you!'

In August ice began to break up around the ship, and Bruce wrote: 'I have been discussing next year's programme with the captain. I have been emphasising the importance of the oceanographical side of the work. He is keen for a high latitude; so am I – *provided always it is compatible with good oceanographic results*. I will not satisfy ocean-ography or other scientific research for the sake of getting one degree – or mile – further than somebody else.'

On the last day of the month they saw Weddell seals which had come ashore to pup. They killed two pups, one in its second day of life, the other five days old. 'They looked very beautiful on the sledge with their great dark eyes and their soft, long, furry coats. They were bleating like lambs. The smaller one had almost a human infant's cry.'

On 1 September, they fired up the engine. But the cold returned, and the sea re-froze. One pup was kept alive. It would suck everything except the milk bottle. They only succeeded when they sucked the milk into a football bladder and used a tube to expel the milk into its stomach. They used the phonograph to record the seal's cries, and Kerr playing the bagpipes. The seal died of convulsions later that day.

It wasn't until 27 November that the ice allowed the *Scotia* to return north. Four days later Bruce took a break from his usual post monitoring the fathom-counter on the derrick. One minute later the derrick broke and smashed through the ship's rail right where he had been standing. The *Scotia* safely reached Stanley in the Falklands where Lt. Marriott from HMS *Beagle* came over to tell them that Otto Nordenskjöld (see next chapter) had not been seen for thirteen months, but Argentine and Swedish ships were looking for them. It hammered home how lucky anyone was to return home from Antarctica. The *Beagle's* officers asked what culinary treat they would like after their dietary deprivations; they chose beer and any lunch with fresh potatoes. Bruce hurried ahead to Buenos Aires on the SS *Orissa*. They saw the ship *Français* heading south, but did not know it was Charcot (chapter ten) or his purpose.

Ashore they met the head of the Argentine Meteorological Office, Walter Davies, who agreed to take over Omond House if the *Scotia* would take down their men and stores. They met the *Uruguay* which had just rescued Nordenskjöld and the *Frithjof*, the Swedish official rescue ship begrudgingly sent down too late to help. On 21

January they left Buenos Aires with new passengers on board: naturalist Luciano Valette, and Hugo Acuña and the German-Argentine Edgar Szmula as meteorological assistants. Calling at the Falkland Islands, the Scots felt more homesick than last time; with each visit it looked more like the west of Scotland. At the South Orkneys, they quickly dropped off the land party at Laurie and sailed on 21 February. The waiting shore party said it was the first day in five weeks when it would have been safe to land a boat.

The Scots party that had remained on South Orkney for the rest of the summer was commanded by Mossman, supported by Pirie, Cuthbertson, Ross, Martin, an Able Seaman trained up as a meteorologist, and Smith, the cook. Their orders were to make hourly meteorological observations and conduct as much other science as they could. It was a comfortable base. Initially there was enough water to be able to take regular baths. They had a year's food supplies, not counting penguins. This was not as long as the supply of yarns held by Bill Smith, the second steward, who filled the evenings with so many reminiscences the others calculated he was at least 143 years old.

When the bay ice broke up it revealed an unpleasant surprise. The crack they had assumed was the shore line was in fact some way out to sea; they had built the hut just yards above high tide. The shore ice now ended in a fifteen-foot ice wall into which they had to cut a ramp for the boat. They took the first Antarctic macaroni penguin specimens to make it home, and the first ever eggs of pintado petrels, a single pure white egg, rather large for the bird. The naturalists found that the flying sea birds produced more heat and maintained a body temperature similar to temperate birds: 108-110°F, while penguins, despite having up to one inch of blubber, maintained 103-105°F. Other observations reveal dubious attitudes to wildlife: the leopard seal 'cannot be played with in the same way as Weddell seals, on whose backs we used to ride ... but is best approached behind a loaded rifle.'

By January the men were eagerly looking forward to the return of the *Scotia*. They ran a sweepstake on the likely date; the loss of Nordenskjöld's *Antarctic* was fresh in memory. As January drew to a close they began, like de Gerlache in eerie anticipation of Shackleton, to consider their options: 'our chances of making Cape Horn or the Falklands, 800 miles away and against contrary winds, were small enough.' February came, the ship didn't. They began surveying their food stores, and calculated they would have to go onto reduced rations by 15 February. They practised repairing their boots with sealskin. Pirie, mindful of the long slow nights, started to make a chess set. On 14 February, just before the last full rations lunch was served, the ship came into the north bay. They waved and returned to eat lunch, suddenly self-conscious about their anxiety, wishing to keep it to themselves.

Ship-based work resumed. One day, sounding with a 60lb weight when surrounded by sperm whales, the lead paused at 6000 feet then descended to 15780 feet. They could think of no other reason except it had landed on a whale's back, over a mile below, but they could scarcely believe it. It was the first indication of how deep that species dives for its prey. The summer of 1903–04 was one of low ice. Under canvas, the *Scotia* sailed in open water past the latitude where the pack had stopped them the previous year. They regretted that the lateness of the season stopped them exploring as far as they might. They met dense pack at 72°18´S and 017°59´W and sounded 6786 feet instead of the usual 15,000 feet. The masts were surrounded by large numbers of birds, as Weddell had also recorded in this area. The skipper went straight to the crow's nest and saw the edge of a large ice-shelf and, he believed, land. It was 3 March, and they named it Coats Land after their principal sponsors. Land had not been expected here. James Clark Ross had sounded 24,000 feet and found no bottom, causing Sir John Murray, back home, to calculate that the coast was four hundred miles farther south. Bruce proved the Weddell Sea was smaller and shallower than previously thought. It was their first sight of the ice barrier, the near-permanent cliffs of multi-year glacier ice forming shelves fast to the shore. The *Scotia* battled to within two miles of it then followed the face for 150 miles. Many explorers might have logged a sense of excitement and wonder, laced with speculation. Bruce's reaction is to make a sounding of the bottom and record: 'I had two water Buchanan-Richard bottles and thermometers, and attached one for a bottom sample. A screw of one bottle broke and I had to get another.' Bruce can be safely read without your cardiologist standing by in case of intolerable excitement.

Their dredges lifted glacial boulders of granite, gneiss, schists, quartzite, sandstone, limestone and slate: all typical of continental land. Bruce correctly guessed it would join up with Enderby Land seen farther east by the sealer John Biscoe in 1831. This deduction was one of the most important geographical discoveries of the expedition, since it was evidence of continuous and extensive continental land. It also explained why Cook and others were consistently obstructed in this area by heavy ice; the continental land mass was drained by huge glaciers despatching vast fleets of bergs northwards.

As Shackleton would discover to his cost, this is a sea where currents press the ice against the shore. It was soon piling up as high as their deck. The ship was pinched by the floes and lifted four feet: disconcerting, but it relieved the pressure. Two days of gales drove them into a bight in the ice barrier. When it eased they were at 74°01′S and 022°00′W. It would be their farthest south, four degrees beyond the previous season, and fourteen miles past Weddell.

As they listened to the grinding and groaning of the pack, the spectre of overwintering haunted them. Three days later it looked worse. The *Scotia* was lifted up by the lateral pressure of the ice, there was no open water to the north, and the pack was freezing hard. Captain Robertson brought down the topgallant spars to reduce the wind stress on her top gear. Bruce ordered an inventory of their stores, and reduced the use of lamps to a minimum. To maintain spirits they played football on the ice. After the gale, the weather turned clear, crisp and calm, and they experienced the 'awful silence' of the barrier.

The zoologists captured emperor penguins weighing up to 80lbs. They had now concluded strangling was the best way to kill penguins, as it minimised the risk of getting blood on the feathers, and was preferable to hydrocyanic acid, which stopped the blood coagulating and made skinning messy. One emperor featured in the cruellest picture in Antarctic history. OS Gilbert Kerr dressed himself in full highland rig and played the bagpipes to it. The bird displayed 'no excitement, no sign of appreciation or disapproval, only sleepy indifference.' In the photo (there's a copy near the dartboard in the bar of Vernadsky Base) the bird stands six feet away looking happy enough, until you look carefully and see there is a line tethering it to Kerr's foot. Some of the emperors were intended for Cape Town zoo. Like many birds, they need a very precise stimulus to feed, and would not eat fish from a bucket, though they would swallow them if hand-fed. For unstated but bizarre reasons the crew did not persevere with this although fresh fish were brought up with each trawl. They tried giving them preserved fish, but the emperors grew thin and died. The sheathbills they tamed should have been easier to look after, being scavengers, but they were killed by their own curiosity; one drowned in a barrel of tar and another suffered death by inebriation in methylated spirits. One live sheathbill was accidentally washed clean in a solution of 50% alcohol, an error highlighted after it preened its feathers and fell over drunk. It survived both the alcohol and the hangover.

On 12 March a south-west wind eased the pressure of the ice, and at 20:30 the ship slipped back down into the water. The spectre of overwintering receded. Said Bruce, 'never during the whole voyage had I seen everybody in such exuberant spirits.' At 16:00 leads opened to the north-east, and they tried to free the vessel with Tonite explosive, by hacking with poles, and jumping up and down. On 13 March they took risks to drive the ship through the pack, and the ice took a bite out of the propeller. Next day they had escaped into brash ice with fresh pancake ice forming on the water. The wind changed to the north. In such conditions the engines were vital in escaping up wind. They decided it was too dangerous to re-enter the pack that season and headed for the 'Ross Deep'. On 18 March they made their richest trawl, lifting many deep-sea fish. They noted that many of them were coloured with reds and purples, and speculated on why creatures living beyond sunlight still made use of colour.

On 23 March they arrived at 68°32´S and 012°49´W over the Ross Deep where Ross had found '4000 fathoms no bottom.' The winch began lowering the 60lb weight and they were surprised when it hit mud at 2660 fathoms (15,960 feet). The current had carried out Ross's line sideways, misleading him. Soundings and deep water sampling, carried out by lowering several miles of wire, were strenuous and sometimes dangerous affairs, with four to six' tons of tension on the cable. The wire could kink, break, and jam, or be taken away by currents. Sometimes seven hours work revealed that the sampling bottles had not worked, and nothing had been learned. But Bruce was doggedness itself, and redrew both the boundaries and bottom contours of the Weddell Sea.

The summer over, they laid course to Cape Town via the sub-Antarctic island of Gough. The *Scotia* rolled heavily, making sleep impossible; the worst roll took them 56° to starboard then 43° to port. Harvey Pirie wrote that although the Roaring Forties had a reputation for wild weather, comparing the Forties with the Furious Fifties was like comparing a lamb to a hyena. Their soundings would reveal a sea floor ridge, emerging above water in various islands: South Georgia, the South Sandwich Islands and South Orkneys, curving from Cape Horn east then back west to the Antarctic Peninsula. This is now known as the Scotia Arc, after the ship, and the tectonic plate to the south is the Scotia Plate.

Returning to Scotland they made such good progress from the Azores they had to sit our a few days in Dun Laoghaire, Ireland, on 15 July as their reception on the Clyde was not ready until 21 July. They had sailed thirty thousand miles in twenty-two months.

A few of the men had remained ashore in the South Orkneys. The second winter, under the command of Mossman, was a tougher affair. The comforting ship was not lying a short walk away, and the island was not brisk with the duties of a full ship's crew. The Argentine party included a 'youth named Acuña, whose profession was hard to define.' He was from the Ministry of Agriculture, not directly relevant to the Antarctic, but he brought a letter franker and some books in a mail bag so the Scots called him the Post Master General. Before the *Scotia* continued south beyond the South Orkneys, Omond House was improved and extended. A shed and coal store was erected alongside and the passage between them was roofed.

Since November they had realised that Omond House was precariously close to the sea, but the prevailing winds gave them shelter. When early March brought onshore gales they had undermined the seaward walls. From 8 to 29 March they toiled to erect a breakwater in front of their only shelter. The biggest blocks weighed over one ton, and took five men seven hours to drag into position with a block and tackle. On 30 March there was a spring tide which they hoped would strengthen their breakwater by washing shingle into the voids. The night of 3 April mocked those hopes. A high spring tide coincided with low pressure, which draws the sea up higher, and hurricane force winds driving right into Scotia Bay. It sounded as if the waves were beating at their door. They looked outside. They were. Waves were sweeping past them and up the beach, threatening to pass right over the storm beach to the other shore. They evacuated Omond House. Masses of ice had been hurled a hundred yards above the high water mark. Cases of stores had been thrown all over the beach. They made what shelter they could. Next morning at 11:30 when the tide had fallen, they re-entered their house and found the sea had broken in but, by some magic, had not put out the fire. However their only shelter for the coming Antarctic winter was precarious: the porch undermined and collapsed, the aisle roof torn off. The corner of the house had gone and the reinforcing buttresses were only standing because frozen spray had cemented them together. Bags of stones and boxes were shoved underneath. The next tide was lower and the weather calmer; the sea merely lapped at the walls. Fetching new rocks for repairs was made difficult when snow froze up the scree-slope where they quarried their stone. They put a sixty-ton dyke around the buttress, finishing it on 22 April. Three days later came Argentine Independence Day, and whatever their nationality they celebrated it with feeling. On 29 April they suffered a hard gale from the south-east. They braced themselves for another beating but big seas did not form, suggesting the sea offshore was beginning to freeze. At 02:00 next morning the night watch observed pack ice advancing, and by 11:00 Scotia Bay was full. They harvested late penguins to store and caught shoals of small fish.

Smith and Mossman suffered from poor health in the mid-winter days. Compared with the previous winter's bustle, it was harder to maintain morale with just a handful of men, three of whom spoke limited English. 'Life had become very dull. The social atmosphere was by no means brilliant,' Mossman wrote. 'There were no quarrels, but during the winter, conversation flagged because there was nothing to talk about.' Even Smith, the garrulous cook, remarked 'Life's too slow for a funeral.' They noted that in great cold, minus 18°C, pockets of air escaping from crevasses looked like smoke. It had been observed at Queensferry on the Firth of Forth in the great frost of 1814.

On 3 August they recorded minus 40°C, 7°C colder than the previous year's minimum. The morning of 8 August brought a thunderstorm. They noted with irony that the ice was hard, dense and rigid, ideal for the sledging they'd had to perform in terrible conditions the previous year. But spirits lifted on 17 August when the first snow petrels returned to their nests. The health of Smith and Mossman improved as the days lengthened. No one suffered the severe nutritional problems experienced by the crews of de Gerlache and Charcot. On 28 August a Föhn wind raised the temperature by 22°C, which was a mixed blessing as they suffered 'silver thaws' when rain froze as it landed. They froze shut the door of the meteorological hut; the met men had to cut the ice so as not to tear out lumps of the wood. To make magnetic observations, Mossman developed a routine: first wiping frost from the instruments. Some days the observer's breath misted the mirrors, and he had to leave the door open. The wind could be too loud for him to hear chronometer's beats from two feet, but if one of the timed observations was missed, the whole series had to begin again. As winter went on, the snow built up. The morning dig-out grew from a fifteen-minute job to two hours.

Further signs of spring began on 2 September when the first Weddell seals came ashore to pup. 11 October brought a cold snap, the last of the winter, and repeating a pattern they had seen the previous year, the first penguins arrived immediately after. On 27 October the ice in Uruguay Cove broke up and went out to sea. They were glad of fresh eggs when the penguins began to lay and were ruthless in their take: eighteen hundred eggs in all. Penguins can relay if eggs are lost immediately, but success is lower for the second batch. The skuas, curious and intelligent birds, were getting used to their new neighbours, and enjoyed cleaning up after the seal-kills. Mossman came across two tern eggs which he put in a bag. He put it down to search a penguin rookery for new chicks, and returned to find a skua had taken the eggs out and eaten them. Trying to take the skuas' own eggs launched open warfare. They bombed him so vigorously he was knocked off balance and fell eighty feet down a steep ice-shelf, escaping injury only by great luck.

Though in 1903 the *Scotia* had sailed out on 23 November, in 1904 Scotia Bay had not thawed by 31 December. The ship was due 'about the end of the year.' When Mossman climbed the hill above Omond House on New Year's Eve and looked south-west it was 'very wintry: nothing but heavy pack to be seen, with very few lanes of water among the floes. As usual, I crossed over to the east side of the glacier to get a view of the conditions to the north and east.' He saw a ship. It was not the *Scotia*, it was the *Uruguay*, the Argentine vessel deputed the work of tidying up.

The *Scotia's* scientific results were published in six volumes from 1907–20. Then the money ran out and the log of the *Scotia*, the popular narrative usually used as a vehicle to promote the men as heroes, was not published until SPRI did so in 1992. Bruce failed to raise money for a second Antarctic trip to achieve the Pole, and instead went north to Spitsbergen with Prince Albert. In 1907 he used much of his own money to set up the Scottish Oceanographic Laboratory with the aim of it being co-opted by Edinburgh University, but the outbreak of the First World War stopped that and it closed for lack of funds in 1920. From 1915–16 he managed a whaling station in the Seychelles, but he didn't enjoy the tropics. He died in 1921 after a long illness followed by depression. The whaler *Smyrna* scattered his ashes in the waters off South Georgia. In 1957, the Commonwealth Trans-Antarctic Expedition closely followed Bruce's planned route and took his Saltire (the Scottish flag) from the 1902–04 voyage and flew it at the South Pole.

In his career he made eleven trips to the Arctic and two to the Antarctic. His Antarctic discoveries were economical, original, and dove-tailed effectively with other contemporary expeditions. His expeditions were conducted with much bravery and no recklessness. When Bruce studied the fossils, he correctly concluded that the South Orkney *graptolites* they had collected fitted biological evidence, gathered by many authors, of historical land connections between Antarctica and New Zealand, Australia and South America, South Africa and South America, and the Auckland Islands near New Zealand. Between Bruce's gathering of the fossils and his paper, a man called Alfred Wegener had from 1906–09 conducted research from a small, sturdy hut I have visited in Danmarkshavn, East Greenland. He postulated a theory which earned him controversy and ridicule but which is now the organising thesis of how we understand the face of the planet on which we live: continental drift. Antarctic fossils would provide dramatic evidence that plants and animals had thrived in environments quite different from their present locations. His oceanographic results added greatly to the geography of the sea floor.

Let's return to where we began: the portrait of Bruce. Genuinely self-effacing, and valuing science more than adventure, he received little recognition outside the circles where the scientific disciplines he helped to advance are valued for their own sake, not as vehicles to fabricate heroes. Robert Rudmose Brown wrote of his old chief, 'Not only did Bruce hold a remarkable record in the number of polar expeditions he had led or accompanied during the last 30 years, but he was also acknowledged to be the highest authority on polar exploration of his time. It was only his intense dislike of publicity and his natural shyness that prevented him becoming one of the outstanding personalities of his generation.' Although nationalistic for Scotland, he was happy for Argentina to continue his science, and Omond House, now Orcadas Base, has the longest history of continuous use of any Antarctic Base. He achieved new standards for science and his zoological collections set the benchmark for decades. Yet he was never a public figure, never remotely famous, which was exactly what he would have wanted.

## HOW MANY ANTARCTICAS?

If you ask scientists what defines a continent, the answers will reflect their discipline. Some geographers define a continent strictly, as the main landmass but not the islands or seas around. Geologists may see them as part of the same thing, just separated by a little local flooding. Antarctica is the most awkward of the seven.

It is the only polar continent: the Arctic is sea surrounded by land. Antarctica is also covered by up to two miles of ice. Remote sensing has revealed the details of the continent's two surfaces: the ice which forms 98% of the visible surface, and the rocks lying beneath. The familiar shape in an atlas, a disc with a tail coiled up towards South America, is the ice Antarctica. If you could lift off this icy lid to reveal the rocky landscape beneath, it would look very different. West Antarctica, that is the Antarctic Peninsula side, would dissolve before your eyes. The Peninsula might be attached by a slender strip of land to the main disc, but the coast between around 80° and 180° west would retreat so far towards the pole that Byrd Land would be left as a large oceanic island.

If we carefully replace the lid, the familiar shape still does not include the sea ice which rings the coast all winter, doubling its size in a cold year. In the twentieth century the pack ice twice reached as far north as South Georgia, equivalent to polar ice appearing off the English Lake District.

In ecological terms, the most important boundary is not on the land but in the sea, which is the home of nearly all Antarctic life. The Polar Front, previously known as the Antarctic Convergence, is a well-marked change from cool waters of the main oceans to the icy. Its line and location vary with the seasons and currents, but it lies mainly between 50°S and 60°S. Each side of this temperature boundary has distinct sea-life which can seldom survive on the other side. The Polar Front therefore defines Antarctica physically and ecologically.

These moving boundaries cannot be used to define the legal limits of Antarctica for the purposes of international treaties. It has been agreed that for such purposes only, Antarctica is everything below 60°S.

# 9

# The Great Escape

## 1901– 03: Otto Nordenskjöld

*Can the Antarctic night wear you down so much that when
you encounter men on the ice by chance, you do not recognise
them as members of your own expedition?*

Otto Nordenskjöld (the *skjöld* approximates to *shelt* as in
shelter) was born on 6 December 1869 in Småland, in the
centre of southern Sweden. His uncle, Baron Adolf
Nordenskiöld (that side of the family spelled the name
differently) had completed a voyage which had defeated the
most determined navigators for over three hundred years,
completing the North East Passage over the north of Russia.
In the steam whaler the *Vega*, he nearly made it in one
season, but was forced to overwinter from 1878 –79,
before completing the first circumnavigation of the
Eurasian-African landmass. Young Otto gained a doctorate
on the geology of Småland and became a lecturer at the
University of Uppsala, but he had inherited his uncle's
hunger for adventure, and led a Swedish expedition to the
Magellan Straits in 1895–97, studying Ice Age deposits in
Tierra del Fuego and estimating how much larger the ice

caps had once been. In 1898 he took part in an expedition to Alaska, and in 1900 was geologist under Admiral Amdrup on the Danish East Greenland Expedition.

Aged thirty-two he was ready to conduct a polar expedition of his own. In contrast to other jingoistic expeditions, his was to be science-led, privately funded, and low-budget. No one had penetrated the ice to the south shore of the Weddell Sea so it wasn't known if the Antarctic Peninsula and Wilkes-Victoria lands further east were connected, though he candidly admitted it was probable that the problem of how much land was connected might never be solved. Nordenskjöld's ambitious plan was to explore new land east and west of the Antarctic Peninsula: to go as far south as possible in the Weddell Sea, stay with five other staff to overwinter, continue work the next summer, and be picked up before the second winter. In the meantime, the ship would ferry various staff to Tierra del Fuego, Staten Island and South Georgia to pursue other projects.

Their ship, *Antarctic*, was formerly the sealer of Henrik Bull (see *The Cheek of Mr Borchgrevink*). It left Gothenburg on 16 October 1901, and paused at Falmouth, in the south west of England, while Otto dashed to London. He met Scotsman William Speirs Bruce who was preparing his own compact, low-budget Scottish National Antarctic Expedition in the *Scotia*. They agreed to offer mutual support if either got into trouble. Crossing the tropics, some of Nordenskjöld's sled dogs died of heat. He had an offer of support from the Argentine Government, which was beginning a major political and diplomatic drive, that still continues, to establish claims on sub-Antarctic and Antarctic territories. In return for donating supplies of food and expensive coal, Argentina wanted one of their own nationals to be a full member of the expedition. Nordenskjöld was sympathetic to their ambitions, but he was wrong-footed on his departure to Buenos Aires when he received messages making it clear that Argentina expected their man to be one of the small overwintering party, jeopardising Nordenskjöld's careful plans to take only those few judged to have the temperament, as well as the need in scientific terms, to endure two months of continuous night. Tactfully, he delayed responding until he met the man: Lt. José Maria Sobral. Nordenskjöld was relieved to find him 'so unaffected and affable, so interested in the [project] and so intrepid [that] the matter was definitely decided the very same day.' Sobral was qualified to assist with meteorology, magnetism, astronomy and hydrography. Nordenskjöld's five other selections for overwintering anxiously wondered who would be ordered to give up their priceless bunk in the tiny wooden hut to make way for this late interloper. It was a diplomatic time bomb ticking in the young leader's hands. In all, crew and staff, twenty-nine men began the voyage out of Buenos Aires in 1901.

Nordenskjöld secured as captain the remarkable Norwegian, Carl Anton Larsen. The son of a sea captain, Larsen had gone to sea as soon as he could walk. Enterprising, brave, and a good skier, he was as passionate and informed about science as he was about business. In 1901 he was manager of the great Finnmarken whaling station in Norway, but Nordenskjöld tempted him to return to the seas he had explored in 1892 – 93 on the sealer *Jason*, when he discovered Oscar II Land on the west shore of the Weddell Sea and got as far as 64°40´S, picking up the first Antarctic fossils from Seymour Island. The staff

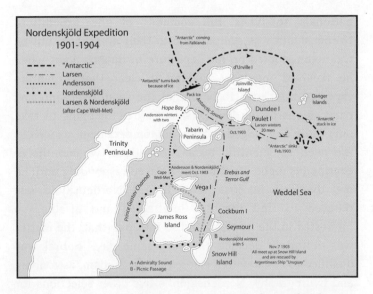

also included the American artist F. W. Stokes, a landscape painter welcomed for his past experience with Robert Peary in Greenland 1893–94. His goal was to record the *aurora australis*, the southern lights, and compare them with the northern lights. They proceeded to Staten Island then east to the Falklands, where they replaced the dogs which had perished in the tropics. These poor beasts are easy to recognise in the photographs; the substitutes are much slighter than the others, and must have suffered dreadfully from the cold. The *Antarctic* arrived in the South Shetlands on 11 January 1902. They began the first part of the mission: exploring islands west of the Peninsula, probing the Bransfield Strait, and going ashore at Nelson Island to sample plants and rocks. They attempted to explore the Orleans Channel trying to determine whether it connected to the Gerlache Strait further south, but they were defeated by dense ice.

They worked their way back north through the pack to the entrance of the sound between the Antarctic Peninsula and Joinville Island. It had been seen when ice-filled by Dumont d'Urville in 1833, but not sailed. The *Antarctic* made the first passage of the sound, naming it after their ship. On the way they observed Hope Bay, an inviting snow-free valley on the mainland shore. They continued and landed on Paulet Island before crossing the Erebus and Terror Gulf to leave a depot of fuel and food on Seymour Island. They continued south down the east coast of the Peninsula, following the Oscar II Coast a decade after Larsen had named it, exploring and mapping until they met sea ice at 66°15′S. They had hoped to push much farther south, but this season conditions would not allow exploration of the south shore of the Weddell Sea. Nordenskjöld's assessment that it would be difficult to link up previously explored sections of coast proved correct: most of the easy discoveries had been made. In February, with the brief southern summer ending, and thin ice coating the surface of the sea each morning like a film of grease, Nordenskjöld was set down on Snow Hill Island, with five companions, sledges and supplies. Nordenskjöld's problem of whose bunk Sobral would take had been solved by Antarctica. Since they arrived they had not seen the *aurora australis* once. The artist Stokes decided an Antarctic winter with nothing to paint was a trial he didn't need. He would return north with the ship. We now know that the Southern Magnetic Pole, which draws in the solar particles that create the aurorae, is on the opposite side of the continent, and the Peninsula seldom enjoys displays.

# PEMMICAN

Pemmican sounds like, and is, a North American Native word. Made by the Cree nation, it was a paste of meat and fat which they took on hunting trips as high-energy rations. Men like John Rae from the Hudson Bay Company found it convenient and sustaining as field food. It was adapted for explorers and frontiersmen and manufactured commercially; both Bovril and Batchelors made varieties. It is not a source of carbohydrates and it was often mixed with broken hard biscuits like those served on ships; the British called this mix hoosh. Some later mixes included carbohydrates. Getting this balance right was important to keep healthy and feel satisfied and full. The science of nutrition was poorly understood; even the word *vitamines* was not coined until 1912. Looking back we can see that men endured extreme hardships on an inadequate diet. When Nansen crossed Greenland he did not check the recipe for the pemmican; the variety he bought had little fat, but Nansen had assumed it comprised 50% fat. Although he had other sources of fats, this unbalanced his diet.

| Ideal formula | | Nansen's rations |
|---|---|---|
| 10% | protein | 40% |
| 30% | fat | 10% |
| 60% | carbohydrates | 50% |

A similar food was devised for dog rations though they did not prosper unless it was mixed with fresh meat, usually penguins and seal. The dog food had low carbohydrates and when men were forced to eat it, they suffered diarrhoea if this could not be made good. Shackleton's men, on top of all their other woes, had to switch to dog pemmican before beginning their boat journey from the peninsula to Elephant Island making use of the 'head' or toilet – meaning over the side of the boat – even more miserable.

The Snow Hill hut

From the ship's hold flowed boxes of supplies which took three days to land, using planks placed across two ship's boats to ferry them ashore. Among them was a partially pre-fabricated hut measuring 13´ 6" x 21´ 0" (4.1 metres by 6.4 metres). It had two wooden skins with insulation between. Short journeys were made to set up supply dumps, in readiness for journeys in the spring, and they prepared to overwinter. Nordenskjöld wrote: 'I stood there amid the grandeur of the scenery, while the sun sank slowly behind the haughty, ice-covered crown of Mount Haddington [on James Ross Island] and gilded the ice-field far away on the eastern horizon. Shall we succeed? At the moment I felt a strong faith in the future, everything lay bright and promising before me.'

Nordenskjöld's party comprised Ole Jonassen, the sledder; Erik Ekelöf, a bacteriologist doubling as doctor; a sailor to handle their boats, Gustaf Åkerlundh; Gösta Bodman (hydrology, meteorology and magnetism), and José Sobral. Heating huts in Antarctica is a problem. They had an iron stove but the temperature was 20°C colder on the linoleum floor which was lethally slippery whether wet or iced. They could live without suffering and they planned to be there only for a year, and while a tent is shelter, a hut is home. In March 1902 they went south with winter on their heels, to lay a last depot, and in late April they returned north to Seymour Island to check their depot and cairn, and collect fossils. Science seemed to have been on their minds more than logistics. On many journeys small oversights eroded their safety margins, and Antarctica doesn't tolerate mistakes. On this trip they forgot their lamp and then let the dogs ransack all the butter from their sledging supplies. Fats are very important both in using the other food groups efficiently and making the stomach feel full.

Back at their Snow Hill some dogs died of exposure, and base storms broke their magnetic observations hut to pieces. The wreckage was salvaged to build kennels. One perk of not having penetrated as far south as they had hoped was that it is never wholly dark at 64°30´S, even in midwinter. However it is savagely cold for its latitude, with strong raw winds. The coldest open boat work I have ever done in Antarctica was at Snow Hill in March. A rattling noise on my survival suit told

me the spray from the bow was freezing in flight before falling . ~
on me as hail. That was late summer, not winter.

In midwinter, June winds wrenched one boat free from its
lashings and threw it seventy metres. Come October 1902,
and early spring, Nordenskjöld, Sobral and Jonassen, went
back to explore the Oscar II Coast. Their preparation had not
been encouraging; on a trial run in July to test the gear, the
tent poles collapsed. Impatience gnawed at them and they set
out again on 30 August to lay depots: too early for serious
sledging. Two of the three dogs broke loose and ran home,
and the journey was rescheduled for late September. Few dogs
were now in good condition, and they could only muster five
working animals for two sleds. Men made up the shortfall.

Modern travellers to Antarctica, having bought the latest
clothing and read up about layering and wicking, assume
the earlier explorers had vastly inferior clothing. In fact,
once the Orkneyman John Rae, in the 1830s, and other
workers of the Hudson's Bay Company had learned how to
dress and travel like the Inuit, there was no need for
anyone to be cold. Nansen reinforced the message after
overwintering among the West Greenland Inuit in 1886–
87. Nordenskjöld had an outer wind-breaking layer made
from canvas, and thermal layers of guanaco and reindeer.
They also had a reasonably varied diet. As well as the polar
staple of pemmican, they had meat biscuits, bacon, lentils
and peas, bread, butter, sugar and coffee.

By 8 October they had covered eighty-four miles. They
scaled Robertson Island, a lone vantage point off the east
coast, and found it was volcanic. The visibility was good and
they could clearly see that the Trinity Coast, a relatively well-
surveyed coast facing the South Shetlands, and Larsen's
Oscar II coast were two sides of the same peninsula. They

had accomplished one of their prime objectives and joined up two previous discoveries on the map. They made the first ever landing on the east side of what we now call the Peninsula at 65°57´S next to a towering nunatak which they named Borchgrevink after the first man to overwinter on the continent. It was during this journey that Nordenskjöld's sled dogs disappeared down a crevasse. He was dragged in after them. The other men ran to the lips and saw him tangled up below; his skis had stopped him plunging out of reach. He was badly hurt, and their most expert sledder, Ole Jonassen, had injured his arm. In the confusion, the dogs got at their own rations and gorged all the pemmican that was supposed to sustain them for the rest of the journey.

The party rested up in a tent while a storm raged for two days. They spent their unwelcome leisure considering their chances of getting back to base. 'One feels like a fever patient lying there without occupation staring at the roof and making spots assume different patterns.' It was no fun 'to listen to the howl of the storm and to know nothing but that our provisions are coming to an end and that our poor dogs are becoming weaker.'

It was now that their previous preparations paid off. They made their way to the depot near Robertson Island and, warmed by food and more fuel, they made it back to the Snow Hill base hut five days after leaving their storm refuge. Despite the fall, they reviewed the trip with some satisfaction: they had travelled 380 miles in thirty-three days and pieced together two pieces of Antarctic geography. However, the rations they had carried were not sufficient to support a much longer journey; on average, each man lost fifteen pounds. In December, they sledged to Seymour Island, and collected important fossils, including plants, ammonites, ferns and firs. Many plainly demonstrated that Antarctica's rocks had once enjoyed a much warmer climate. They also discovered that the emperor penguin, weighing up to forty-five kilos in prime condition, was not the largest that had ever lived. They found the fifty million-year-old bones of a giant penguin: *megadyptes*, as tall as a man. I had a nightmare about these birds; they had ganged up with blue tits to steal milk. The penguins kicked my door down, then they stood in the kitchen helping themselves from the fridge.

But when Nordenskjöld's men returned to base only two things were on their minds; why wasn't the ice melting, and where was the *Antarctic*? On 9 January Jonassen climbed a hill and looked around. It was a melancholy panorama of densely packed ice with little water. On 18 February 1903, the sea froze, and they knew they were trapped for another year. Reluctantly they looked at the penguins that had been their companions and started to kill them. They took four hundred. They even killed skuas. If you are what you eat, skuas are foul. Nordenskjöld glumly recorded: 'It was only bitter need which could compel us to this horrible slaughter. It is especially repulsive here, where the creatures have not yet learned to fear man.' Someone thought it would be a good idea to skin them and wash the meat in seawater so the salt could help preserve them.

Their mood would have deepened farther if they had known why the *Antarctic* had not appeared. She had sunk in Antarctica, on her way to them, six days before. No one in the world knew.

The six at Snow Hill settled down for a second winter. Science kept them busy but the isolation of their position began to settle on their souls. Nordenskjöld wrote: 'With what delight should we not have greeted one blade of grass:

red, green and yellow, the colours which have a stimulating influence on the senses. We saw only pale tints. They attract the beholder with wondrous power, although they seem to radiate a something which resembles the chill of death.'

The greatest part of Nordenskjöld's party was on the ship. Sub-groups had variously overwintered in Tierra del Fuego, South Georgia and the Falklands, while Larsen carried out hydrographic work round South Georgia and a shore party of three men studied its biology and geology. They found one of the few fossils ever discovered there: a mollusc. On 1 May, Andersson walked over the top of the mountains enclosing Cumberland Bay and found himself overlooking a bay within a bay. It was a perfect anchorage framed by high peaks, austerely beautiful. When he clambered down to the shore he found he was not the first person to have visited: on the beach was an abandoned ten-metre sealer's boat, and seven try-pots. He named it Pot Cove which in Norwegian is Grytviken. Two of those pots stand in front of the museum today.

On 5 November 1902, the *Antarctic* had left the Falklands, but she met ice four days later at just 59°30′S. After a spell trapped by sea-ice beneath a huge iceberg in a snow-storm, they freed themselves and made Deception Island in the South Shetlands. They continued south and surveyed the west coast of the Peninsula as far as Brabant Island. In doing so they achieved what they had failed to do the previous season, and sailed from the Orleans Channel into the Gerlache Strait. This linked two important navigable channels for the first time. They began to make their way north, intending to pass through the Antarctic Sound once again. Ice conditions were difficult and the weather poor. They forced their way through sea ice dodging the huge icebergs that drift in here from the ice-shelf on the east side of the Peninsula which is still named Larsen after their captain. On 5 December they began to make their way to the entrance of the sound. In dense ice, with little room for manoeuvre, they were struck by a savage storm.

When it eased they anxiously reviewed their position. The ice might not allow the ship to repeat the passage of the sound, and even if it did, there was no guarantee that conditions on the other side, in the Erebus and Terror Gulf, would be good enough to drive on south to Snow Hill. However if the area were unseasonably iced up, an overland party might get there by skiing over the land and the frozen sea. They remembered the beautiful snow-free bay on the tip of the Peninsula. It might make a suitable base. On 29 December, deputy expedition leader Gunnar Andersson, Samuel Duse, and Toralf Grunden were put ashore at Hope Bay (now Base Esperanza). First, Andersson supervised the laying of a big depot in case the *Antarctic* could not reach Snow Hill Camp, and everyone had to overwinter in Hope Bay waiting to try next again spring.

More immediately, Captain Larsen and Andersson determined that each would head independently for Snow Hill. In the days before radio, you had to think through, and plan for, all the likely outcomes. Once they separated, each party would be ignorant of the other's circumstances. If the ship successfully rounded Joinville and Dundee Islands to the north and arrived first at Nordenskjöld's base, they would wait there for the Hope Bay three until 25 January. If they did not arrive, the ship would sail to Hope Bay and seek them there. If the Hope Bay party got to Nordenskjöld but found no ship they would wait at Snow Hill until 10 March. Then both Nordenskjöld's and Andersson's parties would return to Hope Bay to rendezvous with the ship.

The ship sailed out of Hope Bay. As soon as their tents were pitched and stores organised, Andersson realised that in the haste of unloading, he had landed only half of their bread rations. Duse and Grunden did not blame him; such generosity of spirit would soon be tested to the full. The three began to ski the two hundred miles to Snow Hill.

The *Antarctic* retreated from the sound and began to sail round to the north towards Snow Hill. It rounded the tip of the islands lying off the peninsula but when they turned south they met dense ice and were soon trapped. She was a strong ship designed for polar work so they did not worry, but a storm blew up and pressed the pack ice tight against her hill. Carl Skottsberg, writing on 10 January 1903, said, 'the ship began to tremble like an aspen leaf, and a violent crash sent us all up on deck to see what the matter was. The pressure was tremendous; the vessel rose higher and higher, while the ice was crushed to powder along her sides.' Descending to the ice they found the rudder had been damaged. They were held tight for three weeks. When the pressure eased enough to float free into a narrow lead, they found that they were leaking badly. The nearest land was a small island they had visited last season: Paulet. They planned to beach the *Antarctic* there but the ship was so grievously damaged that on 12 February all twenty men plus the ship's neurotic cat were forced to camp on the ice, where they built a crude tent from sails. The whaleboat was lowered and a ton of provisions loaded into her. They began an exhausting journey, sailing and rowing, then hauling across the sea ice when there was no open water. It took fourteen days to ice-hop the twenty-five miles to Paulet Island, reaching there on 28 February 1903.

Meanwhile Andersson's group worked their way south using a copy of a chart drawn by James Clark Ross. Through an error in the surveying or the copying, it was not correctly orientated, and they were led south-west instead of south, taking them into the fractured ice of Crown Prince Gustav Channel. Instead of land they found a frozen strait full of bergs. Their confusion did not overshadow their sense of the marvellous: 'One can actually imagine that a gigantic snow-clad city lies before us, with houses, palaces, and all the wonders of the world.' They headed for an island they could see to the south-east, thinking it was James Clark Ross Island, but it was Vega Island, named after the ship Adolf Nordenskjöld had navigated through the North East Passage, and close to the north shore of James Ross Island. They toiled up the heights of Vega Island, and saw open sea running away south towards Snow Hill. They could not ski to Snow Hill, and had no boat, but it seemed certain that the *Antarctic* would have found it easy to cross such open water and pick up Nordenskjöld and his companions. They returned north to the agreed rendezvous at Hope Bay, arriving on 13 January, and expecting their comrades to sail into view any day, blissfully unaware that the *Antarctic* was then fighting for her life in the pack. Meanwhile they ascended the hill behind the camp, which is one of the best places in Antarctica to collect fossils, and is now named Mount Flora for the richness of its plant fossils. Clambering around the rocks, they found their boots were not up to the job. The seams opened and holes were worn in their socks. Andersson wouldn't let the prospect of frostbite and lameness get him down, there were compensations: 'we could cut our toenails without taking off our boots.' But when there was no sign of ship or companions by 11

February, they realised something had gone terribly wrong. It seemed likely that the ship had been trapped in ice, perhaps destroyed, and that the crew and returning staff who comprised the majority of their party were dead: drowned or frozen to milken statues. It was certain that no one outside knew anything of their troubles, or could learn of them until the only service that could be conducted for them was a belated funeral.

They began to construct a hut, one man digging up rocks, and the other two carrying the blocks on two poles, like a stretcher. They planned a crude cubic structure within which their larger storm tent could be pitched. On 17 February they laid the foundations, over a yard thick, and began building upwards, filling the voids with fine gravel. They hadn't built the roof when heavy snow fell on 6 March. Desperate to have better shelter before winter closed in hard, they continued working while the snow fell steadily, until on 10 March the weather was too harsh to work and they laid up in the tent for a day. The snow could at least make their walls windproof, and they packed it against the outside. The following day they lifted the sled onto the walls to support their tarpaulin roof. They made a tunnel like an igloo's, with an entrance, between boxes of fossils, just seventy centimetres square. The tunnel also doubled unappetisingly as a food store and foul weather winter toilet area. Duse finished a penguin-skin carpet from the skins of the birds killed for the larder. Finally a house-proud Andersson swept out the interior with the wing of a southern giant petrel. When the three lay down side by side to sleep, they entirely filled it; home was a stone triple coffin. On a cold morning the temperature in their inner tent was −14°C near the roof, and −20°C near the floor. They hated thaws which produced

Hope Bay

mud and cold showers of melting rime. In early March they reviewed their stores and switched sharply from eating depot stores to living off the land. They were fortunate that in this area some penguins linger late after their end of season moulting. Their frying pan was a flat tin with a wooden handle nailed on to it. At first they struggled to raise enough heat to cook; it took them six hours to make penguin stew. But with practice they could get a fire roused in two to three minutes. Grunden sang when he cooked, liking folk songs, shanties, and American Negro songs learned on the Florida coast. One began: 'And a seaman's life it took my fancy most, since I turned o' fifteen year.' It sounded more and more plaintive as the long winter wore them down. As mid-winter approached, they calculated their fuel would not last until spring, and after 1 June, they cut their meals from three a day to two. Canned herrings, tinned meats and dried vegetables provided a welcome break from seal and penguin.

There were a few bottles of spirits to enable them to take a dram of Dutch gin once a month, and each had a birthday during the winter. At Christmas they went on a spree, lighting three candles at the same time.

In the evenings they took turns giving mini-lectures. Duse and Andersson tried to remember the plot of The *Three Musketeers* and *The Count of Monte Cristo* to tell to Grunden, who didn't know them. They made sealskin overshoes to protect their boots; it was immensely time-consuming, which was a blessing. The official account says that time slipped by quickly, with no sense of the oppressive slowness of time, before admitting that they suffered from awful 'intellectual nothingness.' Later they were reduced to passing round food tins to read the labels.

Meanwhile Larsen's party found Paulet: a small, volcanic island with a long, steep storm beach on one shore, behind it a stone ridge rising to a lake whose waters are a strong green colour, enriched by the guano washed down from thousands of Adélie penguins nesting on the slope above. They collapsed ashore, acutely conscious that no one in the world knew of their fate, and that the two other groups whose lives depended on Larsen were beginning a makeshift overwintering, with nothing but fear for their companions' fate to feed their thoughts.

Paulet's rocks are basalt, and naturally fracture into blocks a convenient size for building, if not always a handy shape. For their new accommodation Larsen's men chose a site on the ridge behind the beach, commanding a view of the sea, and built a two-room hut, roofed with sails lashed over oars and salvaged wood. One room was a kitchen; they sensibly isolated the cooking area, because Antarctica is dry and windy, and fires easily flare out of control. The other room had two broad, low stone benches running the interior length of the two longer walls. This was to drain the cold dense air into the trench between. They sat and slept on the benches, a few precious degrees warmer than the floor. The floor was lined with penguin skins; they killed 1100 to see them through the winter. They wanted more, but the Adélies moulted and left before they were finished. The biologist Carl Skottsberg described how any disturbance to the rotting penguin skins sent up a sickening odour: 'When one came out of the fresh air into the hut it was at first almost impossible to breathe, so bad was the atmosphere.'

One of the seamen was already ill when they arrived. Ole Wennersgaard 'had been a long time poorly, had violent attacks of coughing as soon as he went into the open air, and, as we thought at the time, showed other signs of consumption. [It was later diagnosed as heart disease]. He would sit night after night, moaning softly and slowly, for he seldom had any rest, and if one happened to look up during the course of the night, one met the terrified gaze of his large sorrowful eyes. We seldom heard him complain; he only moaned softly.

'On the morning of the 7th of June he had said goodnight with a "Now I shall sleep well." And he fell asleep in a sitting posture, the only one possible for him. Then his neighbour suddenly felt how Wennersgaard sank softly down upon his shoulder – a few rattling breaths, and life had fled.' He was nineteen years old. 'It was dim and silent in the hut; cold, clear and silent in the open air. Death, the one guest who could reach us, had laid his hand heavily upon the circle of comrades who had so long striven together for life. Sewn up in his sleeping bag, the only coffin we could give him, he was carried out to one of the boats. A couple of days later we buried his body in an immense snow-drift. Not until the spring came could we build him a lasting resting place. Slowly we wander home and assemble in the hut, where everything speaks of death and corruption; we assemble there – *nineteen* of us.'

His grave is still there, a simple wooden cross on a stone cairn. Adélie penguins nest all around and on top of it. It is some distance from their camp, around the steep flank of a hill that comes nearly to the water. They did not want a daily reminder of their fragile mortality. The days shortened, the last of the wildlife left.

For the three men at Hope Bay, wrote Andersson, 'The winter passed very quickly.' It makes you wonder what he normally did for entertainment in the long nights. He cherished 'the strong power that warmth and honest friendship has to proudly subdue the dark night of isolation and extreme distress.'

On 29 September 1903 they set off sledging towards Vega Island to reconnoitre ice conditions. It was early in the season for a long journey, and cold; Duse and Grunden got frostbite. Grunden's left foot froze until he could not feel pin pricks, and ugly black blisters covered the toes of his left foot. Duse presented some signs on one little toe. The blisters were lanced with a sail needle, before applying disinfectant and wrapping them in dirty bandages, the only ones they had.

At Snow Hill, Nordenskjöld's group had no reason to doubt that all their friends were in a single group returning to pick them up. They maintained meteorological observations all winter and were surprised to find that they differed from the first year's. Until then, it had been assumed that Antarctica's climate was simple: it was cold in summer and colder in winter, unchanging from year to year.

They found the weather was much more complex. It would prompt men like Hubert Wilkins (see chapter six on Deception Island) to lobby for a network of Antarctic meteorological stations to better understand how polar weather systems affect the inhabited continents.

Their dogs were further reduced when the sled expert Jonassen left the two Falkland Islands sheepdogs untethered. They got into one-sided fights with the big Greenlandic dogs and were killed. On the same day that the Hope Bay party set out, Nordenskjöld and Ole Jonassen began a surveying trip towards the Peninsula. They set out in poor weather and forgot half their bread. Their tent was blown down and torn, forcing them to return to the hut. They tried again on 4 October, leaving messages at key locations, including last year's cairn on Seymour Island. By 12 October they had explored the whole west coast of James Ross Island thereby discovering Prince Gustav Channel, which separates it from the continental land. On 12 October at 13:00 they halted beneath a high square cliff called Cape Dreyfus. It appeared there were seals scattered on ice. But two seemed to rear up to an impossibly high posture. Nordenskjöld's tepid writing doesn't capture the drama of the moment but it does bring out the absurd humour.

'What the deuce can those seals be, standing up there bolt upright?' says one of us, pointing to some small, dark objects far away on the ice, in towards the channel. 'They are moving,' cries another.
A delirious eagerness seizes us. A field glass is pulled out. 'It's men! It's men!' we shout.

There was a moment when they wondered whether they had met the first natives, coming out of primeval isolation to meet them. Perhaps, at last, the ancient protocols on meeting Native Antarctic people would be used.

'Who are they? Is it a sledge-party from the wintering station or can it be people from the *Antarctic*?'

Then there was a pistol shot, the other party had seen them.

Two men, [Grunden was sitting down cooking] black as soot from top to toe; men with black clothes, black faces and high black caps, and with their eyes hidden by peculiar wooden frames, which are so attached to the face that they remind one of black silk masks with pierced pieces of wood for the eyes. Never before have I seen such a mixture of civilisation and the extremest degree of barbarousness; my powers of guessing fail me when I endeavour to imagine to what race of men these creatures belong. They hold out their hands with a hearty 'How do you do?' in the purest English.

Their manners become more English than a Duke's.

'Thanks, how are you?' was my answer.
'Have you heard anything of the boat?' they continue.
'No!'
'Neither have we! How do you like the station?'
'Oh, very well in every respect.'
There comes a moment's pause, and I puzzle my brains without result.

Duse worked out the puzzle quicker than Nordenskjöld:

'Don't you know who I am?'
'No, it's not very easy to recognise you!'
'Oh, I am Duse and this is Gunnar Andersson.'

Joyfully they set off for the Snow Hill base hut. They sighted it two years, to the day and the hour, after they had left Sweden. A celebration dinner featured roast emperor penguin. The name of the meeting place was changed from Cape Dreyfus to Cape Well-met, one of the few name changes you cannot argue with.

Back in Larsen's group at Paulet they were eating well; some of the Norwegians and Swedes were experienced hunters who regularly shot seals on the ice. They were also skilled at ice-fishing, providing some welcome variation in their diet. On 31 October 1903, nineteen days after the sled parties met on the ice, Larsen re-launched the whaleboat with five companions and left Paulet for Hope Bay. At Hope Bay he found an empty hut and a note saying the three had left for Snow Hill to see what had gone wrong. The ice had broken up enough for Larsen to try to sail after them, using one of the tent poles for a mast and the canvas roof from the hut for a sail. Despite their isolation and danger, Larsen paused on his journey to collect fossils. William Speirs Bruce said that Larsen, even when sailing on a sealing voyage, 'showed a zeal for extending our knowledge of these regions would that not have been unworthy of the leader of a purely scientific expedition.'

During this time, Nordenskjöld led his reunited group to Hope Bay, hoping against hope to see the ship. Finding nothing, they left a message and returned to Snow Hill.

Perhaps William Speirs Bruce would learn of their troubles and search for them. Perhaps. On 8 November, around the first date it was possible the ship might come, Bodman and Akerlündh were collecting penguin eggs. They stopped when they saw four men coming from the north, and a ship. They thought it was the *Antarctic* but as they hurried close they saw an unfamiliar vessel. It was an Argentine naval sloop, the *Uruguay*, under Lt. Julián Irízar, Argentina's Naval Attaché to Britain. When the expedition had not returned at the end of the summer, those who had promoted Sobral's attachment to the expedition had organised a search expedition, relieving Bruce of his promise to come to aid. The *Uruguay* had reached Seymour Island on 7 November 1903, and seen a boathook Nordenskjöld had set in a cairn to attract attention to his message left two weeks earlier. The shore party were greeted by two figures on the ice; one was Irízar. They led the visitors off to Snow Hill for another reunion celebration. Irízar told them that Sweden had launched a rescue mission using the *Fridtjof*. During the evening, choices began to weigh on Nordenskjöld's mind and his party mood chilled. He was a thoroughly decent man who had to decide quickly whether to look for Larsen now, or wait for the *Fridtjof*, so as not to snub his country's efforts to rescue him. He reflected, 'the thought of the enormous responsibility resting in the decision that would have to be made within the next few hours, seemed, for the moment, to deprive me of all power of motion. Sorrow was depicted on every countenance for everyone saw how small was the hope of ever again seeing the comrades we had left on board the *Antarctic*.' At 22:30 the whole party atmosphere had dampened, with everyone thinking of Larsen and their other comrades. Annoyingly the dogs disturbed their sober reflections with barking and howling. Bodman went outside and was stunned to see six bedraggled men on the ice, he yelled: 'Larsen! Larsen is here!' Nordenskjöld wrote: 'No pen can describe the joy of this first moment, when I saw among us these men, on whom I had been thinking a few minutes before, with feelings of the greatest despondency. We conducted the newcomers in triumph to the building.' Larsen had sailed to within sixteen miles of the base before dense ice blocked him. They had walked the rest of the way.

Nordenskjöld is able to indulge in wistful nostalgia as he takes leave of their little hut. 'I go for a last turn through the rooms where we have experienced so much during the past years, and which now look so lonely and disordered. The door is barred as carefully as possible ... We cast one look back at the house to which so many memories are attached, and then start off along the ice.' They made their way to the shore but the wind had blown up. It wasn't safe to take the boat out to the ship one final time. They sat until on the shore until dusk, watching the surf, looking at the warm lights on the ship. Then they returned to sleep one final night in the hut.

I visited the hut in February 2008 when the Argentine conservation team who had been renovating it over several seasons were preparing to leave. It is a snug, homely place. The technician had just finished restoring the hurricane lamp and fired it up. We sat hundreds of miles from any other human beings. I thought of how it might have looked to someone able, over a century before, to look down on the Weddell Sea and in the warm slate of winter dusks see this yellow light spring up in the darkness, fierce and bright. Moving round it, six wraiths, parcels of human warmth in the ocean of blue cold all around them.

Nordenskjöld sailed the next day and reached Paulet the following morning at 04:00, just as the sun was rising, sparkling each snow crystal, glittering the scene. No one ashore had stirred. Anticipating another winter vigil, botanist Carl Skottsberg was supervising the collection of six thousand Adélie eggs. Nordenskjöld reflected: 'Everything is so different from those remarkable moments when I myself have been the one affected by the event. Here I am nothing but a spectator, but my feelings are perhaps the deeper, that we come as the unexpected rescuers to men, in a position the gloom of which could hardly be surpassed.'

He ordered the ship's whistle to be sounded and went ashore. The whistle scared the cat witless. It tore round the hut then out among the penguins creating pandemonium. Men followed, staggering, gesticulating: 'sooty, dirty, emaciated, in tattered clothes, but with their countenances, on which suffering has impressed its melancholy seal, beaming with joy.'

Anticipating future expeditions might suffer difficulties in this area, the rescuers now cached a large depot. The Paulet men gazed enviously at the boxes of jams, sugar and bread being deposited only when they were leaving. The new arrivals paid their respects to the teenager's grave. 'We stood in silence around the stone heap ... far from our native land and all those dear to us, here upon this desolate shore, where the crowd of penguins would soon be the only watchers around our comrade's grave.' The final task was to sail to Hope Bay and pick up the botanical fossils Andersson had collected from Mount Flora. They included *Glossopteris*, a plant which enjoys temperate climates and beech species, which indicated mild weather in Antarctica as recently as fifteen million years ago. *Glossopteris* is also found in rocks of the same geological period in Australia and South Africa.

It would later be used as evidence in favour of the theory we now call plate tectonics, to help break up the continents and piece them back together as they were hundreds of millions of years ago when they formed part of the ancient continent of Gondwanaland. In the hold, he also had fossils of *Zeuglodon*, an extinct early whale. On Cockburn Island they discovered huge numbers of scallops on a wave-cut platform at 750´(228m) asl, giving the first indication in Antarctica that there had been isostasy following shrinkage of a previously much thicker ice-cap. At that time it was the greatest single contribution to science in Antarctica.

Nordenskjöld never paid off the debts he incurred. The government refused to bail him out because they had already spent money sending the *Fridtjof* south. In 1905 he was promoted to chair of geography at University of Gothenburg, and carried out expeditions to Greenland in 1909 to study geology and glaciology, and to Chile in 1920–21. His only attempt to return to Antarctica was cancelled as war loomed in Europe. He was one of the rounded Antarctic explorers. Travel was a means to an end, not an end in itself. They tended to have longer and happier careers than those for whom a geographical trophy was all, and the science merely a necessary part of the funding package. He also worked on peace between nations, the colonisation of America to relieve unemployment in Sweden, and he founded and became director of the Gothenburg School of Economics. Having survived everything remote regions could throw at him he died in a traffic accident, aged fifty-nine. Friends and family bailed out his estate's debts.

Nordenskjöld deserves better remembrance. There are several reasons for the amnesia. He did not want fame, nor did his funders. There was no professional photographer: no Frank

Hurley or Herbert Ponting to build a myth. The pictures are often of poor quality, and record everyday events without dramatising them. The account of the expedition, published in Swedish, and not translated into more widely spoken languages for some time, was a compilation of the several authors. Carl Skottsberg's writing sometimes goes to the heart of events and makes it come alive, but much of the others' prose, including Nordenskjöld's, is bland. He generalises his feelings so much they feel second-hand. He seldom puts his finger on the telling detail that fixes an event in the mind or makes the people breathe and live. He was the kind of man who could organise

Otto Nordenskjöld

a fine polar conference, but if he were the after-dinner speaker, you'd sneak out to the pub with Shackleton.

The reconnaissance Larsen made in his winter cruising round South Georgia in 1901 – 1902 was the foundation of his fortune as a whaler, despite it being received wisdom that the Southern Ocean was too remote from world markets to make a profitable industry. Grytviken began life as a whaling station on 16 November 1904 with two sailing ships, the *Louise* and *Rolf*, and a steam catcher, the *Fortuna*. The first whale they took was a humpback. On shore were three prefabricated houses for sixty Norwegians. They built the essentials in a month, including the shallow slip, known as a plan, onto which the whales were hauled for processing, and twelve cookers to extract oil from blubber. Larsen became a rich man through whaling, but no mansion would mean more to him than the hut he shared with nineteen others on the lonely shore at Paulet Island. Storms have reduced it; a few walls still reach shoulder height. Penguins have colonised it; the dividing wall between kitchen and dormitory is a favourite nesting spot for Adélies. Some door and window frames survive; you can touch the few timbers of the *Antarctic* which are not now resting on the sea floor in the jaws of the Weddell Sea. The *Uruguay* still sails from her home port of Buenos Aires, a proud part of national naval history.

# 10

## Antarctica with a Butler:

Jean-Baptiste Charcot's (1867–1936)
Expedition

*You secretly find out that your keel had been badly damaged
by hitting a rock. Do you accept defeat and turn for home, or
do you conceal the truth from friends and colleagues and sail
back into the ice and unchartered waters that holed her?*

### THE FRANÇAIS 1903–05

On 26 June 1905 the President of the Royal Geographical
Society in London welcomed his guest speaker back from
the dead: 'You will remember the reports that were brought
back to South America as to the probable loss of all
concerned.' Jean-Baptiste Charcot had returned just two
weeks before. He began by admitting it was 'not without a
certain trepidation that I venture to address you.' This was
not just formal modesty. Scott's *Discovery* and Bruce's
*Scotia* had also just returned from Antarctica, and the
audience included Captain Robert Falcon Scott. Charcot
said that in France 'polar expeditions had been neglected'
but he hoped France would take its place 'in the peaceful

struggle against the unknown.' Because of limited resources 'it would be better to employ all our resources in thoroughly exploring a narrow corner, and thus securing trustworthy documents with accurate observations, than wandering listlessly up and down the seas' in a way 'more satisfactory to our vanity' but 'far less useful to science.'

Charcot was born on 15 July 1867 at Neuilly-sur-Seine, near Paris. His father Jean-Martin was a successful and wealthy pioneer neuro-psychologist who influenced Freud. The dancer Jane Avril, who featured as the flame-haired can-can artist in Toulouse-Lautrec's most famous poster, was one of his patients. His son also studied medicine, and as is common, found it hard to follow a famous father in the same field. Yet even after Papa died in 1893, leaving him 400,000 gold Francs, he continued to play the dutiful son, marrying a grand-daughter of Victor Hugo, and becoming Head of Clinic at the Faculty of Medicine in 1896. Only in 1902, aged thirty-five, did he throw over his old life and plan an expedition to Greenland. He went in at the deep end, contracting a purpose-built polar vessel from shipwright Père Gautier. Charcot consulted Adrien de Gerlache on the design, who recommended he incorporate the modifications developed by Arctic sealers and whalers, employing a heavier frame and bracing it with additional diagonal beams in the parts that took the direct hits from floating ice: the bow and the waterline. The propeller was to be retractable to avoid damage among dense ice. The forty-six-metre-long three-masted 245-ton schooner *Français* took shape in St Malo shipyard. Singleton designs usually run-up singular bills, and Charcot's ate through his inheritance. To equip the on-board laboratories, he sold a Fragonard painting. Even so, there was too little money for a new engine and the 125HP second-hand one which was eventually secured was known to be short on power and reliability.

Early in 1903, as they were readying to go, concern was mounting over the failure of Captain Larsen to return from the Weddell Sea in the Antarctic. Nothing at all had been heard of Nordenskjöld. One of Charcot's sponsors, who had quickly become a close friend, was the industrial engineer Paul Pléneau, who had signed on as photographer. Charcot needed his agreement for a dramatic change of plan. Abandoning Greenland they would go south to search for Nordenskjöld. Would Pléneau come? He breezily replied, 'Where you like. When you like. For as long as you like.'

Public bodies contributed and the Paris newspaper *Le Matin* launched a public appeal for 150,000 Francs. When donations stalled at F90,000 the editor personally donated F60,000, and the Government conferred F90,000 more plus the status of being the first French National Antarctic expedition. Even so, his budget was still only half Bruce's, itself a thrifty enterprise. Aside from seeking Nordenskjöld, Charcot hastily assembled some aims. He made his core project discovering whether Antarctica was a continent or an archipelago: a secret its ice mantle hid well. Only modern remote sensing would solve it conclusively. In particular he planned to explore the north-west coast of the Palmer Archipelago around Liège, Brabant and Antwerp Islands, to study the south-west entrance to the Gerlache Strait, and to establish a wintering station as far south as the pack allowed. In the following spring and summer he would explore Graham Land especially the Bismarck Strait area, and push as far south as Alexander I Island. 'In a word, we had to continue and complete the labours of the de Gerlache and Nordenskjöld expeditions,' gathering botanical, zoological, hydrographic and meteorological data as they went.

De Gerlache took an advisory role but let himself be drawn into the project, and signed on as an expedition member, despite having recently become engaged to be married. There was a team of scientists and someone Charcot found indispensible: Monsieur Paurnelle, his butler. All were French with the exception of the Italian Alpine guide: Dayné. The first leave-taking of Le Havre on 15 August 1903 ended tragically when a stern cable parted, killing seaman Maignan, his only hand with Antarctic experience.

They re-started, and made Madeira and then Pernambuco in Brazil. Here de Gerlache told Charcot he had changed his mind and he felt honour-bound to return to his fiancée when they reached Buenos Aires. It may have been that de Gerlache had been given time to observe Charcot's leadership and thought he lacked the focus and determination to drive through a project under the stresses Antarctica could impose. Perhaps the aristocrat didn't enjoy being under another's command.

Reaching Buenos Aires on 16 November, Charcot learned that Nordenskjöld and Larsen had been rescued, so he waited there and met the returning men in December. Nordenskjöld studied his plans with approval, according to Charcot, who might have wanted to delicately counter de Gerlache's implied rebuke. He decided to avoid the fate of the *Belgica* at all costs. De Gerlache's own account of the first Antarctic night glossed over its horrors, but it rang false alongside Dr. Cook's sober record of depression and breakdown. The Argentine Republic was cultivating a keen interest in Antarctica and Charcot found 'Nothing could exceed its generous welcome.' Buoyed up by the achievements of the *Uruguay* in rescuing Nordenskjöld, Argentina committed itself to going down to the Peninsula to check for messages Charcot might need to leave. Charcot left on 23 December, bunkered coal in Ushuaia, and began acclimatising to the Southern Ocean with two gales in the Drake Passage.

Despite eighty years of Antarctic experience and over three hundred years of Arctic sailing, explorers were still allowing too little time for preparation, and arriving late in the short Antarctic summer. They did not make landfall until 1 February. For four days they coasted the north-west side of the Palmer Archipelago making a rough hydrographic survey, hampered in turn by snow and fog. The ship's engine, so vital for close manoeuvring in ice, suffered serious failures as one boiler pipe burst and others became blocked. Looking for shelter to make repairs, they were driven from Flandres Bay, and ice and contrary winds blocked their attempted passage through the Lemaire Strait. Returning to Flandres Bay they anchored the ship to the ice, and stayed eleven days, making boat excursions in the area while engineer Goudier and his team laboured. Six years before, de Gerlache had found the area largely ice-free, it was now choked enough to suggest there would be little progress farther south. On 19 February they sailed and erected a cairn on Wiencke Island, in the beautiful Neumayer Channel, to act as a post box in case of emergencies. He had almost completed a circumnavigation of the island when he found a small bay at the south-west end of Wiencke Island which formed one of the best anchorages in the whole Peninsula area, naming it Port Lockroy after the French Minister of Marine. But Charcot wanted to overwinter farther south, and they pressed on, making a successful passage of the Lemaire

Channel where Charcot vividly confessed the tension of navigating unchartered channels choked with ice. As they were forced right under one of the black walls of rock rising nearly vertically and disappearing into the clouds two thousand feet above, there was 'an agonizing moment in which one's whole body contracts, as though trying to make the movement' for the ship. The depth of the channel is highly variable. They were lucky; although close to the shore they were in one of the deep areas. When he emerged into the more open waters of the Penola Strait he compared the surveys of de Gerlache and Dallman a quarter of a century apart, and realised that the Belgian had unwittingly rediscovered and re-named Dallman's Booth and Krogmann Islands. Sometimes good exploration is just ironing out past errors. On the seaward side of Booth Island he found a bay he named Port Charcot: after his father, he was keen to stress, not himself. Within it was a tight cove which he named for the ship. With the hydrographer Matha making soundings from a dinghy ahead of the ship, the *Français* edged in. If the coast farther south offered nothing better, they could retreat here.

They pushed on south hoping to make Cape Tuxen at the mouth of the mythical Bismarck Strait, but were stopped by ice in the Biscoe Islands at 65°59´S 066°22´W. Unwilling to retreat all the way back to Port Lockroy, they picked their way through waters spiked with rocks and reefs, and put in at the cove behind Booth Island, which, in their absence, had filled with wind-blown ice. They pushed their way in on 4 March, the very same day the Bruce was discovering Coats Land in the Weddell Sea. They were now at a similar latitude to Nordenskjöld's Snow Hill Base on the opposite side of the Peninsula, which would add interest to their meteorological and other observations.

The ship was anchored fast to the shore with seven feet of water at the bow and twenty astern. To counter the threat of ice driving in and crushing the ship, anchor chains were strung across the mouth of the bay, and a jam of middling-sized ice soon blocked out the biggest bergs. Huts were constructed ashore, including some fitted with sandstone pillars and marble slabs to provide solid bases for magnetic observations. A large whaleboat covered the petrol store. A selection of supplies were off-loaded as insurance against a ship's fire. They even managed to build igloos for meat including freshly caught seal which they killed in considerable numbers, for both men and dogs. In contrast to de Gerlache's loathing of seal meat, Charcot recorded: 'The meat is excellent' and the fat was used to melt ice for water, saving precious coal. The only two men who couldn't stomach seal enjoyed penguin meat. The signs for a healthy overwintering looked good. He also noted the kindliness of another creature: 'The cormorants, which were equally good eating, never left us.' The men were successful at ice-fishing.

They were well-supplied with food, drink, books and music. On Sundays there were concerts, poetry readings and lectures. Charcot himself gave English lessons. The bunks were designed with sliding doors to create a little private space for the men, but the atmosphere could be claustrophobic. Tensions developed, not concealed by Charcot's insistence that 'perfect harmony prevailed, and the best of spirits and good humour were maintained throughout the expedition.' That's too good to be true.

When choosing the harbour, Charcot had been satisfied that it was protected against winds from any direction except the north-east. The first thing his meteorological observations told him was that the prevailing wind, and the only one that brought gales and foul weather, was from the north-east. Such gales often followed dramatic rises in temperature, from −30°C to −3°C in a few hours. During the winter, the sea away to the west and south-west was always frozen as far as the eye could see, but the area a few miles to the south regularly broke up, though the ice never dispersed enough to use boats. This was unhelpful, as they were denied a solid reliable ice-platform for winter journeys, which would have kept men busy and active. The story of the winter months is of frustration which could only be relieved by the temptation to take risks.

To boost morale, on 30 May Charcot led a picnic excursion to Krogmann Island where they cut up the meat

Champagne and cigars alongside the *Pourquois-Pas?*

and butter with axes and ate while dancing up and down to keep warm. In mid-July, the First Officer and hydrographer Matha presented himself to the expedition leader in Charcot's role as medical officer. His symptoms were swollen limbs, palpitations, and exhaustion. Dr Cook would have known all too well what it was. Hanson on Borchgrevink's expedition had reported the same symptoms on the same day in July and been dead by October. Despite the fresh meat, Matha had scurvy. Charcot repeated Dr Cook's stove treatment, and augmented the diet with more fish and tinned milk. By late September Matha was fit for duty.

They began planning a forty-day trip to begin on 15 August but on 2 August the ice broke. They set out for Krogmann a month later but fog came down and trapped them on an islet only twenty metres across. When it lifted they struggled over to Krogmann, found shelter under rock, and dumped a month's provisions before the pack closed up on them. They barely got back alive.

At long last spring came. On 24 November the whaleboat was loaded with twenty days' rations amounting to nine thousand kilos, scientific instruments and a sledge. The plan was to go to Petermann Island then cross the Penola Channel to the Graham Land coast where they thought they could see a slender open lead. The sea between Petermann Island and the mainland was an interesting mix of bergy bits too dense to sail through, separated by sea-ice too thin to be sure of standing on it. They spent a lot of time knee-deep in melt-water dragging the boat and taking what Charcot called frequent baths. Twelve days working up to eighteen hours a day were made doubly miserable when poor eye-protection caused snow-blindness. When they got close to shore the lead was not there; it had either closed over or been an illusion. They finally got ashore on 29 November in good weather south of Cape Tuxen, and were rewarded by long views into the interior and south down the coast. They surveyed and photographed Graham Land from Booth Island to the Biscoe Islands, from where they could see thirty miles south, proving the strait crossing the Peninsula, supposed by de Gerlache to lie south of Cape Tuxen, did not exist. Had de Gerlache got four miles farther south he would have discovered that himself. But the fictional Bismarck Strait still played tricks. 'I can almost say for certain [it] exists in pretty much the spot where he [Dallman] placed it.'

In December the Alpinist Pierre Dayné was able to make it to the highest peak of Booth Island's southern end and survey the road south, but the ship was still held fast, despite the attentions of spades, saws, crowbars, and even explosives. A lead opened to the south and by 17 December it had reached the ship, and a southerly wind took the ice away. They prepared busily, pausing on Christmas Day to celebrate with a Christmas tree brought from home. They sailed on the high water at 17:30 that evening, heading north first to update the message in the Wiencke Island cairn. Ironically, having decided to commend Port Lockroy to the whalers, Charcot was now iced in there. Dayné and Jabet climbed an adjacent peak and Gourdon ascended to a mountain pass which revealed that the de Gerlache Strait was open. A survey of Anvers Island found a new high point, the beautiful and imposing pyramidal mass which they named Français after their vessel. On 3 January they managed after four days to force clear of the ice and coast down the north side of Antwerp Island. By 7 January a fair wind enabled them to put out the boilers and sail south, heading for the Biscoe Islands at 66° south. On the 8 January, in squalls of snow, the visibility improved enough to reveal the *Français* was about to be squeezed between two large bergs, but they slipped between them before they ground together. Charcot pressed farther south until late on 11 January he made a rash decision. He was in relatively open water with large swells. They were on the edge of close pack ice studded with fortress-like bergs and large plate-like ice-floes. He drove into the pack hoping to get close enough to the shore to land, but it quickly tightened until they could barely move. They forced their way out with great difficulty.

They drove through pack ice and successfully completed the channel between Adelaide Island and the mainland. They crossed the Antarctic Circle and on 11 January 1905 gazed on the dramatic landscape of Alexander Island. The profile was exactly as de Gerlache had described it, but the charted position was wildly inaccurate, putting it forty miles east and seventy-five miles south of its true position. The whole crew came on deck to enjoy the scenery. On 15 January Charcot handed over the bridge to Matha at 08:00 but stayed on deck as they entered a two-mile channel in which large bergs were slowly waltzing. The ship stopped dead, throwing them forwards, the foremast bent with the impact. Charcot wrote: 'We were about a mile from land when, passing approximately a cable's length from a large tabular iceberg more than 150 feet high, the ship received a terrible shock, the bow rearing almost vertically.' The ship fell backwards, and they saw ahead of her a single rock; the extent of the damage was unknown, but water was flooding in. The engine was running so poorly that the pumps had to be operated by hand. The engineer, Libois, lowered himself into the water in the bow and spent several hours working on the damaged hull. Officers joined the men on the hand-pumps. The coast offered no safe landing, and they had seen no wildlife on which to subsist. They did not know what other rocks lay in wait, and the pack was tightening up on them, hampering navigation of the crippled ship. A fault in Gautier's design of the watertight compartments now became apparent. The hole had been punched in a compartment ahead of their main bunkers which had no pumps, and no connection to any pumpable area. Men had to break open the front wall of the bunker to release the water. Charcot climbed on to the yards to direct her course. Out of the pack, but still fighting the leak, he asked his men to make one final sally south to join up, in his concept of the geography, two stretches of mainland coast. They agreed, though what the carpenter thought of this, below decks, waist-deep in freezing water, is not recorded. Charcot did not realise that one of these stretches of 'mainland' was in fact an island – Adelaide.

A north-west wind came, helping them exploit small channels and re-trace their route towards open water. They judged the leak was under control but the damage made it inadvisable to take risks among the ice. They set course north for the Biscoes and sat out a gale there on 19 January. Heavy seas and a three-day fog followed. Charcot stuck to his surveying plans and tried to complete survey work on the Schollaert Channel between Brabant and Anvers Islands, but in storms the propeller key, which locks the propeller to the drive shaft, sheared off. They limped into the shelter of Port Lockroy with relief: *'Oh! Etre au calme, savoir le bateau en securité et pouvoir dormir!'* (Oh to be in calm water, to know the ship is safe, and to be able to sleep!)

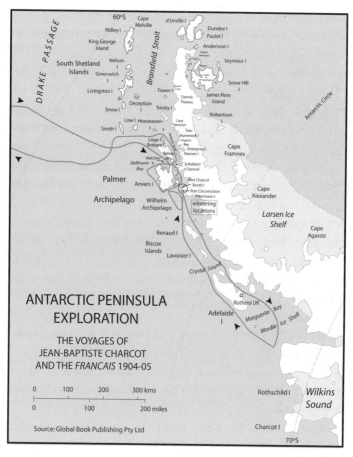

ANTARCTIC PENINSULA
EXPLORATION

THE VOYAGES OF
JEAN-BAPTISTE CHARCOT
AND THE *FRANCAIS* 1904-05

| 0 | 100 | 200 | 300 kms |

| 0 | 100 | 200 miles |

Source: Global Book Publishing Pty Ltd

The men were showing the strain. Charcot's comment
that 'nearly all were enfeebled and ate little; but none
complained, and they kept in good spirits' sounds like
wishful thinking. From 8 to 11 February, they enjoyed the
first good weather they could remember. The sunshine
brightened spirits and refreshed tired bodies, but the clear
water round their anchorage revealed that the damage to
their bows was greater than anyone had thought. On 11

February, when the engineers had done all they could, they tried the engines, and they 'worked almost satisfactorily', which must have been almost reassuring. They went to Biscoe Bay, and completed their survey of the Schollaert Channel, but the summer was ending. It was time to go. They saw their last iceberg by Low Island, the southerly outpost of the South Shetlands, and on 4 March they made the windy open spaces of Puerto Madryn, in northern Patagonia, where they were greeted as if back from the dead. The *Uruguay* had come looking for them but failed to find the cairns, and been stopped by ice short of 65°S before turning home, presuming them lost. Charcot found his wife had made efforts to organise relief, before divorcing him for abandonment. De Gerlache's return to his fiancée looked like a good call. At Buenos Aires the *Français* could at last be inspected in a dock; she had lost seven metres of keel. She had been a brave vessel, the smallest of the era to go south, but she needed some tender loving care. The Argentine Government made a generous offer to purchase her as a supply vessel for her new bases, which Charcot accepted. He returned home a hero, met by the Minister of Marine bearing the *Légion d'Honneur*.

Charcot lost no one, and the expedition recorded successes in all areas of study. They drew new or improved maps of one thousand miles of coast, and made the first good chart of islands along the west coast of the Peninsula. From Booth Island southwards they achieved accurate latitude and longitude fixes for the outside of the Palmer Archipelago and the Schollaert Channel, for the Biscoe Islands, and two thirty-miles stretches of Graham Land that Biscoe had thought to be ice-joined islands. When Charcot delivered his preliminary paper at the RGS, one of the first comments from the floor came from one of Scott's companions, Dr H. R. Mill, who thanked him for nailing down 'the Biscoe Islands [which] have been drifting about on the chart.' In zoology they took a hundred bird specimens and fifteen species of fish, mostly from the top two hundred feet of the water column, which complemented the deeper water samples of the *Belgica* expedition and others. One scientist who received specimens noted that the sea urchins, *crinoides*, and starfish were not only all new, but highly interesting, and there was a 'superb collection of sponges.' In botany they had discovered both of Antarctic's only two flowering plants: *Deschampsia antarctica* on Booth and in Biscoe Bay, and *Colobanthus crassifolius brevifolius* on Antwerp Island.

The *Pourquois-Pas?*

There is a small island called Petermann just south of the Lemaire Channel. For some cruise ships it is their most southerly point, as they pass through the Lemaire then continue just far enough south to see Adélie penguins. Petermann has the most northerly colony of this cold-loving penguin in the Peninsula islands. There is a small Argentine hut and on the shore just south of it, a cross remembering three young British men from the old Faraday Base who lost their lives returning from a late-winter sled journey when the ice broke up under them.

The smooth limbs of silver-grey andesite rocks offer a choice of landing places, the more popular being just north of the hut, at the painfully named Port Circumcision, christened for its discovery on the day of the Feast of the Circumcision, 1 January 1909. But the more humorous part of the name is really the word 'Port'; it is a very small rocky inlet.

When the President of the RGS introduced the returning hero to the membership for a second time, with Shackleton in the audience, he emphasised that his French guest was no less successful for having left the most glorious and high-profile destination to others. 'The fact that Dr Charcot has not reached the South Pole is perhaps sufficiently accounted for by his never having tried to do so.'

In his paper, given that night of 19 December 1911 Charcot set the scene:

The exploration of the Antarctic has been set going, and the movement ought not to slacken until the conquest – still only just begun – is complete. Captain Scott has just set out once more for the final attack on the South Pole itself [how Shackleton, who had fallen out bitterly with Scott, would have striven to appear impassive; none of them knew Amundsen had made the South Pole a few days before] and great expeditions are being talked of in Germany, Norway and Japan, while the Argentine Republic is maintaining a permanent observatory in the South Orkneys, and means to establish another on the west coast of Graham Land – the site of our winter quarters.

It was perfectly natural that Sir E Shackleton should return to this region, with the exploration of which his country had become so intimately connected, and it was equally natural, since he had announced his attention of so doing, that I should refrain from entering the same field, however tempting it might appear. The Antarctic is, besides, vast enough to permit many expeditions to work in it side by side with good results, and I decided to return to the region which I had begun to study in the *Français*, in 1903– 5, continuing the labours of de Gerlache. My object – a thoroughly definite one – was to study from all points of view the greatest possible expanse of ground in the Antarctic without consideration of latitude. I had no hope of getting anywhere near the pole.

Specifically, was Alexander I Land really mainland or was it an island, and, unproven from his first expedition, was there an Antarctic continent?

Charcot led a crew of twenty-two, including eight former shipmates from the *Français*, and a talented scientific team. Second-in-command Maurice Bongrain was in charge of astronomical, pendulum and seismographic observations, and hydrographic work. Third Officer Jules Rouch directed meteorological measurements, atmospheric electricity, and physical oceanography. Godfroy covered tidal observations, coastal hydrography, and the chemistry of the atmosphere; Gourdon, geology and glaciology; Senouque would conduct magnetic and actinometric studies (the science of rays) and the scientific photography. Liouville and Gain were zoologists.

He took advice from all the experienced Antarctic hands of the day: Bruce, de Gerlache, Shackleton, Nordenskjöld and Drygalski. He met Scott to trial experimental motor sledges and was impressed enough to accept three as sponsorship, though he would never find terrain suitable to even land them. For his vessel, Charcot first hoped to buy back the purpose-built *Français*, now the *Austral*, but Argentina was too pleased with its investment to part with her. Charcot went back to Père Gautier's St Malo shipyard and with an expedition budget of F800,000, swollen by public and private pride in his success, commissioned a larger vessel of eight hundred tons, forty metres long at the waterline (ten more than her predecessor) and with a 9.2 metre beam. He gave it the same name as his boyhood model yacht: the *Pourquois-Pas?*, launching her on 18 May 1908. Her frame was even heavier than that of the *Français*. It was reinforced by diagonal braces below the waterline, and the wooden hull was sheathed in iron, then zinc. She had three laboratories fitted out courtesy of the Duke of Monaco, and an electrical generator would add to daily comfort and convenience, and assist greatly in the scientific pursuits. Her brand new engine was four times as powerful as the makeshift antique in the *Français*.

They left Le Havre on 15 August 1908. Poignantly, as Charcot passed the Banco Chico shallows in the River Plate in spring 1907, he saw the *Français* stranded on it. He reached Punta Arenas on 10 December, and departed for Antarctica on 16 December. They made good use of their contacts to collect coal at the Magellan Whaling Company at Deception. Entering the caldera through Neptune's Bellows they saw three whale catchers, one with a whale in tow. Two turned to pilot them through and into Whalers Bay where they surprised Charcot by heading out to sea again; they had turned back in the breakneck high season of whaling purely as a courtesy to him.

It was a strange meeting. The shore was a slaughter-house. They were invited aboard the largest factory ship, the *Gobernador Bories*, but to make room for them to tie alongside it, the whalers had to move six waiting carcases, some of which exploded like cannon. 'The smell,' wailed Charcot, 'is unbearable.' The cabins of the *Pourquois-Pas?* were cold, to save coal no stoves were lit, but they were greeted in the *Bories's* ward-room by a parrot preening itself in front of a roaring coal fire. With satisfaction, he found they were using charts he had surveyed on his previous expedition.

Formalities and bunkering done, they removed themselves from the shambles of Whalers Bay and retreated up to Pendulum Cove, but found the tidelines hedged with whale skeletons still with enough meat on them to stink out the air. They climbed to a cairn and found a memento inside: a broken bottle containing a message from Captain Galindez of the *Uruguay* dated 9 January 1905, when she had ventured south seeking news of them, and supposed them lost. Galindez had stated his intention to press on to

Wiencke to look for them. They read it like Lazarus reading his own death certificate. They studied the layout of Pendulum Cove with interest. Foster's *Chanticleer* illustrations from 1829 showed a little creek running away to the right as you approach the shore. Seventy-six years later this had gone, as the *Uruguay's* 1905 sketch-charts showed, the cliffs apparently having collapsed and filled it. The cove was now an open bay.

The scientists spent the week before Christmas running loose over the island: 'the zoologists Liouville and Gain are scouring the neighbouring area, collecting and classifying all they can.' Late on the evening of 23 December Charcot realised he had not seen Bongrain and Boland for some time. He found them in a field tent using the midnight light to continue their pendulum observations. Charcot returned to ship and brought them cakes and Mariani wine, a patent tonic in which Bordeaux wine was fortified with cocaine. Rouch took soundings in the harbour and compared them with Foster's. In one spot where Foster had found 582 feet, Rouch found only 378 feet. The caldera floor had risen up around two hundred feet. Their medical expertise was now called into use when a whaler's steam slicer cut off four fingers from the operator's hand. The machine was surrounded by blood and guts so gangrene was likely; they operated to tidy and clean up the wounds. He recovered well. The whaling manager Andresen promised to keep tabs on the *Pourquois-Pas?* and visit the Port Lockroy cairn, if possible in their first season, or failing that, a year thence, in January 1910. Charcot admitted past arrangements had not been perfect: 'I was keenly reproached over the last expedition for not having made sure of a shelter in an emergency.' Before leaving, Charcot recommended, as the whalers went farther south, that they use Port Lockroy as the best harbour in that area. They left Deception on Christmas Day 1908, heading for Port Charcot.

As they departed down the Gerlache Strait Charcot remarked 'About us an innumerable quantity of whales are plunging.' The contrast with modern ships, where passengers and staff scan for whale blows for fruitless hours, is heightened in irony by Charcot remarking: 'I personally claim to have done my small part' in reviving Southern Ocean whaling. They first went to Port Lockroy where they opened the message cairn to find it contained just one message: their own from 1905. On 27 December they neared their old overwintering site at Booth Island, and sent ahead their motor launch to see if their Port Charcot anchorage was clear. Its engine failed when they were in the northern mouth of the Lemaire Channel. Bitterly cold, they were forced to row most of the way back before it finally started.

Reaching Booth Island on 29 December, they man-oeuvred the ship into their old anchorage in Français Cove at Port Charcot with some difficulty, since she was ten metres longer than her predecessor. They lodged the bows onto the beach before anchoring her to shore. They strung the steel hawsers from their drag nets behind the ship to try to protect her against wind-blown bergs, but this time the cove first filled with small ice which did not stop large bergs driving through them right up against the ship. They rigged up a hose running meltwater directly to the ship, a fuel – and time-saving luxury – and killed penguins, Charcot rather hypocritically musing: 'Why is man bound to do evil as soon as he visits any place?' before passing them to the cook.

The whaleboat from their previous visit was full of ice but otherwise intact; the magnetic hut was as good as new. Their temporary house had slid off down the slope and then been bombed to destruction by falling ice. They soon saw that the hawsers were not keeping out the bergs the way the chains had: they drove over them or under them. On New Year's Eve the swell rose during breakfast and they heard an ominous grinding noise above their heads; a large berg had broken through and was working against the rudder. With poles they forced it away. At 20:00 the same evening another large berg armed all round with ugly angles and edges made its way straight towards them. The men's nerves were frazzled, fearing the rudder would be destroyed. At the last minute, the wind died and the current bore it away. Following a Spanish custom, continued in South America, they took out a surprise luxury with which to welcome the midnight chimes and the New Year: a small supply of Malaga grapes: 'they tasted as if they had just been picked.'

They realised that Français Cove was a hazardous anchorage, and they had been extremely lucky on the previous expedition that the ice had come to shore in a way that fortified their own protective measures. The luck did not recur. They had to relocate.

On New Year's Day they moved a short distance to Petermann Island where, on the shore facing the Penola Strait, there was another inlet where they could lodge the ship which would not be so vulnerable to large bergs. They had seen it on their previous expedition, but that year it had been iced up for eleven months. They named it Port Circumcision. If you veer to starboard before landing and look to the right, you can see, except at high spring tides, a horizontal line incised roughly into the rock. In a crisp light you can also see two initials: PP, the abbreviation for a small ship whose name reflected the character of the man: the *Pourquois-Pas?* – the *Why Not?* Charcot would note that: 'Throughout the whole remaining ground covered by our expedition we did not discover a single spot at which one could think of wintering with a ship.' Antarctica was a tight-fisted host.

As on the first expedition, they found that the Grandidier Channel between the Biscoes and the mainland was always fraught with dense ice crammed with large bergs. On 4 January 1909, Charcot, Gourdon and Godfroy took the launch to Cape Tuxen, surveyed that coast and the Berthelot Islands. They struggled to return to ship, and had to be rescued by the *Pourquois-Pas?* The launch party had no time to recover from that danger before the ship itself was imperilled. They struck a rock near Cape Tuxen. The stern settled lower in the water. The hull had been torn open, and she was sinking. Charcot ordered cargo to be moved forward, the pumps began to gain on the in-rushing water, but she did not lift free. They had to hope the next high tide would provide that last nudge to raise them clear, but tides in Antarctica have a small range, often no more than a metre and a half. The tide crept up and the ship just rose up enough to free itself. Investigations back at Port Circumcision found that although the hull was leaking, Gautier's super-strength specifications for her hull had left them structurally sound.

Charcot's response was to push south and drive his ship south of the Antarctic Circle and into the narrows where Hansen Island lies in Hanusse Bay tucked in the south of Crystal Sound. In this freezing alley between Adelaide

Island and the Arrowsmith Peninsula, where I have sailed my farthest south, it was not, they found, too cold for an Adélie rookery. The elegant birds stood with the line of their chic black headscarves running below the plump cheek and down through the front arc of their flippers, their white eye-rings giving them a mad stare.

They went back eastwards then south, finding Adelaide island was much larger than John Biscoe had supposed. Despite good weather, Biscoe had wrongly guessed he was close to its shore, estimating there was an ice-edge ten feet high when it was actually one hundred-foot cliffs. Its area had been similarly underestimated; it was seventy miles long not eight. They discovered that in this locality the ice was much less than in 1905, when they had met dense pack seventy miles north of Alexander I Island. Now they passed south of it before meeting the pack. Charcot thought Jenny Island in Marguerite Bay, jointly named for Bongrain's wife and his own, might prove a good site for a base, and the modern British Rothera Base lies just to the north-east of the site he had in mind.

From 73°W to 80°W they sailed to south of the track of the *Belgica*, at times following the path she had drifted when gripped in the pack. From 82°W to 87°W they re-crossed to the north of it as far as Peter I Island, and were also to the north of Bellingshausen's route in this area. They correctly assessed that Peter I seemed to be an isolated island with no other land close. From Peter I they were able to hold a course to the south of Bellingshausen and to north of *Belgica's* ice-drift as far as 103°W, where the latter escaped. In the area of 73° to 80°W they sailed with caution since Knox, sailing on the Wilkes expedition, had reported seeing an ice barrier here. There was nothing.

Charcot supposed it to be another one of the mirages, caused by refraction through thermal layers in the air. Around 71°S and 107°W they crossed Cook's path, and met pack thirty miles north of his farthest south. It would have been possible to steam a little farther south and better his latitude but Charcot thought it was pointless to burn coal to pursue an egotistical goal of no likely geographical importance, and went on his way. Dwindling supplies of coal and an outbreak of scurvy forced Charcot to regroup.

Looking round at the shelterless shores and the huge bergs that seemed to reassure them of deepwater whereas in reality they were snagged on reefs, he pondered: 'A ship overtaken by a storm in this region would find itself in an almost desperate situation.' In this area they surveyed 120 miles of new lands, and saw decisively that Bellingshausen's Alexander I Land was an island. Attempts to land on it were all foiled by ice. Having decided it was impossible to overwinter in this area they returned to Petermann Island and spent the autumn making excursions in that area. They formed the first Antarctic Sports Club running sled and ski races. To occupy minds, there were back copies of *Le Matin* from their sponsor, and fifteen hundred books, with another on the way: *L'Amant de la Dactylograph*, or the *Typist's Lover*, which Third Officer Jules Rouch wrote and read out in instalments. They set up four huts ashore, filled with scientific instruments and powered from the ship's electrical generator.

The winter was trying, with gale force winds for most of the nine months they were iced in. Despite the stores of fresh seal and penguin meat, several members developed severe scurvy. At the end of the winter, from August onwards, the sea ice became heavier and heavier. In spring, on 18 September

1909, a party attempted to cross Graham Land to the Weddell Sea, to join up the west Peninsula observations with the eastern ones of Larsen and Nordenskjöld. But it proved 'impossible to surmount the perpendicular wall of granite and ice which seems to bound the whole region.' Charcot was not well enough to travel, and stayed on board until mid-October, suffering from 'Polar anaemia.' This diagnosis was derived from Dr Cook's reports on the de Gerlache expedition, when reports of anaemia, a side-effect of scurvy, were frequent. On 31 October they decided to break out of the cove and take the *Pourquois-Pas?* north to Deception for coal. With great difficulty they reached Deception in late November, where they learned of two historic journeys. Ten months before Shackleton had got within a hundred miles of the South Pole, and seven months before, Peary claimed, he had reached the North Pole. His claim would soon be seen to require an elastic view of the truth.

Charcot asked a Norwegian diver at the whaling station to look at the damage to his ship and report privately to him; the diver reported that it was unsafe, and they should get north while his luck held. Charcot swore him to secrecy, obtained one hundred tons of coal, and sailed on 7 January 1910. South.

In their injured ship, they returned to the south-west of Alexander I island and surpassed all previous farthest souths in that zone. He called the new land Charcot, again after his father, and his officers and crew might have wondered why he did not try harder to get close to shore and land; only he knew their hull could take no more shocks. They followed the edge of the pack, running along the latitude of 70°S as far as 124°W. 'The ice now became more abundant, the coal was exhausted, and the general health unsatisfactory, so that it was necessary to turn once more to the north, and after ten days of somewhat eventful navigation.' They reached Punta Arenas on 12 February, and were fêted by France on their arrival at Rouen on 4 June 1910.

His main account of the voyage was published in 1910. They had surveyed 1250 miles (2000 kilometres) of unknown or partly known coast, and drawn the most accurate map for decades to come. They returned with three thousand photos and would publish twenty-eight volumes of reports. In eight months of observations at the winter station, his team recorded two earthquakes and five seismic storms. From Deception, on 23 December 1908, they had observed the last contact of the moon departing the sun during a solar eclipse, valuable in measuring astronomical distances. The geologists had shown that the same diorite and granite formations known from Graham Land continued farther south. Collating their results with those of *Belgica*, they established the existence of continental shelf, defined its western limits, and linked up Nordenskjöld's work to north and de Gerlache's to the south. They had made some surveys inland from the heights of the Graham Land glaciers, and throughout the trip the timing of their magnetic observations had been co-ordinated with independent observations on Staten Island and South Orkney for future comparison. The zoologists had collected embryos of all penguins at all stages, and by ringing birds had established that penguins do not breed until they are two years old, after which pairs return to same rookery and the same nest. They collected specimens of the embryos of all the species of seal, including the first ever embryos of the leopard seal.

When Charcot finished giving his paper to the Royal Geographical Society in London, the President said, 'In opening the discussion, it is natural I should first call on those Englishmen who are best capable of expressing the thought-out opinions on the value of this work.'

Sir Ernest Shackleton took the floor: 'When I heard the accounts of the gales, and saw the efforts that had been made to keep that ship safe and quiet during those long months of storm, I came to the conclusion it is better to have a wintering party and no ship in such quarters; and keep the ship for navigation during the summer. What Dr Charcot has gone through to my mind must have been one of the hardest experiences possible.' The French Ambassador Cambon diplomatically complimented both countries in a phrase: 'You have Shackleton, we have Charcot.'

A great friend and fellow-traveller of Shackleton and Scott on the *Discovery* was there: Hugh Mill, born near John O'Groats, as he said of himself, where 'no land lies between the shore of my place of birth and the North Pole.' Mill observed, 'Now Dr Charcot has, in the most interesting manner, connected together all the earlier related discoveries, and showed how much greater they were than the discoverers themselves had supposed.'

Louis Bernacchi, physicist on the *Discovery*, said 'this quiet, unostentatious, and really solid scientific work of Dr Charcot compels our deep admiration and recognition,' and added, 'I think probably the climatic conditions and the general conditions are more severe in the latitude in which Dr Charcot wintered than in the corresponding latitude in the Ross Quadrant.'

Outside France, Charcot is now little known to the general public, but contemporaries often rated him the greatest explorer of his day. Amundsen summed up Charcot as 'the French savant and yachtsman', 'opening up a large extent of the unknown continent.' He thought 'the scientific results were extraordinarily rich' and 'the point that compels our special attention in Charcot's voyages is that he chose one of the most difficult fields of the Antarctic zone to work in.'

Charcot never returned to the Antarctic. During World War One, despite poor health, he worked in the anti-submarine force and was awarded the DSC. On 15 September 1936 he was sailing on the *Pourquois-Pas?* when it was wrecked in a gale on the coast of Iceland. There was only one survivor; Charcot, and forty-two other men died.

# CAPE HORN

People who have never seen the sea know Cape Horn's reputation as a destroyer of ships and men. Why, among all the seas, has this cape come to represent all that is wild and deadly dangerous about the sea?

The Horn was not discovered until 1616, when two small ships under the commands of Willem Schouten and Le Maire came down the east coast of Patagonia, bound for the Pacific. It was nearly a century since Magellan had first found and sailed through his strait, but since then, it had proved a graveyard for shipping. It was nearly sixty years before Francis Drake became the second person to force a route through and get home westward. These two Dutchmen from an insignificant port called Hoorn missed the eastern entrance to the strait, where the coast is sandy and backed by low hills, and continued south along an increasingly rocky and wild coast, where islands send out ridges into the surf, long-toothed like a log-cutter's saw, which the sea breaks into stacks, then rocks, then spume-smashed reefs. They kept far enough out to sea to stay safe on their southward course until they saw the coast begin to curve away towards the west. It was impossible to tell whether the land to starboard was a land mass or a constellation of islands. When, in the 1820s and 1830s, it was eventually surveyed properly by Captain Stokes, an earlier master of the *Beagle*, it drove him to such despair that he shot himself in the head. His successor Captain Fitzroy gazed at the charts he had made and said the myriad rocks and islets looked less like the sea and more like the stars of the sky. One high headland, brutal, simple as a stone axe, rising nearly thirteen hundred feet straight out of the water was rounded, and the coast began to run north. They named it, like one of their little craft, after their home port: Kap Hoorn; it became Cape Horn.

The cape is dangerous because south of it, below 56°S, there is no land to obstruct storms, or check the waves. It is open ocean, all around the world. There is a west-to-east ocean current running through the Drake Passage, and the prevailing winds are westerly. A square-rigged ship was poor at sailing into the wind, so the passage from east to west had both wind and wave stacked against it. It was nothing to take a month to round it. At that distance from Europe, scurvy would now start to sicken the crew unless their diet had been carefully managed. Men were washed overboard, ripped from the rigging, or left helpless in the hammocks with broken bones. A sailor who fell from the top mast hit the deck with the same impact as a motorcyclist coming off at 50mph and hitting a house. Others simply slipped off into the night when feet became too cold to feel a rope and fingers too numb to grasp one. Captain Bligh, who would later suffer mutiny on the *Bounty*, began the practice of sailing east to get to the Pacific: a much longer route, but with the wind behind them, driving them on. Many skippers also sailed with poor charts and limited navigation equipment; they saw land here only when they were too close to escape from being dashed upon it.

If it was this bad, why sail round the Horn at all? Why not stay in the shelter of the Strait of Magellan? Firstly, the strait is a winding S-shape round which clippers, not very manoeuvrable ships, had to thread a path, tacking in limited space, always looking for stray rocks and reefs. Although much of the channel is very deep indeed, there are isolated peaks rising up from the cold of the lightless depths to prick the hull of passing ships. There are local katabatic winds powerful enough to flatten a sailing ship, putting her on her beam ends, in other words, her masts horizontal. These go by the misleadingly cute native name for them: willi-waws. Seamen and owners preferred to fight the open sea, rather than the sea and the land together.

# 11

# Red Water: Whaling

*Herman Melville, writing in* Moby Dick, *argued that whales would never be exterminated by hunting. How wrong he was.*

Whaling was the only commercial activity successfully pursued for any time in Antarctica. Other chapters, particularly chapter six on Deception, have dealt with some aspects of whaling. This short chapter provides context for those sections and describes some sites you may visit where whaling was significant.

In *Moby Dick* Melville dismisses fears that the great whales could be hunted to destruction. His final reason was, 'They have two firm fortresses, which, in all human probability, will forever remain impregnable ... whales can at last resort to their Polar citadels, and diving under the ultimate glassy barriers and walls there, come up among icy fields and floes; and in a charmed circle of everlasting December, bid defiance to all pursuit from man.' Melville was quite wrong.

The small but very sheltered harbour of Neko, tucked deep in Andvord Bay, is a favoured place to set foot on the mainland. The shingle beach only becomes difficult to land on when ice blows hard against the shore. The presence from 1911–16 and 1918–24 of Salvesen's factory ship the *Neko* in the area became notorious. She was not, as is often assumed from name, part of the Japanese fleet. She was a 3,576-ton former passenger liner in the *Kosmos* fleet, and was converted to a factory ship at Leith, before commencing Antarctic whaling in 1911.

The British feared the 'whaling industry may come to a natural end by the reduction of the three species of whales on which the industry is based.' In the June preceding the season 1921–22 they issued a ban on hunting sperm, right and humpback whales. There was outright mistrust between the Norwegian whalers and the British officials. That season the *Neko* reported no humpbacks caught, but two of its labourers transferred the following season to rivals A/S *Hektor* and personally confirmed to the British Magistrate and Whaling Officer, Arthur Bennett, that the *Neko* had taken forty-three humpbacks. It had chosen Andvord Bay because it was remote from the officials in Deception Island, and used the isolation to flout new regulations requiring more efficient use of carcases. The *Neko's* English master, Thomas Sinclair, was renowned, Bennett reported, for continually 'shifting ports and selecting ports for anchorage remote from, and most difficult of access.' Even among the grossly inefficient Norwegian whaling ships she was one of the worst. Her condition was filthy and her catch reports unreliable. She continued at this game until 1923 when she spent the season in South Georgia, before foundering on the Brazilian coast, returning at the end of the season in 1924. Beneath her decks a still worse practice went on. Whalers coming south called in at the Cape Verde Islands for water and fruit. The islands were, and still are, poor compared with other Atlantic islands. Misguided young men would stow away, perhaps hoping to get to America, or maybe simply to try to force a master to employ them. Salvesen's response, and doubtless some other companies' too, was to put them to work poorly fed and clothed, at shovelling coal. If they only worked ordinary shifts they were not paid at all. Opportunities to transfer them to company ships going north were spurned. Bennett believed Salvesen ships called at Cape Verde intending to entrap men. Whaling Officer Hardy's end of year report concluded: 'The company's intention was without doubt organized slavery, and the same could be said for Salvesen's South Georgia station at which large numbers of stowaways are stated to be working without pay.'

Today at Neko Harbour the only noticeable remains on shore are of a much later Argentine refuge, which fell into disrepair following severe fire damage to the Argentine navy's principal support vessel the *Irízar*, named after Julian Irízar who captained the corvette *Uruguay* when it rescued Otto Nordenskjöld from Snow Hill. In the winter of 2009 the hut was destroyed by storms.

Another whaling centre was Wilhelmina Bay between Emma Island and the Peninsula. It is usually visited only by ships which bring passengers to dive the wreck of the *Guvernøren*, a state-of-the-art whale factory ship which caught fire and was beached there. But a Zodiac cruise along the shore reveals many industrial relics, beginning with the wooden navigation marks used to guide vessels through the reef-filled bay. Along the shore you see metal posts and chains used to anchor ships and, in the days before factory ships, hold whale carcases securely in the shallows to be flensed. When snow melts towards the end of the season, some of the small islands reveal abandoned boats and barrels, and the foundations of huts and storehouses.

On the south shore of Trinity Island is Mikkelsen Harbour, skirted by steep, thunderously grumbling glaciers. In the middle of it is a small island, unnamed on marine charts but christened D'Hainaut Island in 1952 after Chilean lieutenant Ladislao D'Hainaut. You can stun your expedition staff with this unimportant information.

It's a horrible landing for Zodiac drivers because the shore is guarded all the way in by rocks deep enough to be out of sight and shallow enough to wreck a propeller. The shore has several old water boats on it, and a sea of whalebones dating from 1910 – 1917. The factory ships *Bombay* and the *Ørn* and *Ørn II* were regulars here.

Port Lockroy off Wiencke Island was an early refuge harbour for whalers and a few remains are still visible. If you step ashore at the landing site nearer the hut, rather than below the boathouse, there are heavy chains stapled to the rocks. At the head of the bay are more, and the remnants of painted graffiti on the rocks above. Hubert Wilkins was responsible for some of the Lockroy graffiti when he persuaded the master of the *Solstreif* to take him and John Lachlan Cope home from their disastrous expedition. The chains were fixed there by the factory ship *Solstreif*, which means the *Sunbeam*. She used the mooring regularly until the crash of 1931, but her name, painted on the rocks, and the date 1912, are now fading. She was owned by A/S *Norge* and at 4637 tons was the third largest factory ship in the Falkland Island Dependencies before World War One.

She was one of the first ships to successfully run a guano drier at sea. In whaler's jargon, guano is the dried meat and bone ground up for fertiliser. British policy was to press for more efficient use of carcases but owners and captains didn't like the cookers on board. Guano was tricky to process but not highly priced, and it took up storage space that could otherwise be used for much more valuable whale oil. This didn't stop the *Solstreif* doing so well in its first season that its owners paid dividends of 50%. One of its captains, Thorvald Andersen, personally harpooned over five thousand Antarctic whales. The whalers also bequeathed another gift, stored in the whaleboats whose outline can still be seen below the front door: dynamite. They carried it for blasting their way out of ice.

You might have thought that the twentieth century was a period of change towards more responsible management. It wasn't. Whaling is a perfect example of the problem of the commons, first stated by the British economist William Lloyd in 1833. It shows how individuals exploiting a shared, unowned resource will maximise their own short-term self-interest and destroy the resource.

To simplify matters, I'll look at the twentieth century kills of the three largest southern whales: the blue, and their less massive cousins, the fin whales, and sei whales. Humpback whales had already been slaughtered out of the equation.

Before the First World War, the British had talks with the whaling companies from the many nations who were using as bases Deception Island, and adjacent areas claimed and adminstered by Britain. Whales were so abundant only the blubber was cut out and the rest of the body, rich with oil and other products like bonemeal, was cast away. It made commercial sense to fill their holds easily with the highest value product, oil, and maximise profits. If they did not, rival companies would out-perform them and shareholders would rebel. In the early days returns for shareholders over a single season could exceed 50% or even 100%.

The First World War virtually stopped whaling, and from 1920-24 catches of the preferred species, the blue, were at about 4,500, and fin catches were around 4,000. Hardly any of the less profitable sei whales were taken. In the following five years catches of blue and fin doubled or more. To the technology of the explosive harpoon, were added stronger and faster hunter ships, feeding a factory ship. The cumbersome business of cutting up a whale in the water alongside the ship or at the beach had been replaced by a stern slipway allowing the carcase to be hauled up a ramp for processing on deck before being dropped into the tryworks, now situated in the hold. Cutting a large whale now took just a few hours. The invention of the reverse osmosis technique to convert seawater to freshwater meant that ships could stay out at sea all season, outside the jurisdiction of the fledgling attempts by the British to impose more responsible practices.

The combined impact of these advances was that the Antarctic whale catch rose from 30,655 whales in the 1929-30 season to 40,201 the following year. The market was glutted, prices collapsed and the 1931–32 season saw catches fall below ten thousand. In the five-year period to 1934, blue whale catches were still double fin catches, with sei whales insignificant. Whaling picked up after the Depression but the five years to 1939 show a shocking turnaround in the species being taken, and it is driven by necessity. The take of blue whales falls, and the take of fins more than doubles, becoming the principal species.

The Second World War gave another respite but whales breed slowly. The blue whale catch fell steeply and declined steadily until 1965 after which none could be found. Catches of fin whales soared to a level far above any past takes of blue whales, totally dominating the catch from 1955–59. By this time sei whales began to form a small proportion of the catch, perhaps 5%. Within a decade little else was being caught. One species after another was annihilated.

Attempts were made to regulate the industry. The International Whaling Commission (IWC) was set up in 1946. In its own words, its purpose 'is to provide for the proper conservation of whale stocks and thus make possible the orderly development of the whaling industry.' Like any authority attempting to resolve the problem of the commons, it faced opposition from operators who had owners and shareholders at their backs. Stocks of whales continued to fall and the IWC decided at its meeting in 1982 that there should be a moratorium on commercial whaling on all whale stocks from 1985/86. Exceptions have been made for scientific research and for indigenous societies with a tradition of whale hunting. Both rationales have been questioned. The Japanese press for quotas which far exceed the maximum numbers needed to inform science, and some native societies like the Inuit take whales like the bowhead whose survival is in doubt. They argue that their hunting did not cause the problem.

Three main countries now wage the political battle to ease the moratorium: Iceland, which manages its own fishery waters independently and effectively, Norway, and

Japan. Part of the problem is a sense of nationalism. Norway and Iceland do not like to be told what to do by nations who have failed to manage their own fisheries. Japan claims a cultural tradition of eating whales, but in truth it largely dates from expediency, in the fat and protein-starved years after their military defeat in 1945. In both Japan and Norway the traditional whaling areas are economically depressed areas with marginal constituencies. Political parties rebuff the whaling companies at their peril.

The integrity of the IWC is now widely seen as damaged. Japan pays the expenses of other delegates in return for helpful votes. Of its eighty-eight member states, all with full voting rights, ten are land-locked, two more border only the Black Sea, and others have only a corridor of territory leading to a one-port coast. Its members include the Saharan wastes of Mali, the Asian steppes of Mongolia, and the intrepid Leviathan chasers of the tax-free haven of San Marino. There is also illegal whaling; South Korea is suspected of tacitly permitting vessels to hunt.

But the real danger in the long term, biologists agree, is pollution. Most whale species recover once hunting stops or is restricted, but if the seas are not healthy, their food and their fate are unsure.

# THE GUVERNØREN

Before World War One the *Guvernøren* was the largest factory ship in the dependencies, at 5459 gross tons. She was built as the Europa to carry cattle between New York and London, before being converted to a factory ship and renamed the *Thøger*, then the *Guvernøren*. She was managed by veteran Leif Bryde, and was the most sophisticated processing ship of her day. She had the new Hartmann rotary cookers available in 1912 which broke up the meat and bone as it cooked them, improving the quality of oil, making it lighter and less acidic. She also had a guano plant, making fertiliser from bones and other by-products. Except on shore stations, it was difficult to make this pay, and few ship owners tried. After unsuccessfully hunting off South Africa she came down to the Antarctic Peninsula in 1913/14 and produced 3500 tons of oil and 2500 sacks guano from 544 whales. She made good profits and seemed to be the future of the industry. Next season, on 27 January 1915, she caught fire; it probably started in her processing machines. All of the eighty-five men on board were saved, but the 2600 tons oil on board were lost; over four hundred whales had died for nothing.

Her bow and bridge are above water, and have been colonised by nesting Antarctic terns. You can look into the portholes, and divers report unused and used harpoon heads are still in the hold. The stern lies under water and you can take Zodiacs over it and, on a calm day, see the outline of its hull diving into the deeper water, where a near-complete whale skeleton lies on the sea bed next to her.

Ernest Shackleton and Frank Hurley (skinning penguin) at
Patience Camp 1915. Photographer: Frank Hurley.
With kind permission of the Royal Geographical Society

# 12

## The Boss: Ernest Shackleton
## (1877–1922)

*The tale of an expedition which barely got under way at all, which never reached the mainland, whose ship was destroyed on its maiden voyage, and whose country, engulfed in war, left them to die. Out of this shambles Shackleton forged the legend of* Endurance.

Headmasters seldom recognise the abilities of children with unconventional talent. They run a system. People who do not conform to the system do not have other talents; they are wrong. In Dulwich College, green and genteel in the leafy London suburbs, a young Irish boy from Kildare was appraised for his school report. The verdict: lacking in motivation. The college was founded in 1619 by the Shakespearian-era actor and theatre manager, Edmund Alleyn, but its greatest treasure is not one of Will's First Editions, but an old wooden boat called the *James Caird* which their unmotivated old boy once took on a two-week cruise from Antarctica to South Georgia, in the greatest open boat journey ever made. The boy was Ernest Henry Shackleton. Aged sixteen he left school for the Merchant

Navy. His first captain had a sharper eye for character: he was the 'most pig-headed, obstinate boy I have ever come across.'

Like many of the British explorers, including his great rival Scott, he did not begin with a great passion for polar exploration. They simply saw it as the best opportunity of the time for a young officer to make a name. Polar expeditions put you in the headlines in a way that being second officer on a cargo vessel or administering an African backwater did not. Shackleton also wanted to impress a Mr and Mrs Dorman, whose daughter Emily he wanted to marry. Mr Dorman was a prosperous solicitor and probably had bigger ambitions for Emily than an officer fresh from his first voyage, bringing guano from Chile. Meanwhile Ernest wrote to her misquoting Robert Browning: 'I hold that a man should strive to his uttermost for his life's set prize.'

Shackleton first went south in 1901–03, serving under Scott on the *Discovery* Expedition to the Ross Sea; in fact Shackleton had been pressed on Scott by a sponsor the Irishman had charmed. Whilst resenting Shackleton's charisma and natural leadership, Scott recognised his physical power and took him on the final three-man push south with the doctor, Edward Wilson. Shackleton did not respect Scott's leadership and the two fell out. They suffered badly from scurvy; Shackleton was coughing up blood, and was a passenger for part of the journey back. Wilson told Scott that Shackleton would not survive the journey. The patient overheard and muttered, 'I'll outlive the pair of you.' He was sent home early on the relief ship. As it sailed away, he stood on deck sobbing his heart out at the humiliation. From now on, he would run his own expeditions. He would define himself by being everything that Scott was not. But one thing he could not blame Scott for was the scurvy. The man in charge of diet was Ernest Shackleton.

He returned in 1907 in the *Nimrod* leading his own expedition funded by sponsors. With two companions he made it to 88°23´, just ninety-eight nautical miles from the Pole. Then he turned back. He knew he could reach the pole, but they did not have enough fuel or food to return to base. Wracked by starvation and lacerated by cold, they got back by the skin of their teeth. Had they gone on south for even one more day, they would have perished. He wrote to Emily, now his wife, 'I thought you would rather have a live donkey than a dead lion.' At his side for this and every future expedition was Frank Wild. Wild was not an immediate fan of his leader, but an incident on the return journey bound him to 'The Boss' forever. They had sat down to a meagre supper of stew and a few biscuits. Wild soon finished and sat suffering still from cold and hunger. Shackleton had one biscuit left. He forced it on Wild. In his journal, Wild wrote in his diary, underlining every single word with emotional emphasis: 'I do not suppose that anyone else in the world can thoroughly realise how much generosity and sympathy was shown by this; I DO by GOD I shall never forget it. Thousands of pounds could not have bought that one biscuit.' On return, Shackleton was knighted. He would never set foot on the Antarctic continent again.

That was Shackleton's last chance to be first to the Pole. Others would be ready to build on his achievements before he had time to launch another expedition. December 1911 saw Amundsen triumph. In January 1912 Scott reached the Pole but died on the return. His party was scurvy-ridden, and out of fuel and food. Most of all Scott was paralysed by his failure to get there first. For nine days they lay dying in their tent eleven miles from a huge supply depot. The weather was normal for that area. Scott showed enormous courage but he and his followers died of poor planning and bad leadership. He is an easy target, and to some degree a fair one. He persisted, to what now seems an absurd degree, in believing polar travel was a test of character where Englishmen would pull through. For ten years British expeditions persevered with man-hauling sleds. Amundsen called it stupid after one day. He was a polar fanatic and had learned and applied every hard-won lesson from Arctic exploration and Native peoples. On his way back from the Pole he left half a ton of excess food on the ice and fed his dogs chocolate for fun. Amundsen put on weight during the trip. Scott starved and froze to death.

Shackleton too had his faults, and these are now glossed over as part of re-writing history and its heroes to suit our times. When news of Scott's death reached Britain, his incompetence in the sanitised white wilderness was re-fashioned to make him a saint to self-sacrifice, a perfect message for a nation going to war. Shackleton's character was flawed in ways we now find it easier to relate to, even if we do not condone it. He was a heavy smoker and drinker, was unfaithful to his wife, and a poor provider for his family. His men would learn to trust him with their lives, but not their money or their wives. While Scott was a man who relied on rank and uniform for authority, Shackleton wielded it by force of personality, including moments of breathtaking generosity. He never asked a man to do more than he would do himself. Although he could be bad-tempered and moody, the worse things got the better his temperament became: a priceless virtue in an expedition leader. For precisely this reason, Sir Edmund Hillary said he was the explorer he would most like to have met.

This background is necessary to know how much Shackleton had staked on the Imperial Trans-Antarctic Expedition of 1914–17, now usually referred to by the ship whose name summed up the ordeal: *Endurance*. The plan was to cross the entire continent, via the Pole. One party would land on the Australian side of Antarctica and follow Shackleton's 1907 route to the point where it left the Ross Ice Shelf at over 83°S. Their task was to lay depots for Shackleton to pick up. The other, under the Boss himself, would begin on the South American side and land in the south-east corner of the Weddell Sea. They would pioneer a totally new route to the Pole, then descend (the South Pole is two miles above sea level), picking up those depots.

The expedition was funded by sponsors, and sailed in debt. The photographs, cine film and every man's journals were Shackleton's property to be sold to pay the bills when he returned. By 1914 enough had been scraped together, but war was looming. If it was declared, they would be morally obliged to offer both ship and men for service. The decision would fall to the Admiralty, and a man with known scepticism for Antarctic adventures: Winston Churchill. When affairs couldn't get worse, Sir Ernest's brother Frank Shackleton was accused of stealing the Irish Crown Jewels. Frank was a homosexual Guards officer whose confidants included the King's brother-in-law, the Duke of Argyll. The potential for scandal affecting the Crown was enormous. Sponsors and money melted away.

Ernest lost £23,000 of £30,000 committed. He managed to coax £29,000 from a Dundee jute magnate called James Caird. That was just enough to sail. He accepted a present of a Bible from Queen Alexandra and with an almighty sigh of relief gave orders to depart. That very day, war was declared. Shackleton cabled Churchill offering his ship and men for war service. He received a one-word reply: Proceed. Churchill probably thought the best place for a maverick during a war was out of the way. At Buenos Aires, slack discipline under the maverick Captain Frank Worsley led to dismissals, hirings and, they found out after sailing, a stowaway, a teenager from Newport, south Wales: Perce Blackborrow. Shackleton admired his pluck, and made him steward.

At South Georgia, they received news that the spring ice was the worst any of the old whaling captains had ever seen. He respected their judgement and delayed a month. But when they did sail on 5 December they met pack ice just three days later at 56°S, hundreds of miles north of its usual limit. They already had eleven thousand miles of sailing behind them. They were still a thousand miles away from the planned landing in Vahsel Bay. From now on, every yard would be fought for.

They had auxiliary steam engines and the ship was strong enough to batter through ice: it had been built as the first purpose-built polar cruise vessel, with Adrien de Gerlache as one of the partners, but others withdrew and the project foundered. This was the *Endurance's* maiden voyage, and she was filmed and photographed in her progress by Frank Hurley, an ambitious Australian who, with Herbert Ponting, was one of the two greats of early Antarctic photography. He sat hatless and gloveless astride spars, exposed in the rigging, toting his forty-pound camera, to expose the glass plates. The sailors admired his toughness, but his high opinion of himself earned him a nickname: The Prince.

But ice-breaking gobbled up precious coal, and it was vital to retain stocks for manoeuvring in shifting ice, in those times when the winds were low or from the wrong quarter. On 18 January 1915 exceptionally cold weather fell on them and the sea froze them in tight. When it relented, they fought free but could not get closer than sixty miles from Vahsel Bay. They stared south over ice ruptured into badlands by colossal pressures created by the slow clockwise rotation of the ice in the vast bay that encloses the Weddell Sea. There was no way of moving their stores and equipment across such terrain. The men watched Shackleton closely to see how he would cope with seeing all his preparation, done under constant financial strain, mocked by the unforgiving continent before he could even step ashore. The sole member released by the Government, the eccentric marine Thomas Orde-Lees, recorded that it was 'a catastrophe which hardly bears thinking of from either a sentimental or financial point of view.' The surgeon Alexander Macklin had a professional interest in Shackleton's morale and wrote: 'He did not rage at all, or show outwardly the slightest sign of disappointment; he told us simply and calmly that we must winter in the Pack; (he) never lost his optimism.'

One special problem faced Shackleton that only a few others like de Gerlache and Nordenskjöld had faced: the ship's officers and men, who formed the greater part of his companions, didn't want to be there. They had never signed on to stay in the Antarctic. Shackleton's Merchant Navy experience put him in a good position to manage this. He understood the regular sailors. He was not much interested in science and scientists, they were necessary to justify and promote a polar expedition and attract funds, but he would have gone without them if he could. No one on board needed to feel that one group was privileged over any other. And while he famously appointed scientists on a whim about their appearance or character, he made sure his officers and sailors were technically competent, including one man who would first stage a one-man mutiny, then use his skills to make escape possible. From the outset Shackleton saw him as a risky appointment, but the man was so exceptional at his craft, Shackleton over-rode his own fears, saying, when recruitment was finished, he was 'the only man I am not dead certain of.' He was the carpenter McNeish.

It is important to remember that although the ship is trapped, during this time life is still as comfortable as it can be in Antarctica. They had all the amenities of a ship at sea and few of the discomforts. Boredom is the main enemy; it leads to discontent. The scientists at least have work to do, but some of the seamen spent all their leisure hours sleeping or smoking in their bunks. This apathy aroused contempt in the officers and men. Nor were the sailors impressed by the scientists, many just out of university. Seeing the gentlemen swabbing floors as part of Shackleton's democratic allocations of chores did not make the seamen feel any camaraderie. For their part, the boffins doubling as housemaids posed dutifully for photographs but recorded their resentments in private diaries.

There was one group everyone loved. Shackleton's previous trips had cured him of believing ponies were any use; he brought only dogs. Hugging a big cuddly dog or playing with a puppy was some substitute for the loss of the company and affections of loved ones. There was plenty of time to go out on the ice and train men and dogs in the arts of sledding and skiing. Igloos were built on the ice to shelter the dogs: they were soon named dogloos. Puppies were born and Tom Crean, the hard-as-nails Irish second officer, was more protective about them than their mother was. In May, the days became short; they contemplated the time coming, it proved to be seventy-nine days, when the sun, the source of hope for spring, as well as heat and light, would not show its face. Would they all be alive when it returned? Both the two previous parties to overwinter unplanned had suffered deaths and the crushing of the spirit that went with disposing of a body in that bitter wasteland far from home. Would they all be sane when light returned?

The two previous enforced overwinterings had very different outcomes for the ships. De Gerlache's *Belgica* had been swept round at random then released into the ocean at the very end of the season. Nordenskjöld's *Antarctic* had been crushed and destroyed. Shackleton found they were in a giant clockwise rotation. Where the ice was hindered by dragging along the shore, or reefs and islands, or ran up against large icebergs stranded on the sea floor, huge stresses were created. They would be helpless to save the ship if she were carried into those compression zones. The winter darkness passed but the ship had suffered. She had been tilted and squeezed until the timbers groaned and emitted thin screams. No ship on earth was built to withstand such pressure; Nansen's *Fram* had successfully been designed to slip up above it. The ice itself moaned and growled relentlessly. Captain Worsley wrote at best it was like 'heavy distant surf', at worst like 'an enormous train with squeaky axles' or 'steamer whistles ... underfoot' or even the 'moans and groans of damned souls in torment.'

All through the winter Shackleton talked to all the officers and men, listening to concerns, patting them on the back, disciplining where necessary, lifting spirits. He thought optimism was the greatest of virtues and he had the worst relationships with the pessimists like Orde-Lees and McNeish. Orde-Lees worried so much about protecting his supply of stores that it was hard to get him to issue anything, even food. He became known as the 'Belly-Burglar'. In July the bosun John Vincent was reported for bullying with blows and language, and demoted to seaman.

On 15 October, early spring in Antarctica, the ice opens into a lead and the ship floats upright. Just two days later it closes again. That is the last time they will see the *Endurance* afloat. She is now leaking and by 24 October they are pumping twenty-four hours a day. They begin offloading stores onto the ice, but continue to live on the ship. Two days later the pressure flexes the ship so hard that her planking starts to gape apart. Worsley wrote that the wind in the rigging was 'making just the sort of sound you would expect a human being to utter if they were in fear of being murdered.' The dogs stare at it, howling. Nearly all sailors are superstitious and some more so than others. Tom McLeod refused to eat penguins because the souls of dead fishermen went to live in them. Now eight emperor penguins come to them across the ice, walking with their dignified gait, their flippers to their sides. They pause before the ship and begin singing to it.

The men ate their last meal on board on 27 October and moved hurriedly to the ice alongside. They called it Dump

Camp. It soon became clear that the dogs were not going to be part of any solution. Needing fresh meat to augment the pemmican, they ate three times as much seal meat as all the men put together. That same day those animals too young or unfit for work were shot. The remaining dog pemmican could double as emergency rations. They even shot the cat, Mr Chippy, a favourite of the carpenter McNeish. It was a rare tactless gesture. What it ate was neither here nor there, compared with the dogs' ravenous appetites. The cat was worth its weight in morale.

With the ruins of the ship in the background, Shackleton summoned the men and addressed them simply. 'Ship and stores have gone – so now we'll go home.' But how? They had no radio transmitter; they couldn't afford one. The war begun in August 1914 had been predicted to end by Christmas but they could not rely on anyone looking for them. Shackleton had told friends not to start worrying until February 1916. If he waited for Churchill to start any relief, it would be a long time coming. Sir Winston was writing to his wife 'when all their impoverished & broken-hearted homes have been restored, when every hospital is gorged with money, & every charitable subscription is closed, then & not till then w[oul]d I concern myself with those penguins.'

There are words that after ten years lecturing on Shackleton I can barely speak without tears coming to my eyes: 'For scientific discovery, give me Scott; for speed and efficiency of travel give me Amundsen; but when disaster strikes and all hope is gone, get down on your knees and pray for Shackleton.' It is usually credited to Sir Edmund Hillary. While working with his son, Peter, I asked if he would mind asking his father if he'd actually said it. Peter came back: 'No he didn't, but he said "It was such a damn fine quote that if anyone ever asked me, I never denied it!"' It was actually written by Raymond Priestley, a geologist who worked with both Scott and Shackleton. In the days that followed, Shackleton would show why he deserved such emotional praise.

They had three small ship's boats, wholly open to the elements. They would need freakishly good weather to sail back to South America across the worst stretch of water in the world. I have crossed the Drake Passage over eighty times and spent six months of my life in it. Maybe six times I have seen conditions fit for a boat such as the *James Caird*, and never for the ten successive days it would have taken them to sail it. Their only hope seemed to be in reaching areas on the other side of the Peninsula, or in the South Shetlands, that were frequented by whalers. When Nordenskjöld had been trapped on Snow Hill Island, Shackleton had been consulted on what stores might best be dropped off for him, so he knew that at Snow Hill, Hope Bay and Paulet Island there were supplies. They could haul across the ice, or wait for it to melt and sail there. Worsley wanted to find a big stable iceberg and sit on it until the ice melted. Waiting for fate wasn't Shackleton's style. McNeish proposed taking the three boats apart and building a small sloop they could all sail in. Shackleton refused. He wanted to retain the mobility of small boats that could be lifted as the sea re-froze or the pack closed.

While these choices exercised Shackleton and Wild, the rest of them put up their tents and organised stores. The plan was soon announced. They would head for Nordenskjöld's old base at Snow Hill, 312 miles away. From there, a 130-mile crossing of the Peninsula would lead to Wilhelmina Bay, a popular anchorage for whalers. To emphasise the need to leave behind all excess weight, Shackleton led by example, throwing onto the ice the gold coins kept as emergency funding, his gold watch and the heavy Bible donated by the Queen. First he tore from it the dedication in her own hand, and the page bearing Job Chapter 38 Verses 29–30: 'Out of whose womb came the Ice? and the hoary frost of heaven, who hath gendered it? The waters are hid as with a stone, and the face of the deep is frozen.' One possession was saved: Hussey's banjo. The Boss thought music was good for morale. Three days later the sledges were loaded with provisions and fifteen men began hauling the first boat over the ice. With the stores in it, the load was around one ton. Orde-Lees, the only experienced skier, was deputed to move up and down the line of march, trouble-shooting. Shackleton watched him a while then remarked: 'Do you know I had no idea how quickly it was possible for a man to get about.' Orde-Lees reserved his dismay for his diary: it 'set me wondering why he had not come to this conclusion long before … Amundsen's rapid journey to the pole was enough to convince one of the value of skis.' But that first day's futile hauling taught them a brutal truth. The boats were too heavy; in two days they covered two miles. To ease the loss of face, Shackleton took Wild, Hurley and Worsley to a vantage point, surveyed the ice and announced the abandonment of the plan. Even the curmudgeonly carpenter McNeish felt part of the team decision, confiding in one of the better-spelled parts of his diary: 'We have made up our minds to stop on this floe until the ice opens.' They camped where they were, and called it Ocean Camp.

After their hasty evacuation, they did not have all the

equipment and stores they wanted, but the ship's hatches and companionways had collapsed, blocking re-entry to the hull. The carpenter had only an adze, a chisel, a hammer and whatever nails he could re-use. Hurley proposed breaking in, and more was salvaged, including his glass photographic plates, stored incongruously in the ship's refrigerator, which served to keep them cool but not cold, sealed in soldered tins.

The *Endurance* lingered another month, sinking head-first at five in the evening on 21 November. You might have thought it would be inexpressibly painful to see the ship which was your home and transport disappear, but when her wreckage slid into the depths, reactions varied. Hurley wrote, 'We are not sorry to see the last of the wreck – an object of depression to all who turned their eyes in that direction.' Shackleton felt the hurt deeply and tried to confide his feelings to his journal but could not: 'I cannot write about it.'

Because the shore party stores were being consumed by the crew as well as the expedition staff, they would not last without killing seals and birds. Shackleton's biggest error in leadership was to give disproportionate weight to the demoralising effect that stockpiling seal and bird meat would have on the sailors. He said they must not be seen to be planning for a long stay. First officer Lionel Greenstreet received the news while reading Nordenskjöld's account of the crew of the *Antarctic* setting up camp on Paulet Island after the ship sank. The first thing they had done was stockpile meat.

As Christmas approached, Shackleton's feelers told him that the fickle men were getting restless. Although conditions for hauling were little different, he decided to make work for idle hands. He announced they would celebrate Christmas on 22 December and begin hauling the day after. When they tried, McNeish was missing his cat and suffering from piles. He felt the boat hauling was pointless, and he was frustrated that his suggestion to build a sloop had been rejected. On 23 December they laboured for eight hours and made just 1.25 miles. There was twenty-four-hour daylight but they worked during the night hours when the surface was a little colder and easier to travel. On 24 December leads opened through the ice and they did no hauling. On 25 December they covered 3 miles, and a miserly 1.75 miles the following day. On the 27 December McNeish threw down the harness in disgust and said he would do no more of this stupid work. The ship had sunk and he was no longer subject to orders. This was technically true. However Antarctica is a poor place to found a republic of one. Shackleton knew that McNeish's words would linger in the men's minds. Everyone knew McNeish was good at this job, and hard-working when he saw the point of the task. On another voyage a fellow sailor wrote of him: 'He could work seemingly endless hours, and if he ever knew fear, not a suspicion of it showed on the solid, graven brickwork of his face.' He was also one of the oldest and most experienced men in the party.

Shackleton felt he had to respond to the truth at the heart of the carpenter's argument. He gathered everyone and read out the articles they had signed, but almost certainly not read. He made up clauses that they would be paid after any sinking, while still serving the expedition. He had no funds to cover this promise. McNeish was now isolated, without support, but Shackleton never forgave him. He took his revenge much later, and many of the officers and crew were shocked and angry when they learned what he had done. McNeish's own diary has no word of his mutiny.

Most of the ice was now rotten: too wet to walk on, too dry to sail. They were forced to retreat half a mile to a more solid floe, and stay there three months. Shackleton signalled his revised intentions with the name: Patience Camp. That patience had to last until the ice broke up close enough to launch the boats. McNeish had been right, and they were now doing what Worsley had advocated in the beginning.

In mid-January most of the remaining dogs were shot, leaving just two teams. Hussey was complaining of severe lassitude and stopped his nightly round of visiting the tents playing his banjo. Not everyone missed it. McNeish recorded his relief while enjoying the evening silence once again: 'his 6 tunes is heart-breaking.' On 21 January the drifting pack took them north across the Antarctic Circle. By mid-February, Orde-Lees was judged to be taking too many risks hunting seals on thin ice, and was banned from hunting. Worsley muttered that the letter of the law was becoming more important than whether there was blubber to burn and meat to eat. Perhaps Shackleton's need to define himself against Scott made him obsess about his record of never losing a man. The men were eating around 1800 calories a day, barely enough for a sedentary life, never mind physical exertion in great cold. Short rations demanded risks be taken. The ice-floe that was the limit of their secure world was reduced by splitting and progressive erosion at the margins. Orders required everyone to sleep fully clothed, including boots, for evacuation within thirty seconds.

In early March Orde-Lees received another round of the abuse that he often invited. He announced he was seasick.

He was right, the ice was breaking up. So were some of the men. One wound copper wire round his belly and announced he was going to walk home.

The slow currents of the pack had taken them away from where they needed to be if they were to strike west for Snow Hill, tucked close into the eastern coast of the Peninsula. Likewise it was bearing them away from Hope Bay. Paulet was their last chance to reach anywhere with even primitive resources: Larsen's rough stone hut and the unused stores. On 11 March the ice opened. They were eighty-five miles from Paulet. Two days later it closed. By 22 March the prospect of being locked in for another winter, this time without a ship, was the fear muttered only quietly in corners. The next day tantalised them with a distant glimpse of the Danger Islands at the entrance to the Antarctic Strait: the first land they had seen in sixteen months. Once more there was too little ice to sledge on and too little water to sail in. Soon, regardless of their position, they would have to take to the boats. There was no more use for the remaining dogs; they were shot on 30 March and eaten in a gloomy feast. Wild led the awful work. He remarked there were a great many men he would rather shoot before any of the dogs.

Sailing back west against the prevailing winds would be slow and dangerous. But there was little land left to the north, just two remote outposts of the South Shetlands: Clarence Island and Elephant Island, and they were a hundred miles away across open ocean. They had two sextants, and a chronometer they did not trust. There was no useful information about currents to help them assess their longitude, but they were always borne east of north: away from all known refuges.

By 9 April the ice floe was little bigger than their camp, and was crumbling under their feet, yet the surrounding ice closed up, denying them any water to launch into. Their floe cracked in two, then cracked again. At 1pm they entered the boats. They began the first leg of a journey which de Gerlache had contemplated, when trapped in winter ice, and concluded there would be no more than a 1 in 100 chance of success.

The first night they camped on a new floe, cooking up the pemmican in a stew they called hoosh. They were now eating the dog pemmican. The lack of carbohydrate in it soon gave them diarrhoea. At 11pm Shackleton felt what he described as an 'intangible feeling of uneasiness' and he left his tent to prowl. Their floe was lifted by a large swell and cracked beneath his feet and right through the sailors' tent. Seaman Holness was in the water in his sleeping bag. Shackleton took hold of the bag and single-handedly hauled him from the water. A few seconds later the two halves of the floe, many hundreds of tons of ice, came back together in a terrible thud. The next night they retreated into the pack for shelter and camped on a floe which was eroding rapidly, but in the morning they could not leave it because the surrounding ice had pressed too close to allow launching the boats. Shackleton swore there would be no more floe camps, and the next night only Green the cook was put ashore while the rest rowed all night to keep station. The next day was sunny and clear, and Worsley could take an accurate sextant sighting. They absorbed the shocking news; the current had taken them ten miles backwards and thirty miles east. The wind moved to the north-west making it impossible to head for the South Shetlands, so they ran instead for Hope Bay on the tip of

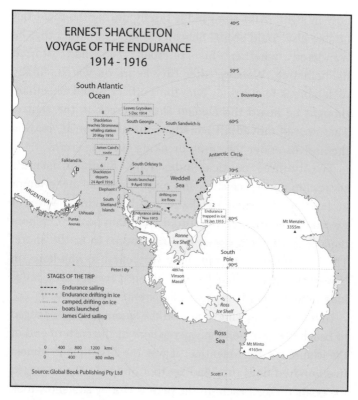

ERNEST SHACKLETON
VOYAGE OF THE ENDURANCE
1914 - 1916

South Atlantic
Ocean

Bouvetøya

1
Leaves Grytviken
5 Dec 1914

8
Shackleton
reaches Stromness
whaling station
20 May 1916

South Georgia

South Sandwich Is

James Caird's
route
7

Antarctic Circle

Falkland Is.

6
Shackleton
departs
24 April 1916

South Orkney Is

5
boats launched
9 April 1916

Weddell
Sea

Elephant I

drifting on
ice floes

ARGENTINA

South
Shetland
Islands

Ushuaia

Endurance sinks
21 Nov 1915

2
Endurance
trapped in ice
19 Jan 1915

Mt Menzies
3355m

Punta
Arenas

Ronne
Ice Shelf

South
Pole
90°S

Peter I Øy

4897m
Vinson
Massif

STAGES OF THE TRIP

- - - - -  Endurance sailing
o o o o o  Endurance drifting in ice
- · - · -  camped, drifting on ice
· · · · · ·  boats launched
· · · · · ·  James Caird sailing

Ross
Ice Shelf

Ross
Sea

Mt Minto
4165m

0    400    800   1200  kms
0        400        800  miles

Source: Global Book Publishing Pty Ltd

Scott I

40°S

50°S

60°S

70°S

80°S

the Peninsula, and the Nordenskjöld three's old camp. On
the following night, 12 April, the wind changed again and
they turned around and set course for their last chance of
land: Elephant Island. The three boats were tied in a line.
All this time Shackleton stood up, to be seen by the
exhausted men to be caring for the cockleshell flotilla every
hour of the day and night. Hurley lost his mittens and
although Shackleton was in the most exposed condition, he
offered his own mittens. When the Australian refused,
Shackleton said he would throw them overboard if he did
not accept. The high exposed mass of Elephant Island was

343

now in sight. Wild glimpsed it briefly during the night but no one else could see it. Shackleton later admitted that he wondered whether his number two had started hallucinating. Worsley, after fifty hours on watch, finally took a break to sleep. At 5am third officer Alfred Cheetham thought he heard the *Dudley Docker* crack in the centre. The men all moved aft to reduce the strain on it, putting themselves under the spray breaking over the stern.

Twenty-three nautical miles long, Elephant Island's shores are mostly ice-cliffs and rocks that repel any attempt at landing. Freezing katabatic winds rip down without warning from the frost-fractured mountain peaks. Offshore reefs snag icebergs which foul the course in to the shore. The large ones may stay there for years; it was here, in November 2007, that I sailed along a twenty-nine miles long tabular berg lying against Clarence Island.

In the dark they almost missed the landing. They managed to beach the boats and stagger ashore at the eastern end of the island at Cape Valentine. It was the first time in almost five hundred days they had set foot on land. They dragged the boats up the beach. In the photos Hurley somehow took amid all this, one man can be seen, sitting apart on the beach. It is the stowaway Perce Blackborrow, whose feet and fingers were so frostbitten he could not assist. Shackleton's bare hands suffered a badly frost-bitten finger. Some men stood shaking helplessly. Many knelt at the edge of the stream running down the beach and guzzled water. Others let the stones of the beach trickle through their fingers like pirates scooping treasure from a chest. The surgeon Macklin said Shackleton 'looked gaunt and haggard.' Another said he looked aged and bowed down. Macklin thought only Frank Wild looked something like himself. He did not, like

Shackleton, feel himself morally responsible for the well-being of twenty-seven men. He sent the two climbers Orde-Lees and Wordie to scale the land behind. They reported no way up for men in their condition. Shackleton saw the vulnerability of the site to storm and rock-fall and immediately began planning to leave. Next day Wild reconnoitred the coast and found a spit seven miles off that looked more promising. It is now Point Wild. The glacier that provided them with fresh water has retreated, exposing the shingle to erosion. It now looks less inviting than Cape Valentine, and I visited it for ten years before I found conditions safe enough to land. But there were penguins and many other nesting birds, as well as seals.

Two boats were upended side by side and made into accommodation. The *James Caird*, Shackleton announced, shouting above the gale that had accompanied them to Cape Wild, would sail with himself and five others north and east to South Georgia to get help. On that course the currents and winds would assist them; they would not if they headed north and west to South America. The whalers would help them return to pick up the other twenty-two. Standing on the narrow strip of shingle with an ice-choked sea for a back-drop, he asked for volunteers to get back into a small boat on their third day on land in six months, and sail off to their likely deaths. There were some volunteers, but his selection epitomises the soundness of Shackleton's man-management. He did not take the six bravest and best. He took Worsley for his navigating skills and uncanny instinct when working blind. He left Wild to be a firm fair hand in charge of the camp. He left both surgeons because it was likely Blackborrow would require his toes amputated to quell incipient gangrene. One would act as anaesthetist for the other's surgery. He was not expected to survive, nor was the first engineer Louis Rickinson who had suffered a heart attack. He took Crean because he needed someone he trusted absolutely, and another Irishman, seaman Timothy McCarthy, who was not only strong and resolute; Worsley thought him the most irrepressible optimist he had ever met. The other two are fascinating choices. He took McNeish for his carpentry skills and to keep the dissident away from a camp where there would be much idle time. Finally he took the demoted bosun John Vincent, another man much happier when active. McNeish now had to improvise a deck in a land without trees. He dismantled additions he had made to the *Dudley Docker*, and cannibalised a sledge and some packing cases, creating a frame over which canvas could be stretched. The canvas was frozen so hard Cheetham and McCarthy had to work the needle with pliers. McNeish completed the work in three working days, sitting out one day of blizzards. The twenty-two-foot boat set sail just after midday on 24 April heading her blunt nose at twenty-two-foot miles of the worst ocean in the world. An albatross picked them out and kept them company. If successful, they expected to be able to return within two weeks. Orde-Lees argued without success that the shore party should kill all the game available in case they were there for the long haul. Wild ridiculed him, though Orde-Lees knew Speirs Bruce had seen a great reduction in South Orkneys' penguins during the winter. Orde-Lees was their Cassandra, his advice and predictions often true, but usually ignored. He also said the pack could delay relief, and the day after the *James Caird* sailed, it closed up the shore and stayed put.

For the men left behind on the shore, the longest walk ended one hundred yards from camp; they were trapped on the beach by mountains steep as cliffs and a glacier to the west, their only view was out to the sea that had nearly killed them, but was now their only hope.

Out in the *James Caird*, the reindeer sleeping bags were moulting and the Irish were keeping their spirits up.

Shackleton: 'Go to sleep Crean and don't be clucking like an old hen.'

Crean: 'Boss, I can't eat those reindeer hairs. I'll have an inside on me like a billy-goat's neck. Let's give 'em to the Skipper and McCarthy. They never know what they're eating.'

The *James Caird* sailed poorly, it was around 25% over-ballasted because Shackleton had overruled Worsley, despite knowing less about boat sailing. They made forty-five miles on the first day as a Force 9 gale blew up creating twenty-foot waves and making all but McCarthy and Worsley seasick. The tiller-men were soaked by breaking waves, the sleeping men were doused by leaks through the canvas decking. When off-duty, three men slept in a space seven feet by five. Worsley sometimes started awake with a dream he had been buried alive. On 26 April Worsley got his first navigational fix. He had both sextants and the chronometer, but he thought the timepiece was not running true. On 29 April he got another fix and they made ninety-two miles, but the next day a confused sea forced them to hove to on a sea-anchor. The leaky deck was cured by colder weather which made the spray freeze on impact; they took turns to chop it off. Whenever anyone began shivering Shackleton ordered hot drinks for all, never singling out anyone as weaker. On 2 May the sea anchor

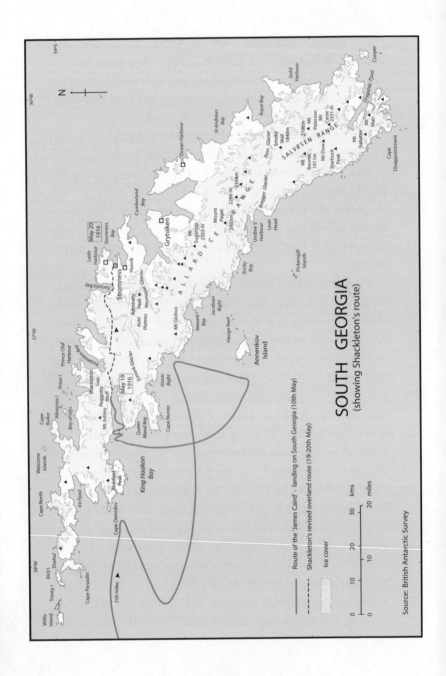

# SOUTH GEORGIA

(showing Shackleton's route)

Route of the 'James Caird' - landing on South Georgia (10th May)

Shackleton's revised overland route (19-20th May)

Ice cover

Source: British Antarctic Survey

kms

miles

parted; a lump of ice had chafed through the painter. The third of May was fine enough to dry out their gear. Worsley got sightings this day and the next, which was very pleasant sailing. Spirits rose; they were two thirds of the way there. The good mood was dampened the next day. Firstly they had finished the first cask of water, and when they opened the second, they found it had leaked and was tainted with saltwater. From now on they were reduced to a quarter-pint of foul water each day. Then Shackleton thought the sky was clearing and remarked on it. Then he shouted 'For God's sake, hold on! It's got us!' as in panic he realised the light was the surf on top of a wave bigger than any he had ever seen in all his life at sea. They were swamped and only after ten minutes bailing did they start to believe they would survive.

One man did not care. A few days into the voyage, John Vincent, who began the expedition as the most physically powerful man of all, had collapsed mentally, becoming a passenger and patient. On the tiller, he did not register the wind shifting north and hitting them almost sideways on, so they were forced to stop sailing and hove to, shipping water. Two days' cloud reduced Worsley to calculating by dead reckoning that they were 115 miles from South Georgia. South Georgia is only one hundred miles long; staying on course was vital. The price of missing it and drifting too far north was discussed secretly by Worsley and Shackleton. The skipper recalled the verdict. Soon 'our water would be finished ... Our food would have lasted a fortnight, but that didn't alter the problem if we had no water, so we dropped the discussion as it was futile.' They had set their course for the Willis Islands at the west end of South Georgia, intending to then slip round to the north-east coast where the whaling stations lay in the sheltered fjords. On 7 May Worsley made sextant sightings guided only by shooting the brightest part of the fog obscuring the sun's disc. He admitted to Shackleton that he could not be sure of his position to better than ten miles. Shackleton re-set the course to ensure they would make landfall at some part of the south-west coast. This made their target bigger but less convenient; there was no habitation anywhere on that coast. At dusk they saw kelp and dreamed of land and fresh water. At eight the next morning a South Georgia shag appeared. Worsley knew they never flew more than fifteen miles from land. It was also the fifteenth day at sea: 8 May. At 12:30 McCarthy called out the single word: 'Land!' After a brief glimpse, the black crag sank back into the murk, a strange emblem of salvation.

Worsley found his latitude was accurate to within two miles, which would be excellent for readings taken from the stable bridge of a large ship, but was plain miraculous in their circumstances. However his longitude, calculated from the faulty chronometer, was twenty miles out. They lay off a large natural harbour called King Haakon Bay. The entrance is guarded by reefs. Even today, only a single safe route in is known to the small cruise ships that on rare occasions visit this site to pay homage to Shackleton's landfall. The only ship, the *Polar Star*, to deviate from the line, to avoid an iceberg, holed itself on a rock. Parched, cold and wet as they were, Shackleton ordered them to stand off for the night. The reward for such brave caution came at 6pm. The wind came at Storm Force out of the WNW, harder than anything they had suffered on the voyage. They bailed all night; even Vincent roused himself to help with the drudgery. Dawn showed them what the night's sound and fury had only hinted at. They were trapped in a triangle of sea between South Georgia and the off-lying Annekov Island. The sea and air united in an unholy marriage, the wind scourging through the waves making the air so heavy with spray a man could drown in it, and the wind so laden with hard drops of ocean it was like raising your face to a sandstorm of small, cruel stones. Down-wind, where the Force 10 gales were blowing them, the uncharted coast of central South Georgia was a wall of surf. The *James Caird* was strained to her limits as Worsley dared to add reefed sails to the main and mizzen mast to help her claw her way off the shore. The planks had been chafed thin by prolonged sailing in ice back on the Peninsula. She hit the waves so hard the planks in the bow flexed open with the shock and shot spurts of water into the boat. When the storm dropped, the wind shifted to the north-west and they could make no progress to rounding the west end of the island and continuing to a whaling station. As they relaxed and changed shift, Crean caught his shoulder and heard a small tinkle. It was the pin which held the foot of the mast in place. Had it come out during the storm the mast would have snapped and dragged them into the sea.

While Shackleton was asleep, Worsley, obsessed with finding an outpost of civilisation, steered for Willis Island. He had taken no account of the fact that they had no water and Vincent and McNeish were barely alive. When Shackleton woke he ordered him to make for King Haakon Bay. They found a cove. It was 10 May, the seventeenth day out. A small stream ran down the beach and they fell to their knees and drank in new life. Next morning they were still too weak to haul the boat clear. They had to dismantle McNeish's additions to drag her up the beach. At

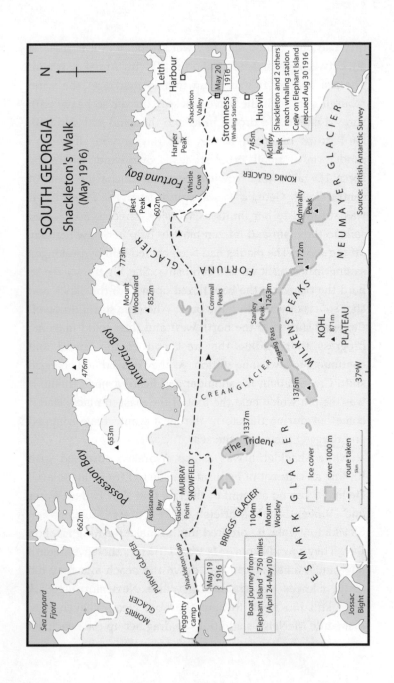

SOUTH GEORGIA
Shackleton's Walk
(May 1916)

Leith Harbour

May 20 1916

Shackleton Valley

Harper Peak

Stromness (Whaling Station)

Husvik

745m

McIlroy Peak

Shackleton and 2 others reach whaling station. Crew on Elephant Island rescued Aug 30 1916

KONIG GLACIER

Fortuna Bay

Whistle Cove

Best Peak

602m

FORTUNA GLACIER

Admiralty Peak

NEUMAYER GLACIER

773m

Mount Woodward

852m

Cornwall Peaks

1172m

WILKENS PEAKS

Stanley Peak

1263m

Zigzag Pass

KOHL PLATEAU

871m

Antarctic Bay

476m

653m

CREAN GLACIER

1375m

37°W

Possession Bay

662m

Assistance Bay

MURRAY SNOWFIELD

Glacier Point

The Trident

1337m

Ice cover

over 1000 m

route taken

5km

PURVIS GLACIER

MORRIS GLACIER

Shackleton Gap

May 19 1916

BRIGGS GLACIER

1104m

Mount Worsley

ESMARK GLACIER

Jossac Bight

Sea Leopard Fjord

Peggotty camp

Boat journey from Elephant Island – 750 miles (April 24–May10)

N

Source: British Antarctic Survey

some point, her rudder had fallen off. She was now too strained to sail round to the north-east coast. So were Vincent and McNeish. Help had to come from the land. The coast of South Georgia was sketchily surveyed; the interior was unknown. They must cross it or die where they were.

They fed on albatross chicks, as big and fat as turkeys, fattened up for the coming winter. Worsley said the first time he killed one he felt like a murderer; after that all he could think of was how good it had tasted. On the third night their rest and recuperation was interrupted in the middle of the night by Shackleton calling out 'Look out, boys, look out! Hold on!' He was pointing at the cliff opposite, black capped with snow, and hallucinating the re-appearance of that one giant wave that had brought them to the brink of destruction. To bring back his optimism, the boat's rudder bobbed ashore. With all the Atlantic to sail over, the rudder came back to the Boss's feet. On 15 May they sailed to the head of the fjord where they had seen a saddle above that offered access to the interior.

They dragged the *James Caird* out of the water and turned her upside down. She was now Peggotty Camp, after that character's boat-house in Charles Dickens's *David Copperfield*. By them on the beach was a pile of timber, all from ships wrecked on the coast or out to sea. This is what happened if you weren't successful. Ever on the lookout for easy money, Shackleton mused to Worsley: 'Some day, Skipper, you and I will come and dig here for old treasure or perhaps sleep quietly with all the other old seamen.' They waited for a moonlit night. McCarthy was judged too weak for major exertion. If they were to cross the island it would be Tom Crean, the Boss and the Skipper who must do it, and do it quickly. Good weather was short-lived, and in bad weather in South Georgia, people were short-lived. At three on the morning of 19 May a bright moon guided them up. From the breaking of the *Endurance* to here had been a journey of fifteen hundred miles. Husvik whaling station and safety for some, if not all, of the party was twenty miles away. They carried a stove and three days' food, but no sleeping bags or tent. The ground was too broken for a sled. McNeish had taken brass screws from the boat and put them in their boot soles to give grip. Only two of them had the best cold-weather boots, Shackleton had given his to one of the men left behind. His adze was their ice-pick. Their one frayed rope was just fifty feet long.

Their weakness, even when starting, may be measured by the fact that they estimated most of the altitudes along the way at two to three times their actual height. When they reached the saddle now known as the Shackleton Gap they were the first people to set eyes on the island's interior. They saw their task spelled out: saw-toothed ridges, cloud-covered pinnacles, near-vertical cliffs, and steep glaciers tumbling in confusion beneath. Snow smothered everything, and they now walked onto a glacier. No one spoke of the condition of the rope holding them together. They saw a smooth even surface below and altered course towards it, looking for easier walking on what must be a frozen lake. Dawn showed them it was the ocean: Cook's Possession Bay, accurately shown on their charts. They re-traced hard-won steps. Their true route took them towards five peaks lying right across their path. They headed to the southernmost of the four passes. Soft snow gave to their knees every step. At nine they ate hot food and before noon they took the last steps that showed them they had laboured, breathless, to a cliff top fifteen hundred feet high, and impossible to descend. Trying to maintain their altitude, they traversed round to the next col and found another version of the same scene. The third pass showed them snow lying over ice. Worsley wanted to try it. Shackleton thought it too risky. It was late in the day and a cold fog was rising from the lower land. When they reached the final pass it was dusk. The fog obscured their footsteps. They began descending but agonisingly slowly. They risked dying from cold and caution. They could slide down but their landing was lost in the mist; it might be another precipice. Crean had been in a similar position once before, on the other side of Antarctica. Short of time and supplies, and faced with a three-day detour or tobogganing an ice-fall, they had taken the risk and lived. Shackleton said, 'It's a devil of a risk, but we've got to take it.' They coiled the ragged rope and sat down, the Boss in the dangerous front seat. Worsley again; 'We seemed to shoot into space. For a moment my hair fairly stood on end. The quite suddenly I was grinning! I was actually enjoying it ... I yelled with excitement, and found that Shackleton and Crean were yelling too.' They slowed and stopped in a bank of snow, standing up in disbelief that they were still in one piece. Shackleton's cautious side re-asserted itself: 'It's not good to do that kind of thing too often,' but 'the risk was justified this time.' They had descended fifteen hundred feet and much reduced the risk of exposure except on Shackleton's and Worsley's legs, as the ride had ripped their trousers. At 6pm they ate. Fifteen hours had taken them half-way. Though the moon had not yet risen they anxiously began walking into the darkness. The temperature sank, freezing the surface and improving the walking. They rested briefly each fifteen minutes and ate at four-hour intervals through the night. They found themselves descending and were convinced they were above Stromness. Then they saw they were on a glacier and remembered there was no glacier at Stromness. They were on the Fortuna Glacier, one bay to the west. Back up they climbed: Worsley suffered a 'hopeless feeling'. One blessing was the weather continued kind.

I cannot know what it was like to make that walk. They began after nine days' rest, following that terrible boat journey. The kind of rest you get on a poor diet, sleeping in old clothes under an upturned boat as winter closes its fist. The lives of twenty-five men depended on those three. In Shackleton's mind, they depended on him, and his mental moral contract to bring them all home. Without knowing it, they were severely dehydrated, weakening the body, befuddling the mind. I have walked for several days in a row, over thirty miles a day, at very high altitude on a poor diet. At the border of exhaustion is a place where the raw physical pain of each moment mingles with distracted thoughts which chatter away in the back of your mind. It is kinder to listen to the mindless chatter, than acknowledge the pain and exhaustion. They passed through that place to somewhere I never want to go, where thoughts impose themselves on your senses.

Worsley's account has no affectation, he says what he saw: 'Each step of that journey comes back clearly, and even now I find myself counting our party – Shackleton, Crean and I and – who was the other? Of course we were only three, but it is strange that in mentally reviewing the crossing we should always think of a fourth, and then correct ourselves.'

Shackleton needed to make it mean something, though he was dismissive of conventional religion. One of the attractions of the polar wastes to him was to experience thoughts and feelings beyond the everyday senses. He might have been interested in Edmund Burke's writing on the sublime: 'When we go but one step beyond the immediate sensible quality of things, we go out of our depth', or as Captain Ahab says to Starbuck in *Moby Dick*: 'All visible objects, man, are but as pasteboard masks.' Shackleton's take was: 'I know that during that long march of thirty-six hours over the unnamed mountains and glaciers of Georgia it often seemed to me that we were four, not three. And Worsley and Crean had the same idea. One feels "the dearth of human words, the roughness of mortal speech," in trying to describe intangible things.'

I have three times walked the final section from Fortuna Bay. It is not demanding if you are fit, rested and well-clothed. They were deficient in all of these: moreover their clothes were held together with safety pins, and their bodies were unwashed in three months. At five in the morning Shackleton broke twenty-two hours without sleep and let them doze. He himself stayed awake, fearing they might sleep so long the cold would take them. After five minutes, he told them they had slept half an hour, and they tramped on. The moon paled. Dawn soon came. It showed them a sea-cliff a few miles ahead in which the rock strata were bent into a huge Z-shape. It was the headland off Stromness. At 06:30, as breakfast was being prepared, Shackleton thought he heard a whistle. Worsley took his chronometer from under his ragged clothes where he was keeping it warm. He knew two whistles sounded at the whaling stations each morning, half an hour apart. The first called them to breakfast, the second to work. At seven they all heard it and Shackleton realised, 'It was the first sound

357

made by outside human agency that had come to our ears since we left in 1914.' They abandoned the empty Primus and began to descend below the major glacier of Fortuna Bay. They saw two signs of man's presence: a seal shot with bullets, and hoof prints in the sand and mud of the glacial outwash. The beach is still trodden by reindeer introduced for food by the Norwegian whalers. Because they live in the southern hemisphere and grow their antlers for the summer breeding season, they are the only reindeer in the world which have antlers at Christmas.

Their luck with the weather still held. Tom Crean found the tarn that bears his name by falling through its ice. Shackleton chose the most direct route: Stromness. Soon they stood by a small outcrop of fine-grained rock shattered by frost into paper-thin sheets. A glaciated valley ran fifteen hundred feet beneath, hidden as it went inland to the left. An open vista showed the route to the right where half of Stromness whaling station is visible beyond the shoulder of the hill, less than two miles away. Against advice, Shackleton insisted on walking down the line of a small stream despite the fact that its line further down was hidden by a fall in slope. The easy route to the right is longer but much faster. They came to a low waterfall and were forced to climb down on the worn rope while icy water cascaded over them. At the foot they picked up the objects they had thrown down before them: the adze and the log. They had sailed into Antarctica with a fully equipped ship. At four in the afternoon on 20 May they walked back into civilisation's meanest outpost, a sub-Antarctic whaling station with the clothes they stood up in and those two items. And one more: a saucepan. They were so tired they all forgot that they had jettisoned the stove.

The different accounts of what happened when three strangers walked off the mountain into a busy factory reflect the exhaustion of the walkers and the stunned disbelief of the whalers, who thought the *Endurance* men long dead. The first two boys who saw them ran away. Shackleton found the foreman who took them to the officer of the manager, a man Shackleton knew. 'Is Mr Sørlle in?' Sørlle had sailed with Larsen to the Weddell Sea in 1892 and had predicted the *Endurance* would never leave the ice.

The foreman told them to wait outside while he asked. 'There are three funny-looking men outside, who say they have come over the island and they know you. I have left them outside.'

The conversation that ensued must have been strange. Men who have undergone stressful isolation tend to be far less lucid and normal than they imagine when they first contact outsiders.

Mr Sørlle came out and said, 'Well?'

'Don't you know me?' said Shackleton.

'I know your voice.'

'My name is Shackleton.'

Sørlle put his hand out. 'Come in. Come in.' Some accounts say he cried.

Shackleton asked, 'Tell me, when was the war over?'

'The war is not over. Millions are being killed. Europe is mad. The world is mad.' No one had a camera with film handy. There are pictures of them later, bathed and shaved. The expression on Shackleton's face is not exultation, or even relief. It is simple suffering, a deep, dark inscription. They lay down in clean sheets on comfortable beds and were so unaccustomed to comfort they slept poorly. In the morning they looked up at the mountains. The night had brought a snowstorm which would have killed anyone on the open mountain. On the other side of the mountain there were still three men, two of them half-dead, and who knew how many still alive on Elephant Island. Worsley went the same evening on the *Samson* to guide the whaler to Peggotty Camp, where McCarthy complained that no expedition member had returned with the rescue ship. After two years in his constant company, they did not recognise their clean and shaven captain. The whalers insisted on picking up a fourth hero: the *James Caird*.

By Tuesday 23 May, Shackleton was already on the whaler *Southern Sky* wondering what he would find on Elephant Island's lonely shore. It took him four voyages to get there. What had seemed like the easy last leg was frustrated by another year of dense pack-ice and then, when he was forced to go to South America to launch the third and fourth bids, unsuitable vessels and the wartime shortage and expensive of coal. Uruguay and Chile were both hugely generous with ships and coal, and it was in a converted tug, working as a lighthouse supply vessel, the *Yelcho*, that an obscure pilot named Luis Pardo brought Shackleton to the savage coast of Point Wild. Or rather Worsley and Shackleton did: Pardo was quite happy to take a back seat. With his usual uncanny skill, Worsley had brought them through ice-clear waters to the north shore of the island when fog closed. Shackleton took them in blind, very slowly. A fourth failure was not countenanced. It was no longer May, when he had promised to return, or even June or July. As they found their way to the jagged stack which lies off the beach, it was the next to last day of August. It was over three months since they had left Wild in charge of a camp mostly comprising invalids, with a heart-attack victim and a case of gangrene.

Marston and Hurley were collecting limpets when an odd ship came into view and sailed past; Worsley had not recognised Point Wild coming at it from the west for the first time. The tough, irrepressible Hurley believed 'by this time we could not have held out for more than a few days.' They tried to halt the vessel by raising a shirt on a pole, but it jammed half way. Then they lit a dirty fire with the last paraffin can. It exploded producing little smoke. In the famous Hurley picture of a smoky fire on the flank of the rocks, the black pall was added in the developing room. But the strange little ship with the Chilean Navy ensign turned around and a boat was lowered. A thick-set man stood in the bow. The camp commander Wild stared to see who it was. Shackleton had seen the shirt at half-mast and assumed it signalled that some had died.

Wild had attracted unstinting praise for his leadership ashore from the prickliest of judges, Orde-Lees. When Wild saw it was Shackleton, he let his larrikin tough-boy image slip: 'I felt jolly near blubbing for a bit and could not speak for several minutes.' Someone on shore cried out: 'Thank God, the Boss is safe.' 'Are you well?' called Shackleton. 'All safe, all well.' 'Thank God.'

Each day Wild had made the men stow and lash their gear ready for departure: for 126 days. Now they were able to board and go in forty-five minutes. The surf was rough and Shackleton did not even walk up the beach to see the camp. Two hours earlier, said Wild, the ice would have blocked them landing. As they left the wind shifted and it again began to drive against the shore. The men began to read the newspapers Shackleton had brought to prepare

361

them for the state of the world. Three million were dead. Orde-Lees noted casualty lists had been renamed Rolls of Honour.

Shackleton went to the Ross Sea and found that his other party had laboured under huge difficulties to lay depots that would never be used, three men dying in the task.

Neither Shackleton nor the world could understand each other for a long time. He could not absorb that the grotesque war had changed how people thought and felt. His saving himself and twenty-seven men was not a triumph; their playlet was an insulting irrelevance to the men laying down their lives in the mud and to the women and children who had lost their husbands and fathers. Many of Shackleton's men signed up immediately and one was killed within the month. Others died before the Armistice. He dedicated his book of the expedition 'To my comrades who fell in the white warfare of the south and on the red fields of France and Flanders.' He knew the two were equal in courage and endeavour.

The Naval establishment implacably opposed his efforts to serve a meaningful wartime role; Scott was their man. The Boss did force recognition of his men's service with the award of the Polar Medal to most members of the expedition. Those who had not lived up to his standards were snubbed, including John Vincent, the demoted bosun, and most controversially, the dour Dundee carpenter McNeish whose brilliantly adapted boat saved all their lives. One moment's challenge to the whole order of discipline would not be forgiven.

Shackleton suffered his own kind of social exile. He had become a poor resident of the non-polar life, and the post-war world. He launched one last ill-focused expedition in

1921. He whistled and most of the old crew came from all corners of the world. As they left Plymouth Harbour with the harbourmaster on board, Shackleton heard a bell-buoy toll and said to him, 'That's my death-knell.' Despite suffering a severe heart attack in Buenos Aires on the way down, he sailed on to South Georgia entering the harbour of Grytviken in improving mood. Grytviken Bay has a desolate beauty to the old whaling station and the small, rusting seal and whale-catching ships add poignant memory. That evening he wrote, 'In the darkening twilight I saw a lone star hover, gem-like above the bay.'

In the early hours of the next morning the surgeon, Macklin once again, was called to his cabin. Shackleton had suffered another heart attack. He was trying to be humorously philosophical about it: 'You're always wanting me to give up things, what is it I ought to give up?'

Macklin replied, 'Chiefly alcohol, Boss, I don't think it agrees with you.'

In a few minutes the great heart died. The men sent his body back home, but when the ship was at Montevideo they received a telegram from his wife, the sufferer of long-time infidelity from her husband. She told them to take his remains back south where he had been truly happy. As you enter Grytviken harbour, the promontory on the right at King Edward Point has a small cross where his men built a cairn and held their own ceremony while the Boss's body was making its way north. The first feature on the left shore is the cemetery, bounded by a low wooden fence painted white. It keeps out the fur seals and elephant seals that loll among the tussock and rough grass below.

Above the grave stands a roughly cut block of granite, taller than a man. On the reverse is written the words from

Browning with which the youthful Shackleton, the obstinate boy, had declared his ambition to his fiancée:

> I hold that a man should strive to his uttermost for his life's set prize.

There he lies among the old sailors, just as he had daydreamed when inspecting the timbers of the ships which had found their way to the head of King Haakon Bay. All the graves in the cemetery face east towards the dawn and the resurrection. For nearly ninety years he alone faced South. In 2011, Frank Wild's ashes, long lost in a crematorium storage facility, were found and returned to lie alongside his great friend.

# 13

## Living in Antarctica: The Bases

*The first generation of explorers brought little, the second brought flat-pack huts. It takes a special person to endure overwintering. Sometimes the selectors get it wrong, badly wrong.*

Before tourism, most visitors to Antarctica were scientists, and the bases where they lived and worked were typically small, with scientists trained to look after themselves as much as possible, to minimise support staff. Early expeditions had taken scientists with them, but essentially they were ship-based, and even if temporary structures were erected ashore, the scientists left when everyone else did. That began to change at the beginning of the twentieth century, and de Gerlache's *Belgica* Expedition of 1897–99 was a turning point. The leaders had taken with them working huts for observing and measuring but no shore accommodation. However they were prepared to overwinter in the ship, and weren't unduly disappointed when the *Belgica* became trapped in the ice. She became the base for the winter and the next spring and summer.

Nordenskjöld's 1901–03 expedition took it a step further, their huts included sleeping quarters and the scientists were intended to be dropped off in the summer and picked up after one winter. The contemporaneous Bruce expedition planned to push south, retreat to the edge of the Antarctic for the winter, and set up a base. He always wanted the base to continue in use, by someone else if not him, and their hut was surrounded by stone walls and named Omond House. Argentina were keen to take it over, and this was the beginning of planned continuity, of having a base to which men would return year after year.

For a long time this was an all-male society. Despite women being physiologically better adapted to withstand exposure, traditional views of gender in universities and institutions were slow to change. Wives accompanied husbands long before anyone employed them in their own right. It is usually said that the first women in Antarctica were the Americans Jenni Darlington and Edith, known as Jackie, Ronne, in 1946, who accompanied their husbands on the expedition of 1946 – 48 led by Finn Ronne which overwintered on Stonington Island, Marguerite Bay. The Filchner-Ronne Ice Shelf and Edith Ronne Land are bequests of this trip. But in the 1930s, the wives of two whaling captains, Caroline Mikkelsen and Ingrid Christensen, accompanied their husbands and had a mountain and a length of coast named after them. Sadly[7] the first woman here was probably a sex worker, the Native woman whose bones were found in a sealer's hut on Desolation Island. Australia began employing women in 1976, when a female doctor overwintered at Macquarie Island, and Britain soon followed. Wendy Pyper of the Australian Antarctic Division kindly provided me the following statement about their staffing. 'Although the Australian Antarctic Division makes a conscious effort to encourage more women to apply for jobs in Antarctica, the ratio of wintering men to women remains at about eight to one and the profile of an average Australian expeditioner is still male, white and aged between 29 and 32. Many occupations, particularly the trade and technical positions, are fields traditionally dominated by men in the Australian community, and so it seems likely that the participation rate of women, particularly in wintering groups, will not increase dramatically unless the jobs change and women can take their children.'

Antarctic visitors soon realise how few places there are to go safely ashore; the wildlife worked this out a long time ago. Most bases are in or next to penguin colonies because people have the same shore needs as penguins: a beach seldom pestered by ice where you can come safely ashore, get clear of the surf, and find ground free of snow and ice. They are usually on islands. This is because the snow and ice on the mainland piles up thousands of feet deep, and where it meets the sea it usually forms ice cliffs or glaciers: no use to man or penguin. Large islands can also produce enough snow and ice to create a hard high barrier to anything trying to come ashore. Small islands give you a chance. In the early days, as the John Lackland Cope fiasco demonstrated so clearly, the price small parties paid for basing themselves on small islands or ledges of land was isolation. Cliffs and glaciers may prevent you from accessing the interior, and small wooden boats are extremely vulnerable to the ice and squalls of Antarctica. Research is then limited to what is in your immediate grasp.

The most popular place to build bases has been in the South Shetland Islands, especially the largest: King George Island. Despite being big enough to support glaciers it is relatively far north and has areas of flat sheltered land, especially in King George Bay facing the Bransfield Strait, which are clear each summer. It is also close to South America and these two factors make it economical and reliable to service and support a base. By Antarctic standards the weather is mild and the seas normally open. I asked a Russian working at Bellingshausen Base on King George Island if he minded working through the winter. He replied, 'Not at all, it's usually around −25° centigrade, maybe −40° in a cold spell. My home is in Siberia, there it's −50° every winter.' It's so comfy, the workers on the Ross Sea side and at the interior bases refer to the Peninsula and South Shetlands as the Banana Belt. Bases are also close enough to share the cost of bringing down fuel and materials: no need for expensive heroics if an accident to your support ship leaves a base short of supplies. There's a high-quality air strip built and operated by Chile but available to other countries. If you have an accident or illness that requires an emergency evacuation during an Antarctic Peninsula visit, the chances are you will be flown out of King George Island.

I shall cover only those bases which are commonly visited and have historic importance. Deception Base has its own section in the chapter on that island, so I'll begin with the most visited place in Antarctica; in 2007–08 it received over 17,500 visitors.

# PORT LOCKROY

On the west side of Wiencke Island lies a small bay called Port Lockroy, discovered by Charcot's first expedition and named after Édoard Lockroy, Vice-President of the French Chamber of Deputies, who had helped Charcot obtain Government backing. Its southern shore forms a low rocky tongue beneath a skirt of mountains rising to the 4735 feet (1435 metres) of the Luigi Peak. This is Jougla Point and just off it lies Goudier Island, named by Charcot after his Chief Engineer. The island is no more than a small stone boss; you can walk across it in two minutes. Once planed flat by ice from the glacier at the back of the bay it is now polished by the patient feet of the gentoo penguins that nest all over it; but in 1944 men scrambled ashore to begin building Base A of Operation Tabarin.

They were not the first men to stay here; it was a popular harbour for whalers up until the industry's collapse through over-fishing in 1931. The Tabarin team landed with their own supplies and some timber salvaged from the whalers' factory at Deception Island. They built Bransfield House, named for the British naval captain who accompanied William Smith back to the South Shetlands. Over time, the building was extended and altered, but it has now been restored to the layout and furnishings it would have had around 1960: more on the restoration later.

After the war, it was used as a scientific base studying the upper atmosphere. Men came down, usually for a stay of two and a half years, learning the ropes from outgoing staff over the summer, and then completing two years, spending the last summer passing on their know-how to the incoming rookies. The great block of valves and dials which sits in the middle of the laboratory room was used for this, and inevitably nicknamed 'Beastie'. The upper atmosphere conducts electrical charges towards the poles and lightning strikes in the southern hemisphere would send signals which were picked up as 'whistlers' enabling this tiny island to monitor electrical activity over huge areas of the earth.

---

**INSIDE PORT LOCKROY BASE A**

The centre is exceptionally well interpreted and manned by knowledgeable staff, so a detailed account of the contents is unnecessary. Do make sure you see these little gems:

- [ ] photo of Prince Philip meeting Raymond Priestley, author of the much quoted 'when disaster strikes and all hope is gone, get down on your knees and pray for Shackleton'

- [ ] poster advertising the Tabarin night club, Paris on wall opposite the door to the sleeping quarters

- [ ] the bath-house on the left as you enter, with rules for collecting water and bathing

- [ ] the sunshine recorder in the laboratory

- [ ] the British Crown Property sign in the Post Office and shop

- [ ] the period foodstuffs in the kitchen

In a small wooden box, on the right hand side as you enter this room, is a piece of meteorological equipment which is elegant in its simplicity. It is a sphere of glass which fits into a light steel cradle. To one side are curved pieces of thin card printed with a grid. This measures hours of sunlight. The crystal ball is placed in a north-facing window (in the southern hemisphere) and each morning a fresh piece of card is fitted beneath it. The ball acts as a lens and whenever the sun shines it burns a line in the paper. At the end of the day the hours of sunshine can be read off against the grid. It has no moving parts and needs about twenty seconds of attention a day.

## THE UNITED KINGDOM ANTARCTIC HERITAGE TRUST

Governments don't usually spend money preserving artefacts and buildings which only their better-off taxpayers have any chance of seeing. The rescue of Port Lockroy is down to a dedicated group of volunteers including former base staff. They formed a charitable trust and rebuilt the base as it was around 1960. The shop and Post Office pay for its operation and maintenance, and enough money is being made to contemplate other projects. Work has begun on the Wordie Hut at Vernadsky Base, and plans are being prepared to restore Detaille Base, and Damoy Refuge hut just north of Port Lockroy. They also have care of Stonington (Tabarin Base E) at 68°11´S in Marguerite Bay, once run by Sir Vivian Fuchs, and nearby Horseshoe (Base Y).

The highest part of the island is roped off from visitors to allow the Base Commander, currently Rick Atkinson, and his team of three, to compare the breeding success of penguins in the undisturbed area with that around the base where people have free access close to the nests. The results mirror those obtained in similar studies elsewhere in Antarctica. The birds in the visited area do as well or slightly better than those in the protected area. This probably reflects two things. Firstly birds become accustomed to the presence of people, in part because their only land predators are other birds, so bulky mammals are not seen as a threat. Secondly humans deter those predators, especially skuas, which in the penguin breeding season feed heavily on eggs and chicks. Of course skuas deserve the same freedom from human interference as penguins, so this is not a neutral outcome. Taking the Peninsula and its islands as a whole, human impact on the predators is very small, and may well be balanced by personnel at other bases bending the rules a little and feeding skuas. These intelligent, curious and fearless birds provide a little animal comfort to people who see only the same human faces for months at a time.

Mail is taken, mostly by cruise ships, to Stanley in the Falkland Islands where it joins Britain's regular postal network. There are many ways of marking nationality and saying, 'This is ours.' For the British, it's having a local Post Office. One Christmas Eve I picked up their last mail sacks before the holiday and ferried them back to our vessel. I felt like Santa Claus.

## FOUR-LEGGED FRIENDS: BAS SLED DOGS

Arctic peoples have used dogs as draught animals for two thousand years, but it was 1899 before Carsten Borchgrevink took the first sled dogs to Antarctica. Roald Amundsen's efficient, if ruthless, use of dogs to reach the South Pole proved they were the best means of travel until mechanical sleds improved in the 1950s. Dogs could haul three times their own weight for thirty miles a day. The best dogs were bred from the four main breeds of Arctic huskies: Samoyed and Siberian from the Russian Arctic, and Malamute and Eskimo from the Americas and Greenland. In 1945 Britain brought twenty-five Labrador dogs to Hope Bay to start a permanent breeding population. They remained an important part of both the logistical and emotional support of Antarctic work.

In August 1963 base men were amused and annoyed to receive a fax from BAS in London advising that with the increasing use of mechanical transport 'no more breeding is to take place on bases except at Halley Bay who must plan to maintain three teams indefinitely.' It seemed premature to men kept busy excavating Eliason motor toboggans from crevasses they had dug themselves into, or repairing their engines and tracks. But in 1957 – 58 Vivian Fuchs and Edmund Hillary had crossed Antarctica mostly using motor-sleds, proving the technology was now reliable.

As scientists became more mindful of dogs as alien species, their management became more cautious. Dogs had been fed partly on seals and penguins to augment the dog food brought in: a direct impact on native animals. They also defecated wherever they went, introducing new organisms and minerals. The import of new dogs was halted in the late 1970s to prevent new parasites or bugs entering the ecosystem. Dogs were bred only from resident Antarctic populations. From 1972 to 1992 BAS dogs were reduced from two hundred to thirty. There were other factors.

In 1991 a new clause was inserted in the Antarctic Treaty the international agreement which regulates activities in the continent: 'Dogs shall not be introduced onto land or ice shelves and a dogs currently in those areas shall be removed by April 1, 1994.' A particular concern was that dogs had introduced, or could introduce diseases like distemper to the seals. 'Had' is unlikely, 'could' is always possible. Perhaps the ban was too cautious, but the Antarctic ecosystem is brutally simple with few checks and balances; one epidemic could be catastrophic. It's too late to be cautious afterwards. By 1993 only two BAS teams remained: named the Huns and the Admirals. One final project was saved for them: to run across the Peninsula to Alexander Island recording the weather on each side. The teams were flown out on 22 February 1994. Most base men would have them back tomorrow, at their own expense. As Antarctic veteran Bernard Stonehouse told me, 'even the friendliest tractor is no substitute for cuddling a dog.'

For an entertaining and informative account of sledge dogs by two men who ran them, read *Of Dogs and Men* by Kevin Walton and Rick Atkinson, a regular Port Lockroy Base Commander. Full details in Acknowledgements.

Just across the Antarctic Circle is a small island rising to a snow dome. On its flank, facing a knoll of eye-catching igneous rock embedded with angular boulders, is a long wooden hut surrounded by the daily junk of Antarctic life. There are cases of tins, rusted almost through, things used and discarded, gadgets superseded and the broken utensils of everyday life. It looks as if it was abandoned in a hurry with hopes to return, never realised. The skuas which nest in the rocks above do not approve of visitors, or indeed other life forms, which they see as just a way of keeping meat fresh until they can eat it. They strafe anyone wandering into an area they think of as their territory, and their ideas of territory are expansive.

This was Base W, built in 1956, and it was large and comfortable compared with the British bases of the 1940s. Detaille was named for the director of the Magellan Whaling Company in Punta Arenas who helped Charcot in his 1908 – 10 expedition by holding stores for him at Deception Island. Workshops, laboratories, offices, a kitchen and dormitories led off a long corridor. A large radio mast stood on the hill behind; its substantial base is still visible. But it was used for only three years because it could not fulfil its planned role. It was intended as a base for dog-sledging parties, and the short documentary *Dog-Sledding in Antarctica* was filmed at Detaille Island. However, they found the sea-ice between the island and the Peninsula was an unstable and treacherous surface to walk or sledge on. Plans were made to decommission it in 1958–59, removing as much of the equipment and garbage as possible. That summer they finally got thick ice, so strong that their support vessel the *Biscoe*, supported by two US ice-breakers, could not get closer than thirty miles to the north. The good intentions of decommissioning base rather than just abandoning it were frustrated. They were forced to load only their essentials onto their sleds and sledge to the ship, leaving on 31 March 1959. They reached there without incident, but as they undid the dog traces to board, one animal called Steve broke loose and they could not catch him. The dog turned back south. They left, unable to tell him that this parting was final. Three months later staff at the British Horseshoe Base over sixty miles south saw a strange dog come bounding into camp; it was Steve.

Because of the way it was abandoned, the camp has a Marie Celeste feel to it. The attic space is full of stores, tools lie on work-benches, magazines on tables, and rusty tins of porridge moulder in the cupboards next to Stephens Navy Pickles (Piccalilli with a picture of a battleship on the label) and Pearce, Duff's lemonade powder in ten-pound tins. The sense of isolation is still strong. I travelled there with John, a man in his early seventies, who as a young graduate had carried out meteorology there. Now retired in Falmouth, in south-west England, he guided us round the rooms, and the half-century's absence had melted away. In the final room he found the blank weather report forms stacked exactly where he had left them.

ESPERANZA

The Argentine Esperanza Base occupies the pleasant, sheltered site on the mainland shore of the Antarctic Sound first seen by Nordenskjöld on his way to the Weddell Sea, and later explored by Gunnar Andersson when he was set down there to seek Nordenskjöld over land. In February 1944 sea ice thwarted the British attempt to set up Hope Bay as Operation Tabarin's Base D. They later came back and set up a station which suffered a fire on 8 November 1948. The Argentines set up five hundred metres away in 1951 and Hispanicised Hope to Esperanza. When the British returned to rebuild Hope Bay a short distance from its original site, it sparked an incident when Argentine troops shot at and expelled British scientists. No one was hurt and when the affair was reported to Buenos Aires the Argentine commander was disciplined and removed. Hope was rebuilt. When Britain rationalised its bases, Hope Bay was transferred to Uruguay on 8 December 1997.

The site's special attraction to science is Mount Flora, first studied by Andersson and his team, and found to be rich in fossils, including ones from warm climates which would later be used as evidence for continents moving between climate zones, helping to confirm the theory which became plate tectonics, governing the fundamental processes that shape the land and sea masses of the earth.

It is one of the largest bases which can be visited. Like the bases of a number of nations, it is not technically a military base, which the Antarctic Treaty forbids, but whenever you go all the staff there happen to be from the military. It has a small dock and jetty, and a heli-pad. Small sections remain of the railway which used to help move heavy supplies from dock to base. The path to the base passes the remains of the hut where Andersson and his two companions overwintered. The Argentines restored the hut in 1966–67. The structure is pitifully small: a very cogent reminder of what they uncomplainingly endured.

The base appears more like a miniature settlement than a workplace, and this is deliberate. Whole families come down here; there is a school, chapel, postal service, and medical centre. Children have been born here including the first Antarctican: Emilio Marcos Palma. Over fifty people commonly overwinter and the carbon footprint of the base is large. The generators alone consume more than 180,000 litres of fuel and year and it has forty-three different buildings. The site is susceptible to high winds. A few years ago the roof was ripped off a building during a storm whose winds exceeded 140mph at which point the anemometer was torn apart.

The huge Adélie colony behind the base is the most northerly continental one.


## VERNADSKY BASE (FORMERLY FARADAY BASE) AND WORDIE HUT (BASE F)

The yellow and light blue flag of the Ukraine flies over Vernadsky Base, a range of buildings on the low-lying Argentine Islands. The archipelago is fringed with rocks and poorly charted reefs, so ships normally stick to safe routes they have sailed before, and anchor a long Zodiac ride away. It's a good place to look for leopard seals along the way.

In a snug channel at the side of Vernadsky is a little wooden hut built in 1947, and the predecessor of Faraday/Vernadsky. It is named the Wordie Hut after the young geologist James Mann Wordie who sailed with Shackleton on the *Endurance*, and went on to enjoy a distinguished career in academic and public life. One of his students recalls asking if the student baths might have hot water, and having his ears blistered by a response that included a reference to the lack of hot baths on Elephant Island. The 1947 expedition had planned to head much farther south to Adelaide Island and build a new base, but was frustrated by poor weather and dense ice. They retreated back north and erected their hut here on the site which had been used by the 1935–36 British Grahamland Expedition. That hut had lasted about ten years before being flattened by a wave from a calving glacier or possibly a tsunami. The new hut originally comprised a single eighteen-feet square building, which was the size of the longest timber conveniently available in the shortages following the war. That building is now the living space, organised around the stove. The base was extended in 1951, adding the workshop, laboratory and extra accommodation.

The men at Wordie carried out meteorological observations; it still has a crystal ball sunshine recorder on the window ledge and a variety of other instruments on the walls. The outdoor meteorological instruments stood on the concrete base a short distance to the right of the front door. A short scramble to the left of the front door is a bare wooden sign announcing British Crown Property, dating from the era before the Antarctic Treaty, when territorial claims were still actively pursued. The little hut closed as a base in 1954 and you may discover why: the channel in which it stands is early to freeze over and late to thaw, making efficient provisioning difficult. There were also fears of further catastrophic calving. The work was transferred to a new base half a mile away on the Argentine Islands, which was later named Faraday, after the English physicist Michael Faraday, then Vernadsky. Wordie was maintained for use as an emergency hut, and as a refuge for

Faraday staff needing to escape from base for a night or two. Ironically it was used again as a base in 1960 by another British expedition which had hoped to overwinter at Adelaide Island, but been unable to get there. Wordie finally closed in 1996 when Faraday Base was sold to the Ukraine for one pound and renamed Vernadsky. The price tag is explained by the fact that Britain wanted to reduce the number of their bases, and decommissioning a base is more expensive than building it in the first place. Ukraine wanted a base following its emergence as a nation after the break-up of the Soviet Union; the coin which paid for it is set into the bar between the handpumps.

The United Kingdom Antarctic Heritage Trust began restoring Wordie Hut in 2009. The small office and bunkroom near the front door still has a filing box in which individual records of sled dogs were kept. The cards have now been removed for safe-keeping. The characteristics of each dog were noted: how well they worked, how quarrelsome they were, their fertility, and for the bitches, their nursing and mothering skills. The cards were used to select mates and improve the breed. The living accommodation includes books, a radio still bearing the old FIDS signature, clothing, and packs of pemmican. The food in the kitchen is mostly modern stores, from Vernadsky.

As you enter Vernadsky Base you take off your boots and heavy clothing in a changing area where there are portraits of past base teams and of Vladimir Vernadsky (1863 – 1945) after whom the base is named. He was a polymath whose greatest discovery was that the Earth had not always had an oxygen-rich atmosphere. Early life had developed at a time when oxygen was just a trace element in the atmosphere, along with many others. He showed that it was not a physical or chemical change that had to happen before life could evolve, it was the other way around. Primitive organisms did not need oxygen, but they did create it as a by-product. This was the first great environmental change created by life itself. Later life found it so useful it developed, through evolution, new forms which used and depended on oxygen.

The main corridor which leads away from the cloakroom has offices and labs on either side and even a gymnasium. Notice how the calendars, magazine photos and computer screen-savers, when they are not pin-up girls, are green fields and countryside. Remember Nordenskjöld, and Bruce's men, pining for colour for his starved eyes. Near the end of the corridor the word Ozone is written above your head and a narrow ladder leads up into a low attic. The original Dobson's spectrophotometer is still up there next to the modern replacement: an instrument that showed us how quickly and perilously we can change a vital part of the environment.

The second most famous room after that housing the Dobson's spectrophometer is the bar, which dates from its British days. Hardwood was sent down for the carpenter to make a new observation hut. He made the hut out of spare wood and built a bar with the hardwood. It cost him his job, but the bar's still there. Look out for the pound coin with which the base was bought; it's embedded between the handles of the beer pumps. The base is said to order more potatoes per head of staff than any other base, and the result is a very good home-made vodka. I thought the year they made it in the fire-extinguishers was a particularly good vintage, though you wouldn't have wanted to be there when a fire broke out.

Women were introduced here for one season and when there was friction, they decided it was due to tensions created by their presence. It might have been better to root out the troublemakers whatever their sex.

Hanging behind the bar is a collection of bras, collected simply by offering a free shot of vodka in return for taking off your bra in the bar. It worries me how many women who can afford an expensive cruise think this is a good deal.

# THE OZONE LAYER

The ozone layer used to be like a car tyre; no one thought about it much until it had a hole in it. Ozone molecules are a rare kind of oxygen. Unlike regular oxygen molecules, they are made from the bonding together of three atoms ($O_3$) not two ($O_2$). In every ten million air molecules, only three are ozone, and they are mostly found high in the upper atmosphere, around twenty kilometres up.

Each element absorbs radiation, including the narrow band of wavelengths we see as light, in a unique way. Ozone is best at absorbing ultra-violet rays. It plays a vital role in reducing the amount of ultra-violet light that reaches the surface of the earth, and is crucial to maintaining the balance of life on earth; however, this defence is extremely fragile. If $O_3$ occurred in a pure band, unmixed with normal oxygen, it would be only 3mm thick: the thickness of a British one-pound coin. Yet we depend on it to survive.

The ozone layer occurs because solar light of a wavelength less than 2.4 nanometres can break up regular $O_2$ oxygen into O-radicals, single O atoms which are very active in combining with remaining $O_2$ molecules to make ozone. At 20 kilometres conditions are ideal to create and maintain $O_3$. Above this, there are a great many energetic ultra-violet rays, but not many oxygen molecules to react with. Lower down, there is a rich supply of $O_2$ molecules to react with, but few rays make it that far.

Ozone is not stable; in time it reverts back to $O_2$, so the ozone layer is not a fixed supply of the same molecules, but more like a pond through which a stream flows: it stays the same size, even though the water in it is constantly replaced.

In the 1930s an English scientist called Gordon Dobson pioneered Ozone Layer studies and created a unit to describe the density of ozone and a machine to measure it. When he was first able to measure it, the Earth's atmosphere at 0°C had the equivalent of approximately 3mm of pure ozone; he designated this as 300 Dobson Units or DUs. During subsequent research this was regarded as the norm. Hand-built measuring instruments were made and, to enjoy unpolluted conditions, put to work in Antarctica at two British bases: Faraday and Halley, which stands on the ice of the Weddell Sea.

They discovered an annual cycle with low levels each spring. Then, in the late 1970s, something funny began happening at Faraday. Every year they detected lower and lower levels of ozone. They did not know why, but wondered if their ageing instrument was becoming less sensitive. Halley's readings also showed the same decline year on year. The problem was, hardly anyone else was measuring ozone levels, so they only had each other to compare results with. If ozone levels were really declining it was dangerous for everyone. Fearing needless controversy they mulled over it for some years before deciding to publish, admitting it might be instrument error. New machines were built and their readings showed the same trend; the changes were in the environment, not the kit. Levels in the Arctic were falling too, though not so fast, and the timing of the Arctic change lagged behind the Antarctic. They pieced together a picture of ozone in the atmosphere. The fastest rate of ozone formation was in the tropics which maintained levels of 400-450 DUs. The stratospheric winds common in those latitudes carry it around the globe and mix it up. Levels at the Poles are lower, averaging 300DUs.

The speed of change had been so rapid that consequences were already evident. In areas where the thinning of the ozone, or the 'hole in the ozone layer' as it soon became known, was greatest, skin cancers in livestock and people increased in frequency and severity. It seemed likely that some human activity was seriously affecting the system. The villains turned out to be two groups of chemicals called CFCs (chlorofluorinated carbons) and hydrochlorofluorocarbons (HCFCs). These gases are designer chemicals used in the compressors of refrigerators, and in air-conditioning systems and aerosols. Ironically, CFCs had been selected because at sea level they are inert, showing no interest in reacting with other chemicals. Twenty kilometres up, that all changes. The chlorides and bromides they contain become catalysts; when they meet ozone, they rip off the third oxygen atom. While ozone continued to be made at the same rate, it was now being broken down more quickly. Each summer the rising levels of radiation created ozone faster, and levels recovered, but because CFCs created an ever more rapid breakdown of ozone, levels couldn't bounce back to last year's levels. There was therefore less ozone to block incoming radiation. To return to the analogy of the pond, the same flow of water entered the pond, but each spring it flowed out more quickly, and the pond became shallower. Ozone levels are lowest in September and October before mixing of air masses begins to restores levels from mid-November onwards.

This theory asked industry and governments to accept that there was a link between current human activity and measurable and hazardous environmental change. There were other chemicals which could be substituted for CFCs and HCFCs. Governments signed the Montreal Protocol for future use in 1987, and most big manufacturers ratified it in 1989. Lows in the ozone layer began to fill, endorsing the theory and the remedy, though some countries, notably China, at first argued that they had only just begun to manufacture such goods and had some credit at the environmental bank where the First World had already exhausted its credit. Since the lucrative western markets for their goods prohibited CFCs and HCFCs, market forces brought the ethics into line. Most atmospheric models predict the atmosphere will by 2020–25 return to ozone levels equal to those first observed.

The differences between the behaviour of the two polar zones seems to be caused by the Antarctic atmosphere being more self-contained. Air circulations called Polar stratospheric clouds carry more nitrite acid and water vapour than most air systems. When that stronger mix meets CFCs it helps switch on the chlorides and bromides, which then strip $O_3$ back to $O_2$. This action is stimulated by light and so it increases in intensity each spring. In winter, Antarctica has an atmospheric current which greatly reduces mixing, allowing Polar Stratospheric Clouds to form in great cold and isolation, creating a stronger brew of nitrite acid and water vapour, freeing more chlorides and bromides to break down ozone.

## MEASURING OZONE: SPECTROPHOTOMETERS

The light that our eyes see is a tiny part of the spectrum of electro-magnetic waves. The violet end of the visible spectrum is the shortest wavelength our eyes can see. Some animals can see even shorter waves: ultra-violet ones. We can't, but they can damage our bodies, causing burns and cancers.

In the 1920s, Gordon Dobson designed a machine which measured the amount of sunlight in different wavelengths within the ultra-violet range. It is useful to measure light levels at two wavelengths: 305 nanometres and 325 nanometres (abbreviated to nm: there are 1000 million nanometres in a metre.) These are emitted in the same quantities by the sun, but while 305 nm light is strongly absorbed by ozone, 325 nm is not absorbed. If you measure the difference in light received at the ground between the two wavelengths, you can calculate how much ozone must have been there to block it.

# GONZÁLEZ VIDELA BASE/WATERBOAT POINT

González Videla is a Chilean base named after a former president. It sits on a small low promontory which is separated at high tide from the mainland rising behind it. However, it is regarded as a landing on the mainland for the purpose of completing a continental landing. The site is home to a small group of leucistic gentoo penguins, a genetic variation which results in muted colouring, so the familiar patter of plumage is still there, but in variations of a pinkish biscuit colour. Eye colour is normal, because the faulty gene does not control the nervous system, of which the eyes are part.

It is often said that history has unjustly neglected someone. This is not true of the man who led the British Imperial Antarctic Expedition of 1920, Dr John Lackland Cope; anonymity is too good for him. He began by proposing to spearhead three teams of 120 men supported by twelve airplanes on a circumnavigation lasting five years. If it had been completed as projected, Cope's expedition would have colonised three-quarters of the continent for Britain by setting up permanent stations. He ended up leading eight dogs with nothing to do and four men who all hated each other. One of them was Hubert Wilkins who afterwards said the only thing to be learned from it was how not to organise a polar expedition. The Royal Geographical Society had examined the man and his plans then declined to support either. He bragged of having $750,000 worth of backing from three governments, yet he soon declared that all the money raised had been spent buying the dogs, leaving none to pay the whaler that was now to take them down instead of the twelve airplanes.

Embezzlement was suspected. Thomas Bagshawe was nominally the geologist, and Maxime Lester, formerly second mate on a tramp, was designated surveyor. The Norwegian whaling magnate Lars Christensen gave them free passage, and on Christmas Eve 1920, they entered Port Foster, Deception Island. Then they begged passage on the Norwegian steamer *Solstreif* to Paradise Harbour, landing 12 January 1921. Even this would not have happened had not Wilkins pledged his expensive photo equipment as security against their expenses.

The base staff are proud of the rather eccentric history of their location: Waterboat Point. They struggled to find a route up from the coast to access the interior, and nearly died trying. They also explored in a five-metre-long life-boat, utterly vulnerable to the weather. When Wilkins, Cope and Lester were caught in a storm in Andvord Bay the boat took in water until they were nearly swamped. Only Wilkins was well enough to move, and he had barely enough strength to cut down their sail. Eventually Wilkins found a Norwegian whaler to take them home, but Bagshawe and Lester wanted to stay. Cope, hoping their adventure might help him raise more funds, not only encouraged them, but discouraged any whalers from checking on them. There was an abandoned waterboat left by Salvesen's factory ship *Neko* in 1913, which they upturned for living quarters. Their food comprised only biscuits, baked beans, pemmican, sweets and alcohol. When they settled down to their first meal they found they had forgotten to bring forks. They had a phonograph and some records. Lester and Bagshawe quarrelled regularly, but the anger was as quick to die down as it was to flare up. Wilkins wrote: 'Two men who can have an angry row in the morning and forget about it by afternoon can get along anywhere for any length of time.' Frank Debenham, the Australian founder of Cambridge's Scott Polar Research Institute, said they 'possessed that quality so annoying to the great Napoleon of not knowing when they were defeated.' Cope never returned. When he reached the Falkland Islands, the authorities were so keen to move him on they got him a job potato peeling on a Scottish steamer. It was the end of his career as explorer. Next year Captain Andersen sent the whale catcher *Graham* with the Deception Island Magistrate-cum-Whaling Officer Arthur Bennett and a prayer book. He expected to read the Burial Service for the Dead over the corpses. He found them alive and reasonably well on 18 December 1921. Indeed Bennett may have suffered more on that day, for in a year, Bagshawe and Lester had taken only one bath.

The site where they stayed is now on the edge of the Chilean González Videla Base. They upturned their boat on a rocky knoll on a rocky shore, just yards from the water. It is a perfect place for gentoo penguins to nest, which is what they have done for ninety years since. Their guano has helped rot down the remains of the wooden boat, but the outline of the gunnels is still visible among the nests, though much fainter than ten years ago.


ARCTOWSKI BASE


Arctowski was founded in 1977 and named after the geologist, meteorologist and oceanographer Henry Arctowski who accompanied de Gerlache. It is located on a triangular shingle foreshore where two steep storm beaches meet at a cluster of rocks. Your arrival is watched over by a shrine to the Virgin Mary, and more practically, by a navigation light. It is a location where, from 1905, the first factory whaling ship in Antarctica, the *Admiralen*, used to anchor. Colossal bones from the head are arranged on the shore, probably from blue whales or fin whales.

The base conducts research into glaciology, meteorology, geology, birds and sea-life, especially invertebrates and parasites of fish. It is a station where staff overwinter, but with a personnel reduced from summer levels of around twenty, as many of the projects are seasonal, studying creatures which only visit to nest, or which are locked beneath the sea-ice all winter.


## BELLINGSHAUSEN AND FREI

Two bases sit side by side above the same beach in Admiralty Bay, King George Island. The former is Russian, named for Admiral Bellingshausen. The latter is Chilean, named for a recent President who visited Antarctica: Eduardo Frei. Frei Base plays a similar political role to the Argentine base, Esperanza. A mother gave birth there in 1984, but it was not until 1995 that they built their first science building, a rather modest affair.

The Russian base suffered from poor housekeeping during the break-up of the Soviet Union, but was assisted in a big clean-up operation by volunteers from other nations. It is not hard to tell which side of the bay is Russian; on a small hill above it is a Russian Orthodox church, built of Siberian pine, smelling richly of resin, and home.

## ALMIRANTE BROWN

In Paradise harbour, within sight of the Chilean González Videla Base, lies a small base, named for the Irish-born William Brown (1777 – 1857), founder of the Argentine Navy. Work on meteorology, marine water temperatures and salinity have been carried out there. Since the support vessel, the ice-breaker *Irízar*, was damaged by fire, there seems to have been no activity. The original base burned down in 1984. There are a few stories about it; my best source, an Argentine I won't name, said it was arson, by a station doctor who received mail telling him his sweetheart had finished with him. He determined to rush home and mend the relationship, and to avoid completing his contract, he made sure there was nowhere to work by burning down the base.

# 14

## Who Owns Antarctica?

*Visitors undoubtedly visit another continent, for some it's the
motivation for coming, but have they been to another country?
And why, in 1982, did two modern industrial countries go to
war over possession of sub-Antarctic and adjacent islands?*

This chapter looks at who claims Antarctica, how it is run,
and why Britain and Argentina went to war over the
Falklands and South Georgia.

When you go to Antarctica you visit a new continent, but
not a new country. Many bases will stamp your passport,
and they never forget to include their country's name, but
it's a souvenir. None of these stamps has any legal validity.
Predictably, penguins feature heavily on them, though not
necessarily with the anatomical fidelity you might expect
given the leisure they have to study them. I like those on
the Ukrainian Vernadsky Station, which look like Cold War
veterans standing to attention, gazing up at a fly-past
during a May Day parade.

In the era of exploration, there were various loose tests
of whether a sovereignty claim was valid; there were

procedures for claiming sovereignty which you followed as best you could. Going ashore was important, although drive-by claims were made when the weather was bad, or time pressing. Cook's 1775 claim on South Georgia was a model. He made a rough survey of the north coast, before going ashore at a place he smartly christened Possession Bay, in case anyone who followed was slow on the uptake. It was claimed for Britain in the name of His Majesty King George III and a volley of small arms discharged into the air. The event was recorded not just in the ship's log, but through materials left behind. Trees, where available, would be carved with due particulars, or have plaques nailed to them bearing the relevant boasts. Caches of coins showing the reigning monarch would be sealed in caskets or bottles: constitutional voodoo dolls to warn off unbelievers in the British values of fair play, in so far as fair play was compatible with world domination.

How seriously other countries took this depended on a number of factors. An important consideration was whether they were able politically or militarily to stand up to Britain. In Cook's time few could stand up to British arms; in the century that followed, virtually none.

When the British began probing around the South Shetlands they did what they always did and claimed it for Britain. In the case of Antarctica claims were simplified by the lack of indigenous peoples. Of course staking a claim was just the prelude to coming back to occupy the territory and make money. Antarctica was different. Whales and seals were two obvious sources of income, but much money could be made without owning territory, and the climate was too hostile to occupy all year round. Most countries never made formal claims. Those who did tended to be the early arrivals, plus two who were geographically closest, that is, Australia, France, New Zealand, Norway and the United Kingdom, plus Argentina and Chile. Notably the USA and Russia were as well qualified as these to lodge claims but chose not to.

These claims and counterclaims were mostly expressed in rhetoric and paperwork, though shots were fired on a few occasions, notably in 1952 by the maverick Argentine officer at Esperanza Base. But usually conflict was expressed in symbols. When the Second World War broke out the Argentines went down to a vacant Deception and painted over the Union Flag with the Argentine. The British came back in the austral summer of 1943–44 with their own paint pots.

It seemed likely that as the Cold War escalated in the 1950s, it might also be fought on the coldest front of all: Antarctica. That it wasn't was the remarkable result of applying scientific co-operation to politics, and it was an idea with a long pedigree. When Clements Markham was pitching a proposal for a new Antarctic expedition to the British Government, F. Sidney Parry, the Private Secretary to the Treasury, advised him to emphasise the practical value of magnetism, and minimise the role of pure science. But he had mis-read his Prime Minister. Arthur Balfour said, 'I take a different view – a view based on the scientific experience of the past. If our predecessors in the last two centuries had taken any narrow utilitarian view of their work, it is manifest that our ignorance of the planet on which we live would be much more profound than it is at present. There cannot be any territorial rivalry between any of the countries engaged in Antarctic exploration; and such rivalry as there may be, must be of a purely scientific character.'

# THE INTERNATIONAL GEOPHYSICAL YEAR (IGY)

The modern scientific venture which guided future politics was the initiative begun in 1950, when US and UK scientists revived ideas of the International Polar Years of 1882–83 and 1932–33. They had been chosen as years of either unusually high or low sunspot activity, when certain atmospheric effects are exaggerated. 1957–58 was

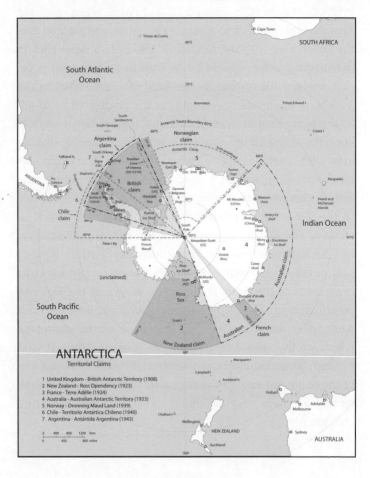

expected to be a maximum sunspot year, so in 1952 the International Council of Scientific Unions set up a committee to organise an International Geophysical Year, which was a long one, running from 1 July 1957 to 1 January 1959.

The focus was to be on Antarctica and space. In both spheres, it was recognised that the expense and danger of research in those areas made co-operation vital, if scientific investment was to be efficient and effective. It galvanised unprecedented activity. Twelve nations established fifty new stations in Antarctica, staffed with over five thousand personnel. They co-ordinated studies on glaciology, meteorology, geology, geomagnetism and the upper atmosphere.

In one harmless sense, the Cold War continued; naturally the biggest contributors were the USA and USSR who built seven new stations each. The USSR had a base at Pole of Inaccessibility. To see the significance of the American choice, you must remember that many Antarctic claims had been made after exploring a length of coastline, then claiming all the land in the sector between those two latitude lines, until they converged at the South Pole. The USA set up Scott-Amundsen, a large shelter right over the Pole, with a toe in every sector. But still it made no territorial claims. Ironically, the Pole itself moves with time, and the ice on which the base is built flows at ten metres a year, so no building can stay over the true Pole for long.

Despite wider political tensions the IGY was a great success, and it was decided that the principles could be extended to future management of the continent. The result was the Antarctic Treaty, signed on 1 December 1959 and coming into force on 23 June 1961. The original signatories were: Argentina, Australia, Belgium, Chile, France, Japan, New Zealand, Norway, South Africa, USSR, UK and USA.

Diplomats and civil servants are often criticised, but the people who drafted the Treaty deserve the utmost praise. Faced with a large and delicate problem in a tense political climate, they devised a solution that has survived intact for fifty years. They began by setting out what was valuable and worthy of protection: it was in the interest of all mankind that Antarctica be used for peaceful purposes, not discord, and to recognise the contribution made to science by international co-operation in Antarctica. The main body of the treaty is expressed in a series of articles which can be summarised as follows. They cleverly avoid requiring anyone to lose face or renounce past claims.

### Article I

It was for peaceful use only, with no military or weapon testing

But military personnel may be deployed for science or other peaceful purposes.

### Article II

Freedom of scientific investigation and co-operation pioneered in IGY shall continue, subject to the provisions of this Treaty.

### Article III

To promote co-operation

a)    future plans should be shared

b)    personnel exchanged

c)    results freely available.

Article IV

Nothing in this Treaty is to be interpreted as

a) renouncing any asserted sovereignty claims

b) renouncing any claims consequent on that country's activities

c) prejudicing views on any other country's claims

d) no acts undertaken while Treaty in force can support or detract from sovereignty claims

e) no new or enhanced claim may be made while Treaty in force.

Article V

Antarctica to be a non-nuclear area, and nuclear agreements signed by signatories to Treaty also apply in Antarctica.

Article VI

Provisions of Treaty apply south of 60°S including ice shelves but without prejudice to the International Law of the Sea.

Article VII

All signatories have absolute freedom of access and inspection. All signatories must inform other signatories of all expeditions, manned stations and military movements.

Article VIII

Clarification of responsibilities for actions of observers and exchanged staff.

Article IX
  Future actions required by signatories to further aims
  of the Treaty.

Article X
  Each signatory monitors others' compliance.

Article XI
  Resolution of disputes through negotiation and
  mediation, or, failing that, The International Court of
  Justice.

Article XII
  Means of modifying Treaty is by unanimous
  agreement. After 30 years, any signatory may call a
  conference to review the Treaty's operation.

Article XIII
  Treaty subject to ratification by signatory states. Open
  to succession by any UN member state.

Article XIV
  Deposition of copies of Treaty in USA for transmission
  to members.

A number of protocols have been added, of which the most
important for visitors is the Environmental Protocol signed
4 October 1991. It designates Antarctica as a 'natural
reserve, devoted to peace and science', and prohibits
activities related to mineral resources except for science,
though the distinction may be hard to make in practice.

The Treaty was put in force for fifty years, and may only be changed unanimously. The current signatories represent 80% of the world's population. It includes those who first came to the table: Argentina, Australia, Belgium, Chile, France, Japan, New Zealand, Norway, South Africa, USSR, UK, and USA, plus thirty-three others, including major powers of the coming era like China and India, plus some countries whose polar credentials seem a bit thin, such as Papua New Guinea.

It has been a huge success. Some political manoeuvring has continued, thankfully without gunfire. But some countries, including Chile and Argentina, have invested heavily in developments which seem to overlook some of the articles they have signed up to, particularly Article IV d) and e), that you can't reinforce your claim after signing the treaty. Both have turned bases into miniature settlements with spouses and children living there. On 7 January 1978, baby Emilio Marcos de Palma was born to Silvia and her husband Argentine Army Captain Jorge de Palma at Esperanza Base. She was flown in heavily pregnant with doctors, gave birth, and took a photo-call before being flown home. In the next five years seven more births followed. Not to be outdone, in 1984 a baby was born at the Chilean Eduardo Frei Base. These are not the priorities of the Treaty, but childbirth is a healthier form of competition than gunfire.

## GOVERNING TOURISM

IAATO is a trade organisation founded in 1991 to advocate, promote and practice safe and environmentally responsible private-sector travel to the Antarctic. It was founded in 1991· by seven private tour operators already operating there and now has over a hundred members. It was a smart move satisfying several important needs:

- [ ] it demonstrated responsible practice to governments with a stake in Antarctica and
- [ ] has allowed the industry to operate and develop without government interference
- [ ] has promoted good practice
- [ ] has promoted management and
- [ ] monitoring to inform future policy

## WHO OWNS THE FALKLAND ISLANDS (ISLAS MALVINAS)?

The Falklands are the principal islands, and the only ones with a significant population, in a number of territories, known as the Falkland Islands Dependencies, that share related issues of sovereignty and administration.

British sovereignty claims over the Falkland Islands and South Georgia are different from British claims in Antarctica proper, because both those territories lie north of the limit of the Antarctic Treaty.

Beginning with South Georgia, in 1775 Cook landed, made a model claim, and drew a chart, but no one came to colonise. When the Norwegian Carl Anton Larsen wanted to set up a whaling station in Grytviken, South Georgia in the first years of the twentieth century, Britain was almost embarrassed to find she had the best claim on the island, and felt obliged to administer it. Since then she has been firm in maintaining that claim, and has been actively governing the whaling and fishing industries, and more recently, tourism.

Two countries now claim sovereignty over the Falklands, remote islands with a total population the same as the crew of HMS *Hermes*, the flagship of the British Falklands War Task Force of 1982. Before relating the British and Argentine claims, it's helpful to give a brief history of the discovery and government of the islands. It may be helpful to read these in the light of three core questions to which the debate returns, put by D. George Boyce in his excellent and concise book *The Falklands War*, which has greatly informed this chapter.

☐ What right has Britain to remote islands 8000 miles from its shores?
☐ What right has Argentina to govern a people of wholly different racial, linguistic and cultural background?
☐ What right does a small population with a dependent economy have to self-determination?

## HISTORY

Several navigators have been credited with the first sighting of the Falklands. Like many remote islands they were chanced upon because a vessel had been blown off course by a storm, as was the fine English seaman John Davis when he saw land on 14 August 1592. Of course the circumstances in which early mariners were least sure of their position was when tossed around in a storm, but it usually taken that he saw the Falklands, though he did not land. The earliest sighting that has been conclusively authenticated was by Dutchman Sebald van Weert in 1600. The first known landing was not made until 1690, by the British naval captain John Strong in the thirty-eight-gun privateer *Welfare*. Strong named the islands after his patron Viscount Falkland, who soon afterwards became First Lord of the Admiralty. A few years later, passing French sailors called the Islands *Les Îles Malouines* after their home port of St Malo. The Spanish translated this as *Las Islas Malvinas*. It remained uninhabited.

In 1764, a small French colony, Port Louis, was established on East Falkland, claiming possession for France. Comically, the following year, a British expedition, not knowing the French were established there, reached Saunders Island, West Falkland, and anchored in a harbour which it named Port Egmont. It took formal possession of it and of 'all the neighbouring islands' for King George III. The following year, another British expedition established a settlement of about 100 people at Port Egmont, and the year after, 1767, France sold Port Louis to Spain for £24,000, who renamed it Puerto de la Soledad. The dual occupation was short-lived. In 1770, the Spanish drove the British out of Port Egmont. Britain negotiated a return but almost as soon as they got back, they evacuated the islands on economic grounds in 1774, but without relinquishing British sovereignty.

In 1810 Argentina declared independence from Spain but it was not yet a functioning state. The Spanish settlement on East Falkland was itself withdrawn in 1811, forty-four years after acquiring it, leaving the Islands without inhabitants or any form of government. The islands continued to be used by sealers, principally British and American, until in November 1820, Colonel David Jewett, an American national, visited the Islands and claimed formal possession of them in the name of the Government of Buenos Aires, but stayed on the islands for only a few weeks.

In 1820 the Government of the Province of Buenos Aires, trying to clear debts, sold the rights to exploit fish and the plentiful wild cattle running free on the Falklands to the French-born, US-trained businessman Louis Vernet. He also sought permission from the British. By 1828 the business was thriving, under the management of Matthew Brisbane, who had been master of the tiny cutter *Beaufoy* when James Weddell discovered the Weddell Sea. They sold fresh and salted beef, vegetables and dairy products to ships, but felt threatened by the visits of numbers of US sealers, returning from Antarctica, who used the islands as their own. When Vernet asked for the protection of a naval ship, Buenos Aires refused, but appointed him Governor. In 1831, after warning the US *Harrier* for unauthorised exploitation of the islands he confiscated the vessel and sent its master to Buenos Aires for trial. In reprisal the United States sent the warship *Lexington*, which trashed Louis Vernet's settlement and declared the Falklands free from all government.

The islands remained without authority until September 1832, when the Government of Buenos Aires appointed Juan Mestivier as Civil and Political Governor on an interim basis. The British Government protested to the Buenos Aires Government that this appointment infringed British sovereignty over the Islands, but Mestivier sailed to the Falklands at the end of 1832 on the schooner *Sarandi* with some convicts and twenty-five soldiers, most of whom had been deported as part-punishment for offences. Four days after arrival he was murdered by his own soldiers. In January 1833, the British warship HMS *Clio* arrived at Puerto de la Soledad with instructions to exercise British rights of sovereignty, and give the remaining Argentines the opportunity to stay or return to Buenos Aires. They left Matthew Brisbane in command. He was murdered by the convicts.

The British naval officer First Lieutenant Henry Smith arrived on HMS *Challenger* the following year to administer the Islands. With four seamen and Royal Marines, he spent four years restoring Vernet's work. In 1841, a civil Lieutenant Governor was appointed and, in 1843, the civil administration was put on a permanent footing by an Act of the British Parliament. The Lieutenant Governor's title was changed to Governor and, in 1845, the first Executive and Legislative Councils were set up. There was a majority of appointed officials in the Legislative Council until 1951, but from 1949, members elected by universal adult suffrage were introduced into the Council.

British rule continued until the Falklands were invaded and occupied by Argentine military forces on 2 April 1982. A British task force was despatched and, following a conflict in which 255 British and 625 Argentine lives were lost, the Argentine forces surrendered on 14 June 1982. British records show that suicides from post-traumatic stress have now exceeded the fatalities suffered in direct combat. Argentine figures are similar. Therefore total casualties now approach the 1982 population of the islands, which was eighteen hundred souls.

# THE BRITISH CASE FOR THE FALKLAND ISLANDS

There was no indigenous or settled population before British settlement. With the exception of two months' illegal occupation in 1982, the Falklands have been continuously, peacefully and effectively inhabited and administered by Britain since 1833. Over many years, international postal agreements have been made confirming British administration with little or no challenge.

Not until 1946 did the Fascist dictator Peron claim the Falklands. In 1947 Britain invited Argentina to subject sovereignty to arbitration at the International Court of Justice at the UN, binding itself to the judgement; Argentina refused. Three further similar invitations were refused.

Many people who live in the Falklands trace their origins in the Islands back to the early nineteenth century. The islands have been listed by name among British dependencies since 1887. Enquiries for leases have been directed to The British Government since the nineteenth century. Argentina was formally notified of Letters of Patent (a legal instrument granting title) claiming the Falklands in 1908; they made no objection, and took no action to contest it.

## THE LINDBLAD EXPLORER: LARS-ERIC LINDBLAD INVENTS ANTARCTIC TOURISM

In the late 1950s, both Chile and Argentina took over five hundred paying passengers on various voyages to the Antarctic Peninsula using naval transport ships. Systematic tourism began in 1966, when Lars-Eric Lindblad wanted to visit Antarctica without working on a base: the usual route for the curious. He found enough like-minded souls to charter a ship and visit for pleasure. The voyage was highly successful and his one-off trip became a business. In 1969 he launched a purpose built ship, the *Lindblad Explorer*; its bright red hull and slightly oversized funnel were familiar to Antarctic travellers for nearly forty years, during which she made over 250 voyages there.

Lindblad devised the model for Antarctic tourism: sail from South America across the Drake, visit the Peninsula and South Shetlands, and use the ship as the hotel. Landings were made using inflatable boats, Zodiacs, which were tough, versatile and stable.

Many other companies followed the model. The big growth came with the break-up of the former Soviet Union during 1990 – 91, which brought many small ice-strengthened vessels into the market for sale or charter. With them came officers and crews experienced in ice navigation.

There was rapid growth and visitor numbers reached nearly fifteen thousand by the 1999 – 2000 season, and were close to thirty thousand as the end of that decade approached. The slump in many developed nations' economies produced a check. At the same time, several incidents provoked discussion about the appropriateness of tourism in a hazardous and pristine environment. In January 2007, the MS *Nordkapp* hit a rock off Deception Island and spilled a small quantity of light fuel oil. Scientists were quick to ask why risks should be taken to allow tourists to come sightseeing in a fragile and unspoiled environment. They had not made the equivalent response when the only severe pollution incident happened on 28 January 1989. The Argentine vessel *Bahia Paraiso* ran aground off the American Palmer Station, after ignoring advice and entering the bay by a channel known to the base personnel to be full of rocks. It was carrying a quarter of a million gallons of fuel for Argentine bases. The men were safely evacuated; the ship sank.

But the most notable incident occurred in the first minutes of 23 November 2007 when the *Lindblad Explorer*, renamed the *Explorer*, made world headlines. She was sailing down the Bransfield Strait east of Penguin Island, and sailed into the edge of an ice field which contained glacier ice as well as sea ice. The captain was experienced in Baltic waters, which have sea ice but not glacier ice. He was not experienced in Antarctic ice. The Inquiry would find he had been overconfident in approaching at speed. The ship came to a halt: not unusual. But at 00:05 an alarm sounded on the bridge indicating flooding in cabin 312. An Able Seaman was sent to look at the problem and confirmed at 00:08 that it was seawater and there was a hole in the hull. The captain went to look for himself, returned to the bridge, and in the words of the official report said, 'Oh [expletive deleted] ... This is serious.' At 00:12 the general emergency alarm was sounded calling all passengers to the assembly point. Pumping could not keep pace with the flooding, which could not be isolated in the compartment that was first breached. At 02:15 the ship suffered a total power blackout. She had a list of 15°-18°, a large iceberg was approaching, and the ship could not move. As a precaution, at 02:35 the order was given to abandon ship. There were several other cruise ships in the area; I was on the *Polar Star* approaching the Peninsula but we were too distant to assist.

The engineers laboured by flashlight below decks to restore power long enough to take the ship into clearer, safer water. All one hundred passengers and fifty-four crew were successfully evacuated to lifeboats, though unlike modern specialist polar vessels, she had open lifeboats with canvas covers, and if the weather deteriorated and rescue was delayed, they would be exposed to the elements. Inexplicably, the crew forgot to put up the covers. There was a Force 6 wind making enough spray to wet everyone in the boats. The lifeboat engines were hand-cranked, cold, and cussed. Three out of the four failed to start, and Zodiacs had to be used to pull them away from the ship.

The Norwegian vessel *Nordnorge* arrived with the *Endeavour* at 06:25 and the *Nordnorge* began to pick up passengers. Two hours after the last person was picked up, the wind had risen to gale force. The ship sank at 19:00 in deep water at twenty-five miles SE of Penguin Island. Passengers were transferred to nearby King George Island and put up at the Chilean and Uruguayan bases until they could be flown out.

The marketing name of the cruise was *The Spirit of Shackleton*, which was more realistic than anyone would have liked. But the captain's precautionary early evacuation, and the engineer's bravery in restoring power, were judged by the inquiry to have saved lives. No one died, no one was seriously injured.

Tourism will always be under scrutiny from unsympathetic eyes, but it has a value far beyond the pleasure of the moment. One of Lindblad's motives for running trips to Antarctica was 'You can't protect what you don't know.' If only scientists visit, the continent has few advocates, and they would be ones with a vested interest, easy for politicians to sideline. Every year thirty thousand new advocates for Antarctica return to their home countries. Without tourism, Antarctica would not just be the White Continent, but also the silent one.

The Falkland Islanders have repeatedly made known their wish to remain British. A poll, conducted in 1994 revealed that 87% of them would be against any form of discussion with Argentina over sovereignty, under any circumstances.

Although the United Nations General Assembly has not debated the question of the Falklands since 1988, the Committee of Twenty-Four has continued to adopt resolutions calling for negotiations between Britain and Argentina. These resolutions are flawed because they make no reference to the Islanders' right to choose their own future. Several members of the Committee have acknowledged this omission. The principle of self-determination is included in every other resolution considered by the Committee. The British position that sovereignty is not for negotiation remains unaltered. There will be no change in the status of the Falklands without the Islanders' consent. Britain notes that Argentina's claim to the Falklands principally depends firstly on a Spanish title granted by Pope Alexander VI in the treaty of Tordesillas in 1493, and secondly on the conquest of the adjacent continental territories. But that treaty was a direct deal between one petitioning country, Spain, and a Papacy whose authority was tainted by Alexander VI being Spanish and having become Pontiff by bribery. At the time, the Catholic King François of France thought the deal preposterous and demanded to 'see the clause in Adam's will which entitled the Kings of Castile and Portugal to divide the earth between them.' The islands were seen and claimed for Britain before Spain had any knowledge of them, and lie over three hundred miles from the coast.

When Jewett claimed the islands for the Government of Buenos Aires, in 1820, that government of Buenos Aires was not recognised by any other foreign power. No act of occupation followed Jewett's visit and the islands remained without effective government. Five years before Buenos Aires had declared independence from Spain, in 1816, the Spanish settlement had been evacuated, leaving the Islands without inhabitants or any form of government. Argentina's subsequent attempts at settlement were sporadic and ineffectual. As for territorial contiguity, says the FCO, it 'has never been a determinant for title to islands (otherwise the Canary Islands, for example, might be Moroccan) and should not be used to overrule the right of self-determination.'

## THE ARGENTINE CASE FOR LAS ISLAS MALVINAS

By the Treaty of Tordesillas in 1493, Pope Alexander VI apportioned discoveries in the New World between Portugal and Spain. The Falklands lie in the area given to Spain. In 1820 the Government of Buenos Aires was the only functional government of that area and had inherited the rights exercised by Spain. Argentina claims sovereignty over the Falklands through her inheritance, on independence, of Spain's possessory title and through her attempts to settle the Islands between 1826 and 1833, and through the concept of territorial contiguity, since she has undisputed sovereignty over the adjacent mainland. On 10 June 1829, the Buenos Aires Government issued a decree setting forth its rights, derived from the Spanish Viceroyalty of La Plata, placing the Islands under the control of a political and military commandant, Louis Vernet. Its remaining occupants were expelled by force by the British.

In March 1967 and again in August 1968 Britain made statements and signed a memorandum of understanding that it would concede and recognise sovereignty subject to certain conditions, and respecting the wishes of the Falklanders. In the early 1970s, the Edward Heath Government made economic agreements that resulted in many Falkland Island services being provided by Argentina at costs subsidised by the Argentine exchequer, a *de facto* acceptance of an emerging Argentine role in administration. In 1994, the Argentine Constitution was amended to include a clause asserting sovereignty over the Islands, which would be pursued 'in accordance with international law.'

The possession of territories remote from the mother country, with populations planted by colonial settlement, is an anachronism in the twenty-first century. (This view is shared by most of Latin America, notwithstanding that a strand of Argentina's case is that it inherited rights from Spain, a colonial power which acquired them by violence.) Foregrounding the rights of a very small number of inhabitants of British descent skews the debate, moving the focus from wider issues of principle to the self-interest of a tiny community. The United Nations has not given precedence to their rights of self-determination in its resolutions about future governance.

The British Government has, under both Labour and Conservative administrations, given strong signals that Britain did not desire governance in perpetuity, and its policy was to manage the transfer of sovereignty in a manner that respected the future rights of Falklanders. From the mid-1970s, British foreign policy was that the best solution was to cede to Argentina's claims, but leaseback the islands for seventy years, so few adult islanders would live to undergo the transfer. In 1981 they withdrew full British citizenship from Falklands passport holders (the status was only restored after the 1982 war). Whenever talks approached meaningful progress towards transfer, British Governments have retreated, and negotiations have been unproductive because they were insincere on the British side.

## THE UNITED NATIONS' POSITION

In 1960 the United Nations General Assembly adopted its Declaration of the Granting of Independence to Colonial Countries and Peoples. A committee was set up to oversee implementation of this resolution. This Committee, which became known as the Committee of Twenty-Four, considered the question of the Falklands for the first time in 1964. Following its recommendations, the General Assembly adopted Resolution 2065 in 1965, inviting the British and Argentine Governments to begin negotiations with a view to finding a peaceful solution to the problem, bearing in mind the interests of the population of the Falkland Islands. During 1967 and 1968 Britain entered into negotiations with Argentina based on a willingness to transfer sovereignty. Britain maintained throughout that any transfer of sovereignty must be subject to the wishes of the Islanders. It was on this issue that negotiations foundered.

# THE FUTURE

The dispute raises interesting questions about historical rights and commitments in the modern world. No part of the British mainland is as fiercely patriotic as the Falkland Islands. Their Britishness and relative autonomy, fortified by their isolation and self-sufficiency, is at the heart of their culture and identity. Living in some future *Malvinas* would not be life. The 1982 war hardened attitudes in the Falklands and the United Kingdom. On 1 April 1982 not one in a hundred British people at home, including me, could have found the Falklands on a map. Many thought they were north of the British Isles, somewhere near the Shetlands, perhaps. But when Britain went to war it was not for economic interest, but for principles of defending citizens and rights; the Argentine government of the day was a brutal, undemocratic, military regime. Now that many hundreds of lives, mostly military, a few civilian, have been given for the Falklands, how could any Government quietly hand them over to the country which began the war?

In Argentina, the war is perceived as a just cause badly handled. Likewise the loss, directly and indirectly, of over a thousand lives means abandoning their ambitions is unthinkable. No single political ambition in Argentina is as unavoidable to tourists as the desire to 'reclaim' the Malvinas. Slogans such as *The Malvinas are ours, and one day we will return*, stand outside every military institution. In March 2009 British Prime Minister Gordon Brown told Argentine President Cristina Fernández (Kirchner) he would not even talk about future sovereignty.

Argentina's greatest writer Jorge Luis Borges said that the Falklands War was two bald men fighting over a comb. It would be beyond farce or tragedy if they fought over it twice. Let us hope another generation of young men and women will not pay the price.

# 15

## The Future of Antarctica

Within a year of its discovery, Antarctica's wildlife was being butchered. The Antarctic fur seal barely survived the onslaught. The last expedition to South Georgia by Captain Budington in 1892 yielded only 135 skins, all taken at small rookeries previously unknown. But once the killing stopped, the seals showed their resilience. They are superbly adapted to their environment, and they fed and bred their way back to prosperity. There are beaches in South Georgia, such as Elsehul Bay, Cooper Bay and Stromness, where in recent years I have had to abandon or cut short tourist landings when territorial males refused to concede passage across the beach. It's a nice problem, coping with their success. There is even talk of culling them in areas like the Bay of Isles in South Georgia where rarer species, like albatrosses, suffer the erosion of their nesting areas in the tussock grass by the crush of seals.

Whales were hunted right into the 1980s. The forests of spouts which welcomed the first explorers may never be seen again. Some species are recovering much better than others, and may now be close to their pre-hunting levels;

others species struggle, and we can only guess why. Blue whales have been reduced to such low numbers that recovery seems difficult. Their social structures, migration habits, and the behavioural savvy passed down by animals over two centuries old, have all been damaged. Scavenging birds probably flourished on the waste of whaling and will have fallen back in recent years. Penguins and the krill-specialist crabeater seals may have stayed at much higher levels than before whaling, exploiting the plankton and small fish no longer scooped up by whales. They may be inhibiting some whales' recovery by harvesting their food. In the future, man may add to that threat. Fishing fleets have eyed the huge tonnage of protein represented by krill, so vast the annual spring bloom can be monitored from space. The moment they die, fluorine from their exoskeleton migrates into the flesh, and the body is useful only for animal feed or fertiliser. So far this has protected them from gross exploitation. One discovery can change all that.

As to current human impacts, the only ones of any importance come from outside Antarctica. Biologists have been shocked at the industrial chemicals which are showing up in animals like seals, penguins and whales which live in the earth's remotest corners. When populations vary wildly, we seldom understand why, because we learned little about the ecology of the animals before killing them or their food. Only when albatross numbers began to crash did studies of their feeding flights revealed that Falkland Island black-browed albatross parents were going to the southern Indian Ocean to feed, and being drowned when they took the hooks baited with squid lowered in their tens of thousands from long-line fishing vessels. For each drowning, a chick starved to death. Techniques have been developed to reduce this tragic by-catch to virtually nil.

People actually working in Antarctica generally have a small environmental footprint, visitors even less. But we must remember that in a simple fragile ecosystem (the two go together) small inputs can have radical impacts. The Antarctic Treaty has steered the continent through difficult times and protected it well, though cynics might argue that Antarctica's climate continues to offer the best line of defence against commercial development and pollution. Antarctica has its share of mineral reserves, and techniques for exploiting them will only improve. If significant warming occurred on the continent exploitation would become easier and more economical as more land was exposed. Current indications are that it is not experiencing any overall change in temperatures, despite some regional trends, such as the warming of the northern and central parts of the Peninsula and adjacent islands, and the cooling of the south. This has been caused by a strengthening of a wind gyre which has drawn in more warm oceanic air to the north, and which is returning from the continent more strongly chilled farther south. As the world's resources become scarcer and more expensive, it will become harder to argue and enforce a view that economic growth should ignore Antarctica's untouched minerals. Then we will find out if a genuine will exists to protect it as wilderness, or if governments have simply been making a virtue out of necessity.

Polar exploration has been consciously used as a theatre to promote individual fame and national status. The stage was huge and the cast small, but many stars were made. The same stories are revisited by each new generation. This book is a step in redressing the balance between the romantic stars and the unsung heroes.

Polar struggle always has an audience. The expedition becomes a metaphor for the struggle for life, and failure becomes death, and death itself becomes some transcendent delivery beyond worldly care. Death is not simply the price paid for ambition; it is a sacrifice, and they are transfigured. Their every moment might have been driven by a selfish hunger for fame, but in dying they are redeemed, they die for their country, for all of us. Even if their bodies are lost, devoured by white winds, the man is resurrected, in stone and bronze and oils, poetry and song, in books, newspapers and magazines; medals are struck, a cenotaph raised, and garlands laid.

A continent cannot be discovered in a moment. Like Columbus, the first Antarctic visitors saw islands, then larger coasts. They made contradictory interpretations of what they had found. Ice stopped them answering with certainty even simple questions of geography, keeping them from the shore, capturing their vessels and carrying them off in a slow-motion fairground ride to madness. The weather could kill in summer, and for many years was unendurable all winter. Slowly their guesses got better, the scale of the discovery was revealed in piecemeal portions, then joined up, until there could be no doubt that this was a continent.

The men who succeeded often fade from view. They did their job, there is no redemption in that. If you have offended no one, a promotion is expected, maybe a mention in an honours list. If the politics changed while you were away, and there is a new King or President, perhaps just a different Admiral in high office, you may be sidelined, made absolute lord of a verandahed bungalow in a pestilential clime. Sometimes it may simply be easier to ignore you.

Maritime historians will always remember the dashing Captain James Clark Ross. Anyone who has looked at a map of Antarctica cannot miss James Weddell's name, written on a frozen sea. Cook's later career has been reassessed but his reputation is worldwide and goes beyond his own sphere, which is true fame. Shackleton seems to have gained an uneclipsable position in the firmament, which probably means he is due for a fall. But two men, Palmer and Bellingshausen, who vie for the honour of first seeing continental land, are famous only in their home towns. De Gerlache, who endured the first Antarctic overwintering, on the edge of madness, is barely known outside his native Belgium.

In the book's opening, I said it was like a conspiracy, the way names have been forgotten. Politics is part of it. The nations who were there at the beginning trumpet their heroes and camouflage the role of rival nations. Heroes who suited the times, like Scott, were embraced, and his despair reinvented as self-sacrifice, while it took different times and different values to canonise Shackleton. Wilkes, the supreme hankerer after recognition and status, was brutally sacrificed for the politics of the moment.

There is a possibility that the first men to see the last continent were the sick and broken sailors of the Spanish warship the *San Telmo*, if their vessel survived the Drake Passage only to be smashed to scantling on Livingston Island. Perhaps only their 644 ghosts looked on.

The name of the American sealer whose boot first trod on the continent may never be known, unless a stray ship's log or paper puts a name to the man who led the boat ashore. Most of all, Captain William Smith deserves to be a household name. He was not an explorer or a scientist, he was a working seaman, earning a tough living, who took time out to be curious, although curiosity didn't pay. He believed in the worth of the land on the edge of the world, which he saw once in a storm. He returned three times and brought the world in his wake. Smith died thinking that wild shore was worth a pension: something to save him from the poorhouse, or from walking the streets of Whitechapel in thin-soled boots. His petition for recognition is a sad paper chain that runs out, leaves him standing cap in hand, ignored by men sitting each day before coal fires in Admiralty offices. His adventure was worth a pension. It was worth immortality. I close with a toast, a hot rum toddy for the real hero: Bill Smith.

# Definitions

PLACE NAMES
Different countries have given their own names to many prominent features. Some have changed over time, sometimes the same name was used twice. Explorers also named land when ignorant or unsure of whether it had already been seen before. Islands seen in poor weather often had multiple christenings. I value clarity over strict contemporary veracity and use the modern names unless otherwise stated. The section on sources and further reading recommends the best guide to Antarctic place names.

UNITS OF MEASUREMENT
When writing of land distances, miles are statute miles of 1760 yards unless otherwise stated. When writing of sea distances, miles are nautical miles of 2027 yards, or 1.15 statute miles. Sea miles are convenient units for voyages because one degree of latitude is precisely sixty nautical miles, and one minute of latitude is one nautical mile. One tenth of a nautical mile is called a cable. Some quotes include distances in leagues, which are three miles.

## ABBREVIATIONS

BAS: British Antarctic Survey, Cambridge, England. A Government institution administering science and other British interests in Antarctica.

FIDS: Falkland Islands Dependencies Service. The arm of the British Government administering the United Kingdom's south Atlantic possessions.

IAATO: International Association of Antarctic Tour Operators. A trade organisation of cruise operators.

RRS: Royal Research Ship.

SPRI: Scott Polar Research Institute, Cambridge, England.

# A Glossary of Specialist Polar and Maritime Words

Binnacle: deck mounting holding a compass.

Brig: a vessel with two masts, both square-rigged.

Brigantine: a two-masted vessel with the foremast square-rigged and the other fore-and-aft.

Collier: a ship for carrying coal.

Confused sea: a sea in which waves come from more than one direction, producing a lumpy unpredictable motion.

Corvette: a patrol vessel smaller than a frigate.

Dead reckoning: the craft, rather than science, of estimating your progress and position from sailing speed, wind, currents and other factors when instruments are lacking or can't be used.

Finnesko: Norwegian for Lapp shoes, soft reindeer-skin boots with the fur worn outside, traditionally lined with an Arctic plant called *sennegras* which insulates and absorbs moisture.

Föhn: a strong wind from mountains, warming as it descends, which can cause rapid snow melt.

Heave to: to turn a vessel into the wind and hold the same position.

Ice blink: a brightness on cloud low above the horizon, occurring when there is extensive ice just beyond what can be directly seen.

Isostasy: when a large ice-cap forms, its weight depresses the land. The rebound when it melts is called isostasy.

Jury rig: a temporary repair to major items of sailing gear, like spars masts and rudders, until proper repairs can be carried out.

Katabatic wind: a violent local wind caused by very cold, dense air flowing off the land, typically from ice-caps.

Lahar: a flow of volcanic ash and water which can travel much faster than lava.

Landfall: confusingly, this means sighting land after a sea voyage, not going ashore.

Lead: a temporary linear opening in the ice.

Nunatak: a mountain peak showing above an ice-cap, usually as a slender pyramid.

Pack ice: dense ice from various sources which surrounds the continent completely each winter and melts back each summer. It is now defined as seven-tenths or more coverage of the sea surface.

Pemmican: a meat product adapted from a high-energy hunting food made by Cree and other Natives of the northern tribes. It mostly comprises meat and fat and needs carbohydrates to be added to make a basic diet. Lacks vitamin C.

Phytoplankton: unicellular plants which are the base level of the Antarctic food chain.

Polynya: a Russian term for a permanent, non-linear opening in sea ice.

Reefed sails: sails reduced in size to cope with high winds by rolling up an edge and tying it down.

Rorqual whales: large filter-feeding whales with pleats in their throats to help gulp and strain krill from the ocean.

Schooner: ship with two or more masts with the aft equal or larger to those in front of it.

Sea anchor: a floating device on a length of rope. In rough weather it is thrown overboard, attached to the bow. It is designed to drag in the water and keep the bow to wind and so present the most buoyant form to the seas.

Sea ice: ice formed when the sea freezes.

Sennegras: boot insulation, see finnesko.

Shallop: a small ship's boat, stored on deck or davits and powered by a sail or oars.

Ship's Officers: captain has three related meanings: a rank in the Navy, the holder of a Master Mariner's certificate, the man in charge of a vessel. In the eighteenth century, discipline problems became serious when officers of the army or marines were on board ship and refused to take command from Navy men or gentlemen civilian officers. The doctrine of a captain's word being absolute clarified this. Under sail, with no engineers on board, the next most senior officer was a man variously called, First Mate, Chief Mate, Chief Officer or sometimes First Officer. The officer below was therefore Second Mate or Second Officer, and so on. Midshipmen were gentlemen apprentices training to become full officers. In navies, there was usually a glass floor between these gentlemen and the men. It was exceptional to cross it, however able you were. Private vessels were more socially fluid. Above this ceiling the English names, like admiral and captain, are Latin in origin via French, because such work fell to the upper classes. Below the ceiling, starting with the bosun (Anglo-Saxon 'boatswain' meaning boatmaster) the men and their titles are all from the underclass.

Sloop: single-masted vessel with fore-and-aft rig.

Starboard: the right side of the ship when you look forward, a corruption of steerboard when most ships were steered by a trailing oar which right-handed people could most conveniently handle on that side. In port, to stop it being caught against the dock or bank, you manoeuvred the other side close in: the port side.

Tabular ice bergs: named for their flat white tops and vertical sides, like table-tops. They break off the huge ice shelves attached to sheltered parts of the continent.

Tonite: an explosive used in the late 1800s and early 1900s consisting of equal weights of barium nitrate and guncotton. The name derives from the Latin verb *tonare*, to thunder.

Zooplankton: small crustacea which drift in the water. The 'plan' part of the word is the same base as 'planet': which means wanderer. The best known is krill.

# Timelines:

## South Georgia and the Falkland Islands

Although longer Antarctic cruises visit both these places, South Georgia is a sub-Antarctic island and the Falklands are cool temperate. Some South Georgia history has been included in various parts of the book to explain Antarctic history, but the Falklands deserve a fuller history than this volume can encompass. For South Georgia, I would especially recommend *A Visitor's Guide to South Georgia* by Sally Poncet and Kim Crosbie, full details are in the Acknowledgements. However, the following two timelines outline key dates in the history of South Georgia and the Falklands.

### SOUTH GEORGIA TIMELINE

| | |
|---|---|
| 1675 | London Merchant Antoine de la Roché sights a large island. |
| 1775 | Captain James Cook lands, claims it for Britain, surveys the north-east shore, and proves it is not part of a southern continent. |

| | |
|---|---|
| 1786 | Thomas Delano of London in the *Lord Hawkesbury* takes the first seals. |
| 1819 | Thaddeus Bellingshausen surveys the remaining coast, and meets elephant sealers camped ashore for the summer. |
| 1820 | The earliest known burial of a sealer, Frank Cabriel, on 14 October. |
| 1881 | First closed season for sealing. |
| 1882 | Scientists base themselves on the island. |
| 1901–02 | Captain C. A. Larsen, employed for the Otto Nordenskjöld expedition, explores the island seeking commercial opportunities in whaling and sealing. |
| 1904 | On 16 November Larsen begins the first permanent settlement, a whaling town, at Grytviken. He negotiates a twenty-one-year lease from 1 January 1906. |
| 1906 | Sandefjord Whaling Company sets up a factory ship in Stromness Bay, paying dividends of 60% and 120% in its first two seasons. |
| 1907 | Argentina builds a meteorological base at King Edward Point. A factory ship is established at Husvik. |
| 1909 | Population reaches 720, including 3 women and a child. |
| 1911 | Larsen's company pays a 50% dividend. |
| 1911–12 | The Filchner Expedition in the *Deutschland* surveys the coast. Third officer Walter Slossarczyk was lost presumed drowned when rowing in the bay. The lower single cross above the cemetery is his. |

| 1912 | twelve men die of typhus brought on a ship. Work begins on Stromness Whaling Station. |
|------|------|
| 1913 | First birth, Solveig Gunbjorg Jacobsen, on 8 October, daughter of the assistant manager of a whaling station. |
| 1913 | Christmas Day, consecration of church, christening of Solveig Jacobsen. |
| 1916 | 24 April Shackleton sails from Elephant Island to South Georgia then crosses the island on foot. |
| 1922 | 5 January death of Sir Ernest Shackleton on the *Quest* at Grytviken. 5 March, burial of Shackleton. |
| 1925–26 | Peak whaling year with nearly 8000 whales. The first factory ship, the *Lansing*, arrives. |
| 1928–29 | Extensive inland survey by the Kohl-Larsen Expedition. |
| 1932 | First marriage, 24 February, between Alfred Jones and Vera Riches. |
| 1932–33 | Market glut closes all whaling stations except Grytviken. |
| 1933–34 | Leith Whaling Station opens. |
| 1949 | South Georgia incorporated in FIDS. |
| 1951–57 | Duncan Carse conducts full and detailed surveys. |
| 1959–60 | Husvik Whaling Station closes. |
| 1960–61 | Leith Whaling Station closes. |
| 1962 | Norwegians cease whaling at Grytviken. |
| 1963–64 | Japanese whaling at Grytviken. Closes through lack of whales. |

| 1966 | Whaling ends in South Georgia. |
| 1969–82 | BAS administers the island. Minimum winter population twelve, maximum summer population: fifty. |
| 1980 | Pack ice extends 110 miles north of South Georgia. |
| 1980s | Fur seals recover to 300,000 breeding females. |
| 1982 | April, Argentinian ships *Guerrico* and *Bahía Paraíso* force surrender of British authorities at Grytviken. |
| 1982 | 25 April, British troops retake South Georgia, and station garrison at King Edward Point. |
| 1998 | South African fishing vessel *Sudur Havid* sinks off South Georgia. The higher cross above the cemetery is a memorial to them. |
| 2003–05 | Clear-up of Grytviken Whaling Station. |

## A FALKLANDS TIMELINE

| 1493 | The year after Columbus returns, Pope Alexander VI signs the Treaty of Tordesillas, assigning rights in the New World to Portugal and Spain. |
| 1592 | 14 August 1592 discovery of the Falklands by master navigator John Davis. |
| 1690 | Captain John Strong, in thirty-eight-gun privateer *Welfare* makes first recorded landing, names Falkland Sound after Viscount Falkland of Admiralty Office. |

| | |
|---|---|
| 1764 | April, French settle in Port Louis, Berkeley Sound, E Falkland, twenty miles NW of Stanley (named for Secretary in Foreign and Colonial Office), and claim for France as Îles Malouines. |
| 1765, early | British military found garrison on Saunders Island, W Falkland, unaware of French, and claim for King George as Port Egmont. |
| 1767 | French sell Port Louis to Spanish. |
| 1770 | Spanish drive British out of Port Egmont. |
| 1770s | Sealers and whalers, mainly American, British and French, use harbours. |
| 1771 | British successfully negotiate their return, but |
| 1774 | abandon because of cost. |
| 1810 | Argentina declares independence. |
| 1811 | Spanish abandon islands. Sealers and whalers continue to use harbours. |
| 1820 | Government of Province of Buenos Aires and British authorities grant rights to exploit fish and wild cattle and grants land to French-born, US-trained businessman Louis Vernet. |
| 1828 | Vernet's business with English manager Matthew Brisbane, thrives. Vernet confiscates US *Harrier*, 1831, for exploiting island without permission. US corvette *Lexington* sacks settlement, destroys Vernet's business, declares islands free of all governance. |
| Sept 1832 | Buenos Aires sends schooner *Sarandi* with new Governor, twenty-five soldiers and |

|  |  |
|---|---|
|  | some convicts. Soldiers mutiny, murder governor. |
| Jan 1833 | Sloop HMS *Clio* deposits Brisbane, soon murdered by convicts. |
| Jan 1834 | HMS *Challenger* arrives at Port Louis and leaves first lieutenant Henry Smith, 4 seamen and Royal Marines. For four years restores Vernet's work. Other naval officers succeed him, until civil administration takes over under Lt. R. C. Moody, Army Engineer, 1842. |
| 1841 | Falklands declared Crown Colony. |
| Post 1850 | Argentina becomes nation state. |
| 1946 | Fascist dictator Peron claims Falklands. |
| 1966 | 28 September, twenty members of New Argentina Movement symbolically 'seize' islands to annoyance of Argentina's President. |
| March 1967 | GB Government says it will concede sovereignty subject to certain conditions, respecting wishes of Falklanders. |
| 1970s | Christian Salvesen buys whaling station leases. From 1978 a Buenos Aires businessman Constantino Davidoff negotiates right to salvage. |
| 1971 | British PM Edward Heath agrees improved air and sea transport between Argentina and islands, and unrestricted visits. |
| 1973 | UN passes resolution asking both sides to expedite solution. Juan Peron elected President. |
| Dec 1973 | *Cronica* newspaper launches an 'Invade the Falklands' campaign. |

| | |
|---|---|
| Oct 1975 | Lord Shackleton chairs report recording economic decline. |
| March 1976 | Military junta takes power unopposed. Buys British military equipment. |
| 1976 | James Callaghan's Government anxious to reduce non-NATO commitments, begins renewing patrol vessel *Endurance's* role in Falklands on annual basis. Margaret Thatcher continues the practice, signalling reduced interest in the islands. |
| 1978 | Chile and Argentina nearly go to war over Beagle Channel, Argentina spends billions on armaments. |
| 1980 | Argentina economy in crisis, wages fall 40% in value, interest rates ruinous. |
| 1981 | UK Nationality Bill takes full British Citizenship from Islanders. |
| Dec 1981 | General Leopoldo Galtieri takes over Presidency of Argentina. |
| 19 Mar 1982 | Scrap metal dealers under Constantino Davidoff land on South Georgia and raise Argentina flag. |
| 30 Mar 1982 | British Joint Intelligence Committee, Latin America Current Intelligence Group, meets under chair of Foreign Office and insists invasion not imminent. Still afraid of provoking what they fear. |
| 2 Apr 1982 | Argentina invades Falklands. |
| 3 Apr 1982 | Argentines seize Grytviken. Margaret Thatcher announces Task Force. |
| 25 April 1982 | South Georgia retaken. |
| 14 June 1982 | Argentine forces surrender Falklands. |

# Acknowledgements

My deepest thanks to all the friends and colleagues who helped me through the many obscure corners of knowledge touched on in this book. Charles Aithie drew the fine, clear maps. Special thanks to my patient editor Kathryn Gray, who added creativity and imagination as well as controlling my text. More thanks to Rick Atkinson, and all the Port Lockroy staff, and Laura Baker, Robert Burton, James and Sharon Lowen, Tan Pearson, Richard and the Monday Drinks Club, Wendy Pyper, the Foyle Reading Room staff at the RGS, John Sparks, Callum and Jane Thompson, Josef Verlinden, Nancy Watson, Richard Williams and all my friends on the *Polar Star*.

I met Celia Ansdell in Antarctica and I knew she understood me when she suggested that we meet up in the UK, and coaxed me by saying, 'I have a little place ten minutes walk from the Royal Geographical Society and twenty minutes from the British Library and the British Museum.' Her version is that despite knowing souvenirs of Antarctica are forbidden she brought me back and it's too much trouble to return me. Thanks for everything.

A reference and reading list is on my website: www.cloudroad.co.uk but the following sources were especially useful.


## BOOKS

*The Falklands War* by D. George Boyce (Palgrave Macmillan, 2005). I derived some of my core arguments on sovereignty from this book.

*From Venus to Antarctica: The Life of Dumont d'Urville* by John Dunmore (Exisle Publishing, 2007) is a very readable biography.

*Sea of Glory* by Nathaniel Philbrick (Viking, 2003) is an entertaining account of the Wilkes Expedition.

*A Visitor's Guide to South Georgia* by Sally Poncet and Kim Crosbie (WildGuides Ltd, 2005)

Kevin Walton's and Rick Atkinson's *Of Dogs and Men* (Images Publishing, Malvern 1996) tells you what it was like to run dogs. Great photos and text.

## WEBSITES

Antarctic Treaty Secretariat www.ats.aq
British Antarctic Survey www.bas.ac.uk
Falkland Islands Government www.falklands.gov.fk
Scott Polar Research Institute www.spri.cam.ac.uk
South Georgia Government website www.sgisland.gs
South Georgia Museum www.sgmuseum.gs
www.south-pole.com is a quirky site with twin interests in polar discovery and philately.

United Kingdom Antarctic Heritage Trust www.ukaht.org
Save the Albatross rspb.org.uk

MAPS

Antarctic Peninsula and Weddell Sea (Scale 1:3,000,000) and Graham Land and South Shetland Islands (1:1,000,000).
BAS (Misc) 13A and 13B. One sheet, map each side.
South Georgia BAS (Misc) 12A and 12B (1:200:000).
Falkland Islands OS (1:250,000).

Special thanks to Dr Adrian Fox, Head of Mapping and Geographic Information Centre, British Antarctic Survey for advice on the Shackleton route across South Georgia and the British Antarctic Survey for allowing us to use information from their 2004, 1:200,000 scale South Georgia, map. BAS (Misc)12. Cambridge. British Antarctic Survey.

We would also like to acknowledge the Royal Scottish Geographical Society for their permission to reproduce Laurie Island from the Scottish National Antarctic Expedition of 1903.

And lastly we are especially grateful to Global Book Publishing Pty Ltd, Australia for giving us permission to use cartography from their book Antarctica: The Complete Story 2001, Global Book Publishing, as an important source for our maps.

# Index

450

High defenition Pdf versions
of all the maps may be viewed
free online at John Harrison's
website: www.cloudroad.co.uk